Mid-Century Men

Mid-Century Men

by

ARTHUR HOPCRAFT

HAMISH HAMILTON
London

First published in Great Britain 1982
by Hamish Hamilton Ltd
Garden House 57–59 Long Acre London WC2E 9JZ

Copyright © 1982 by Arthur Hopcraft

British Library Cataloguing in Publication Data

Hopcraft, Arthur
  Mid-century men.
  I. Title
  823'.914[F]   PR6058.058/

  ISBN 0-241-10782-2

Photoset by Rowland Phototypesetting Ltd
Bury St Edmunds, Suffolk
Printed in Great Britain by
St Edmundsbury Press, Bury St Edmunds, Suffolk.

Book One

CHAPTER ONE

Craddock could remember a time when his hangovers were trivially unpleasant: thick head, loose bowels and a feeling of self-reproach, all of which could be adequately treated with plenty of tap water and a day's abstinence from alcohol. It was like that when he was on his first paper at the age of sixteen; when he was in khaki doing his National Service; when he was on one, two, three more provincial papers; when he was on his first national paper, and his second; when he began to freelance; and long after that. When did it change? Recently. Well, yes, but what was recent? The last two years, say? Could it be longer? On second thoughts, perhaps much less. Was it a matter only of months? He would try to count the number of days on which he had felt as he did now. At the rate of, say, twice a month as a fair average he ought to arrive at a definite distance of time, if he concentrated. Today was the thirteenth of December, a Wednesday. Now, working backwards . . .

'Christ,' he said aloud, after a few seconds of silent counting. Hearing his own voice embarrassed him, since he was alone, but he decided to complete his comment audibly, as an act of defiance. 'That's quite enough of that.' The utterance made him smile, not happily. It was the nervous smile of someone frightened. The defiance was a bleak joke against himself.

He was frightened of his hangover because it would consist of fear: fear as a force in itself. It would not be manifest in intimations of illness, such as an irregular heartbeat or swimming vision or swelling legs, all of which symptoms and more he had heard discussed among drinkers, boastful and forlorn alike. He would not see non-existent intruders in his house, as poor old Hector Brunskill had the day he was carted off to hospital. Craddock would suffer no delusions. There would be gaps in his memory of the past twenty-four hours, and the incidents he could recall would in part be blurred. That was of no concern to him. The cost of one of his lost days would have to be paid, and that was that. He would find startling bills in his pockets; an entry on one or other of his credit card statements would surprise him in due course. A doorman might regret he was not, until further notice, to be admitted. A barman might refuse to serve him until he apologised. It would all happen again.

But instead of remorse, nausea or ghostly visitation he had a day of dread to face. He entered it as if it were a cold sea, one foot dangled tentatively. The foot wore a sock. Otherwise Craddock was naked. He was irritated by the sock, being fastidious about not wearing clothes in bed. The burst of annoyance sustained him all the way to the bathroom.

★

'I'm not sure whether I'm relieved or disappointed. I thought you'd have the shakes like a quivering aspen. Or be in a catatonic trance with your head up the chimney. Or *something* visibly pitiable. You look a bit faded, but don't we all sometimes – having me on, aren't you, darling?'

Liz Ellison was sitting upright in one of Craddock's armchairs, the afternoon winter sunshine giving the bay window glancing blows now and then and each time making her turn her head to catch the warmth. And the light, of course, Craddock noted. Liz was an actress, and although Craddock liked her for her unusual lack of vanity and the uncalculating way she sped through life, he had come to realise that Liz could never resist being lit. She had an apparently careless trick of finding the right position in any room, day or night, so that the slender face with its light skin taut on the bones could be tilted in a subtle variety of angles to be shown at advantage. Was that unfair to her? Probably it was, he thought. It was not a case of showing herself off. She seemed to have a running love affair with light: light of all kinds – sun, candle-light, stage-light. She toyed with light, as if asking, 'Are we still friends?' Yet she was not coquettish. The love affair was not conscious, perhaps; just a compulsion which, being Liz, she was able to meet without being aware of it. Certainly without caring if anyone else noticed. Craddock liked Liz very much. He could think of no one else who could address him as 'Darling' without irritating him.

He gestured at the fireplace, tiled in shiny brown, its aperture covered by a big electric fire. 'I knew a bloke called Hector Brunskill. He *did* stick his head up the chimney. Tried to get his whole body up, actually. Trying to escape from all these people who'd invaded his bed-sitter – policemen, the mayor and half the town council, all after his blood. Nobody there, of course, poor sod. That was the drink. Hector was one of the most intelligent men I've ever met. One of the nicest, too. A total failure. He thought journalism fell into two categories: either corrupt or ridiculous. I'll tell you about him one day.'

Liz's laugh was incongruously raucous for so elegant a body. 'Darling, you just *have*.' Craddock studied her profile as again she turned it so that the sun could brush the flesh. The side he was looking at now had the delicate shadowing of a pencil sketch. 'He sounds a love,' she said, and he nodded faintly before she was once more looking fully at him.

'There was a bit more to him than that.' Craddock got up from the chair where he had been sitting, with his elbow and fist propping his head above the dining table, and went across the room towards her. He was a compact man with the slow movement of someone heavier. He was wearing slippers, cord trousers, open-necked shirt and a sweater. 'Really, Tony, you look like a new pin, shaved and bathed. I was expecting a derelict,' she said. 'Why did you give me all that piffle on the phone?'

The room was long and narrow. The previous owners of the house had knocked out the wall which had divided a small square sitting room from a small dining room, conforming with general practice in the street Craddock lived in. Once the houses would have been known as artisans' cottages. Now there were fitted carpets in plain colours, Indian rugs from the Oxfam shop, pine coffee tables, drinks cabinets with shelves that swivelled out, bunk beds for the children, full central heating. It was middle class South-West London. Craddock had lived in Parton Street for nearly six years. He had no children, so no bunk beds. His drinks cabinet was in white laminated plastic, and the shelves did not swivel. Otherwise his house was much like the others. With the price had come the carpets; and he had felt no need to change the decoration from white, off-white, fawn and French grey paint which covered the walls in an entirely inoffensive 'scheme', as the young man from the estate agent had called it. Craddock knew it was unimaginitive, and had no interest in changing it. The place was clean, and Mrs Readhead had no difficulty in keeping it so in her twice-weekly visits of two hours. (She had her own key, and Craddock was usually out when she called. If he was not they were polite and even attentive to each other, although not using Christian names. Craddock imagined their relationship was not unlike a substantial number of Victorian marriages. Mrs Readhead was roughly Craddock's age.)

*

Craddock and Liz were born in the same year, on the same day. Eighteen months from now, in 1980, they would be fifty. Neither had ever married.

'It wasn't piffle,' Craddock said. 'I was trying to describe exactly how I felt – just terrified of nothing in particular.'

'Feeling sorry for yourself.'

'Very. Wouldn't you?'

'Well, we all do sometimes.'

'Feel terrified of nothing in particular?'

'No. Self-*pity*, darling.'

He had paused beside the drinks cabinet, with its glass doors. His voice rose angrily. 'I feel sorry for myself because I feel scared to death. Of nothing and everything.' The voice subsided. 'It's irrational, and I've always thought I was a rational human being.'

'I've seen you impenetrably drunk. When you're like that you don't know whether you're Oscar Wilde or John the Baptist.'

Craddock shrugged. 'Being drunk's different.'

'Certainly changes *you*.' Liz gave him a smile which mixed fondness and regret.

'I'm going to pack it in altogether,' Craddock had turned to open the cabinet doors as he spoke, so he missed the look of alarm on Liz's face. He took out two glasses and placed them on top of the cabinet. 'I don't mean right this minute. I shall have to have a couple today, just to get myself under control. What can I offer you? I'm going to try a very thin whisky and water.' He looked at her, holding the whisky bottle.

Liz said slowly, 'When you said "pack it in" then, the way you said it, just for a moment I really thought you meant something else. It was the tone of voice, when I couldn't see your face. Like on the 'phone, I suppose.'

There was a silence of five or six seconds, before Craddock grasped her meaning. 'It's called "doing something silly", ' he said at last. She nodded. 'No, Liz. I keep telling you I feel scared. I've never said I was in despair, have I?' He put on a voice of exaggerated mock-patience. 'You see, you haven't been listening. I'm talking about the mysterious awfulness of my hangovers. That's all.'

'Right. Exactly. Thank you.' Liz was now very brisk. She rummaged in her shoulder bag, made of some multi-coloured woven cloth and acquired on one of her tours of distant places, and produced cigarettes and lighter. 'Self-pity. Self-dramatisation. Self-inflicted wounds.' She inhaled, then held the cigarette away from her face, the lovely hand splayed and almost transparent against the sunlight. When she blew out a little cloud of smoke it hung in the air, and as she turned once again with that tiny tilting of the profile towards the window she completed the composition of such a theatrical portrait that Craddock laughed aloud. It was the laughter of genuine pleasure.

Liz fluttered her free hand. 'I'm sorry,' she said. 'I shouldn't have said that last bit. Sounds too much like the other thing, and I never thought you *were* self-destructive – that's why you upset me at that moment. But I'll tell you what you *are*, Tony. You're terribly wilful . . .'

'Over-cautious,' he cut in sharply, 'unwilling to get involved. That's the usual complaint.'

'Whoever says that doesn't know you. Or only knows you sober. Even then it's not true. I wouldn't call you a cautious writer. You give great offence. Look at all those potty women's libbers. After that last character of yours I played, they tried to drown us both in vitriol. I couldn't have got more publicity if I'd done it topless. *What* are you, an antediluvian sexist? Didn't you force me to do dirt on my gender, or some such offensiveness?'

Craddock grinned. 'There were one or two shrill Fleet Street bitches of both sexes who didn't much like that particular telly play,' he said. He was slightly bemused to find he was still holding the unopened whisky bottle. Now it was Liz's turn to laugh as he seemed to ponder the bottle's function. 'Christ,' he said, and quickly took the stopper off and poured two incautious measures. 'Join me?' She nodded, and he carried both glasses out to the kitchen to top them up with water.

The kitchen had a light smell of scouring powder; Mrs Readhead had been conscientiously at work the day before. 'It's all terribly sanitary.' Liz had followed him, and she stood in the doorway looking over the cups on their hooks, the white cooker, the white tiles, the white refrigerator, the white cupboards. She opened one of the cupboard doors: plates neatly stacked. She closed it, and took the glass he held out to her. 'Do you like it as orderly as this? You know what *my* place is like. Cheers, darling.' She drank, the cigarette smoke curling above the glass. She was wearing trousers and loose-fitting smock-like top, open at the neck. Her hair was gathered up at the back. It was fair, not quite blonde with no grey in it. She had little make-up. The only ornamentation about her, without the shoulder bag, was on her wrists: several thin bracelets in coloured plastic. A very young girl would choose them. But Liz did not pretend youthfulness. She liked whatever of its trappings suited her, and she never made the mistake of overloading herself.

'Your place is a cheerful dump,' said Craddock, who was still standing at the sink, unwilling to leave it until he was sure he had the mixture right in his glass. He turned the cold tap to add a short splash, then sipped. He was satisfied. 'I can't work in clutter. And that's what this house is for. To work in.' She looked at him with an expression of sympathy. 'Well, for Christ's sake, I've got to *have* somewhere to work.' He turned to lean against the sink, feeling that he was explaining, or apologising, unnecessarily. It brought a wave of tiredness.

Liz moved a few steps to the white pedal bin, flipped up the lid and tapped cigarette ash into it. She said, 'If you've been in this state before, and you say you have, is there someone else you usually call on?'

'No.'

'Do you mean there's no one you feel you *can*?' Craddock shook his head irritably.

'You just sit it out.'

'Sort of. Yes.'

'And it goes away.'

He shrugged.

Liz persisted. 'Like pins and needles or back-ache or something.'

'If you say so, Liz.'

She flicked more ash into the bin. 'Was it much worse this time then?'

He started back towards the living room. 'You happened to 'phone me,' he said. 'You said, "How are you?" So I told you. I don't know that I was all that much worse this time. I think it's just that it's happened once too often. If you hadn't called perhaps I *would* have 'phoned somebody.'

'Like the Samaritans?'

'No. And I thought we'd dealt with that.'

'Sorry. It was a joke.'

'Now you see the seriousness of my predicament. I missed a joke. That's a grave matter. Must give cause for concern.'

They were sitting in the two armchairs in the bay window. The sun had gone. The light was a flat grey. He put his glass on the floor, hitched up both sleeves to bare his wrists and started counting his pulse rate. He gave it a full minute. Liz giggled at him, because he looked so solemn.

'Eighty-nine,' he said.

'What should it be?'

'I'd prefer about eighty-four or -five, in these circumstances.'

'But you don't think it calls for medical attention?'

He shook his head, still not smiling, and then sipped from his glass.

'Have you ever been to your doctor about these hangovers?'

Craddock studied her face. 'I'm not missing another joke, am I?'

'Darling, I'm taking you seriously.'

'What could he possibly say, except tell me to stop drinking?'

'He might diagnose some allergy to a particular drink. Some special susceptibility. He might put his finger on it in a trice.' Liz had a tendency towards quaintly-dated English when she was being earnest. She pointed at his glass. 'I mean, he might say the evidence points conclusively to the demon whisky, and if you touch nothing but the grape you'll be as right as twenty dear old shillings to the pound.' Craddock was mesmerised by her. It was as if some old-maid aunt from his childhood had taken possession of this sensual body he was looking at. The thought flickered across his mind that there must be times when she talked to her young boyfriends like that. Surely not. But yes, she certainly would if the mood took her. The idea held a sad comicality. Did they ever call her 'Auntie Liz'?

'It couldn't do any harm to ask. Are you listening?'

'Of course I am.'

'You'd gone a bit vacant. They say horses can sleep standing up. You had that look.'

'Liz, let's face it. It's not what I drink, it's just how much. These stupid bloody great benders. I seem to need them. About once every ten, twelve, fourteen days I set off on the same old beat and get catastrophically plastered.'

'Well, the right kind of doctor might easily tell you why.'

'I know why. I like it, that's why. It's just that recovery is such an agonising process nowadays. Takes so long.' He lowered the glass as he was about to drink. 'The right kind of doctor. Are you suggesting a head-shrinker? I really can do without that kind of talk today.'

'I'm simply trying to be practical, Tony.'

He raised his glass to her. 'I love you for it.'

'Who would you have 'phoned?'

'What?'

'If I hadn't given you a ring. You said you'd have 'phoned somebody this time for an encouraging word. Who?'

'Oh, I don't know. I hadn't got round to thinking about it. Perhaps that's all I would have done – thought about it. Once I'd considered what I was going to say: "Look, er, listen. You see, I've got these funny feelings, and I just thought I'd give you a buzz and tell you about them . . ." See what I mean? Perhaps I'd have settled for a few hairs of the dog and a little weep over Mahler's "Song of the Earth". That's been the usual way lately. I've got three different recordings. Do you fancy hearing one?'

'If you feel the need.'

'Not really. You're better medicine. Have I actually said thank you for 'phoning?'

'I think it was implied in all that babble.'

'Piffle, you said before.'
'I've retracted that.'
'Thank you for 'phoning.'
'My pleasure.'
'I'm feeling a bit more human now.'
'Good.'

Craddock stood up; his glass was empty, and he went to the drinks cabinet. 'I called you about a fortnight ago, just on the off chance. I had to see someone who lives near your place. I thought we might have a meal. Some young man at your flat said you were still on tour. New Zealand? New South Wales?'

'You mean the young man?'

'No. Where you were at the time.'

'Could have been either. We played them both. I have an impression of a certain uneasiness Down Under, where Chekhov is concerned.'

'They didn't get the jokes?' She shook her head slowly. 'I've had the same problem with the television critics of the *Aberdeen Evening Angst* and other stern-minded provincial publications.' He proffered the whisky bottle at her, and she considered briefly before placing the palm of her free hand over the glass. Craddock poured himself an inch or so, then on reflection another. 'Won't be a minute.' He wandered out to the kitchen. When he came back he had a jug of water as well as his glass.

Liz said, 'Does that jug indicate you're going to get properly stuck into the scotch?'

'I hope I'll get just enough.'

'For what?'

'For getting my perspective back.'

Liz was abruptly busy as she made a show of irritation out of lighting another cigarette. 'Does that mean half-pissed, or completely out of your mind?'

Craddock disliked having disturbed her. 'Honestly, it just means quietening down enough to be able to get some sleep and some food, then a proper *night's* sleep and resume normal life tomorrow. Back to work. Penitence and reform. That was one of Hector Brunskill's catchphrases.'

'I think you made him up.'

'Not at all. I assure you.' He drank, standing in the middle of the room. She blew smoke towards him, and flicked ash carelessly on to the carpet. 'Born in Mexico City. English parents. They sent him over here to school – one of those scandalous little Dickensian boarding schools that apparently were a growth industry around the Home Counties in the Thirties. Staple diet, educational and nutritional, the stick and the carrot. Both early experiences – Mexico and this Berkshire Dotheboys Hall – made Hector a lifelong revolutionary. All forms of authority should at all times be opposed, preferably with violence, Hector believed. He did a bit of it, as well. In a modest way. The odd brick through a borough engineer's window. A pee in the editor's potted begonias. Left quite a trail of petty vandalism as he went from one sweatshop of a local paper to another.' Craddock drank to the past, and took his mouth from the glass as if from a kiss.

'Is he still around?' Liz asked the question gently.

'No, went early. On the other hand, having laughed his way out of the psychiatric ward of an extremely squalid general hospital, he did see Mexico again. Stayed off the booze and bought himself a package tour. He sent me a postcard. Portrait of one of his great heroes, Benito Juares, Mexican people's revolutionary par excellence. On the back Hector had written one of his Thoughts For The Day, the sort of slogan he used to burst out with suddenly in the pub in the old days. This one was, "If they won't learn from life let death be the teacher". A couple of exclamation marks. I suspect he'd surrendered to the tequila.'

'Sounds as if he might have been giving you the gypsy's warning.'

Craddock laughed. His eyes lit up as he looked at her. 'Do you know you've just spoken a real Hector Brunskill line?'

She was immediately suspicious. 'Are you sure he's not a character in your next play?'

'If he was, why should you think he never existed? It wouldn't be the first time I've borrowed from flesh and blood.'

He could see that she was troubled. More than that: moved. He sensed why, and for a moment felt it would be wiser of him to let the matter rest. Was it the whisky that was bringing a burn to his neck and face? Only partly, he knew. 'Everything I've told you about him is true. The man was real.'

'Suppose you write about him.' She faltered and he waited

without taking his eyes from hers. 'I never know how to take you. When you were talking about him you sounded as if you loved him. Really loved him. But then the next moment you seem to just . . .' She flicked one hand in the air: a dismissing gesture. 'Suddenly he's just another character. But if he isn't – well, could you write about him with love?'

'Obituaries make unrewarding reading.'

'That's the sort of "get lost" answer I hoped you wouldn't give me. I suppose I came too close, did I?'

'I invited it.'

'And then you . . .' Again the dismissing flick of the hand.

In the silence he smiled at her. Not an admission. Not an apology. More than an acknowledgment. A recognition. An understanding. It was dusk now, and they were both aware of lights in the street; in a couple of the houses opposite children's voices and the banging of front doors merged. Liz asked, 'Can you safely be left on your own now? Won't start swigging from the neck of the bottle?'

'You've worked wonders. Thank you, nurse.'

She stood up, gathering cigarettes, lighter, shoulder bag. Her topcoat, a strikingly odd garment, like a Victorian cloak, lay in a heap between the two armchairs.

'Do you want me to call a taxi for you?'

'No, I'll use the tube.'

'Right, I'll walk you to the station.'

She gave him a look of mock alarm. 'Are you sure you should?'

'I can quite reasonably take my umbrella. Steadying influence.'

She said she would use his bathroom first. While she did Craddock stiffened his drink and took two gulps. His legs were more firm than he knew he had a right to expect.

He had changed into shoes and was buttoning a sheepskin coat when she came back into the room. He held her cloak for her, and as she settled comfortably into its shoulders he kissed her cheek and murmured, 'Thanks for coming round.'

She turned and put both hands to his face, then kissed him on the lips. 'Yes, well, you look after yourself and stop being daft,' she said. 'You gave me a fright.' He nodded solemnly.

In the narrow street, as they walked towards the brighter

lights and the increasing noise of traffic, the air had a still, damp chill. Her eye was caught by the switching-on of a Christmas tree in the house they were passing, and she paused to smile at it and the young woman with a child in her arms beside it. She looked back into Craddock's face. 'Sweet,' she said.

'Yes, I suppose so,' Craddock answered, and they walked on.

Liz wanted to know where and how he would spend Christmas, and he gave a shrug of indifference. 'I'm going to be in San Francisco,' she said.

'Sounds nice, if you like that sort of thing.'

'Well, there are these friends and the cheap flights, and I'm doing some work in Canada in the New Year.'

'Sounds like an awful lot of time in big iron bird.'

'Why don't you take a little jaunt somewhere? Come to California.'

'Not me.'

'You'd love it. It's full of eccentrics; you'd fit in perfectly.' He shook his head. 'You used to travel all the time, didn't you? India, Africa – all those magazine things you used to write. Why don't you just take off somewhere? Be a tourist. Everyone's doing it; hadn't you heard?'

'Liz, if it's outside Europe I've no wish to see it ever again. And when I say "Europe" I mean the disinfected, temperate zones too.'

'All right then. Amsterdam, Rome, Lisbon, Paris . . .'

He cut in quite sharply. 'I'm too busy.'

'You could have fooled me, darling.' Then her tone changed to match her shift to eager professional curiosity. 'Work? What is it? Who's it for? Just a one-off or another series?'

They were turning into the main street, with its haphazard mix of shops selling clothes ahead of chain-store fashion (and those behind it), books both honourably rare and bulgingly pornographic, high-class fruit and veg, pets and pet food, family-pack meat for the deep freeze, lampshades, grass seed, screwdrivers, pots and pans, fish and chips, typing paper, wallpaper, fishing rods, door knobs, drink; everything an urban villager could need. Craddock seldom shopped anywhere else, although he bought frequently by mail order in a random way as offers of crates of wine, the odd chair or reissues of old records of the 'Classic Performance' kind waylaid him in the weeklies and the newspapers. Browsing in this bazaar of a street, as through pages of classified advertisements, always provided an indolent calm. It probably came from the security of the familiar. The items in the Sex Shop window – dildo, vibrator, glossily photographed breast and buttock – commanded his inquisitiveness, just as the lonely hearts columns did with their appeals for *someone, anyone*. How frantic; how poignant. What he got from both kinds of display included a mild sexual excitement, as he was ready to admit to himself and anyone else who cared to ask, but mostly he felt a sad wonder, a melancholy. He knew this feeling nourished him in some way. He did not understand why that should be; but he accepted it. Would he ever know why? Did he need to?

Liz had to repeat her questions as Craddock's mind wandered, aimless but compelled, in and out of these shop doorways and blind alleys. 'It isn't television,' he said. 'It's a book. A novel.'

'Darling. Wonderful. What's it about?'

'Oh, the state of the nation. Nothing ambitious.'

'Be serious.'

'I do try.'

'Well, tell me what it's about?'

'Politics.'

'I always thought you hated politics.'

'Quite.'

She had stopped abruptly, and he was a few paces ahead before he realised it. 'Good *heavens*,' she said loudly as he turned. Several people walking past them were startled and looked at her. She took no notice, her voice retaining its ring. 'I'd completely forgotten. That's why I 'phoned you in the first place. You and politics. Now you can see how much you worried me.'

The walking had begun to tire him, because of the accumulated alcohol. He could summon little interest in whatever Liz had forgotten. He looked along the street towards the tube station, and she knew at once what was in his mind. 'Listen, darling, you don't have to go another step,' she said, standing close to him and talking quietly now. 'But before you crawl back to bed just let me ask you a favour. A friend of mine wants to talk to you. Wants to interview you. I said I'd prepare the ground. Just tell you he's very straight and nice, and I'm sure you'll like him.'

Craddock shook his head weakly. He had spent many years of his working life interviewing others and felt uncomfortable in a reversal of the roles. Not that he was often approached. When he was, usually by reporters looking for gossip column material about actors and actresses he knew, he was inclined to declare ignorance even if he happened to be well-informed. Such instances gave him a sense of disloyalty, which annoyed him because objectively he could see it was without good cause. But he had done that kind of journalistic snooping in his time, much in need of the help he would nowadays refuse to give.

'It's not the usual showbiz piddle he wants,' Liz said.

'Was I thinking aloud then?' Craddock was alarmed. Surely he wasn't so fuddled that he had been talking without knowing it?

Liz was very patient, steering him along the thickening thread of shoppers and placing him against a stretch of wall between a delicatessen and a driving school office. 'It's you and *politics*,' she said. 'He's writing a series of articles about the way television handles politics and he wants to talk to *you* about political *drama*.'

'I don't write any.'

'Exactly. He wants to know why.'

Craddock sighed. He wondered whether he would be able to suppress his embarrassment sufficiently to take a passing taxi the short distance home – the drive could hardly be longer than two or three minutes; then he decided he certainly could, as he spotted a lighted cab sign moving towards him. He stepped forward, raising the umbrella, and the cab swerved on cue. Liz's voice carried easily above the traffic sounds. 'His name's Peter Franklin.'

CHAPTER TWO

The next morning's mail included the mild encouragement of a cheque from Craddock's agent for twenty-three pounds and seventeen pence, his cut of the sale of one of his television plays to Brunei, Malta, Nigeria and Zanzibar. Such driblets of income always pleased him out of all proportion to the amount received because they were so improbable. This particular play had concerned a group of cyclists squabbling on a weekend tour of North Yorkshire. What was its appeal to Zanzibar? The answer was beyond imagination, which made its sale all the more flattering. Further, Craddock reflected that twenty-three pounds would pay for some of the excesses of his day and night in town, now surfacing in clearer detail in his memory.

Events had come to a bedraggled end in a cellar club off Shaftesbury Avenue at approximately three in the morning, he now recalled. Recognising the face of an actor he did not personally know, and whose work he disliked for its exaggerated mannerisms, he decided to interrupt the man's conversation with his friends and gave him some advice. With uncommon restraint, as Craddock now saw, the actor had chosen to deal with the abuse by pretending he was not the man Craddock thought he was. To this Craddock had replied, 'Of course, if you *were* Julian Thomas you'd have every reason for denying it, wouldn't you?' This got some laughs, but not from Julian.

The resultant scuffle was a feeble confusion of pushing and pulling, from which Craddock was extricated by an old friend, and his drinking companion for much of the night, called Donald Bennett. Donald put Craddock protectively first into his sheepskin and then into the Gents, while tempers were cooled and a cab called.

Craddock and Donald had helped each other out in this way many times over the years. They met infrequently now, making nostalgic lurching journeys around the pubs and clubs that used to be favourites when Craddock was still a newspaperman. Donald was a football reporter, with burly good looks and an East End accent to echo the gas-lit music hall. Craddock shared his passion for soccer, and their enduring friendship was fuelled by eulogies and disputes on old heroes long-retired and scores that should have been different. The talk was balm and intoxicant, like the drink.

Frowning over the remembered little tussle with Julian, who was entitled to drink with his friends unmolested, however bad an actor, Craddock acknowledged to himself that he was lucky the incident happened where it did. He could think of no other drinking club where at three a.m. he would be so indulged. And it was not because he was popular with the management. He was not, but Donald was. Donald went home to bed now and then with Dorothy, who ran the place. She called it Michelle's and entertained her customers with exclusively French singers, taped. She attracted mostly theatre people and the staff of bars which closed before hers. She reigned over a very profitable little den. Forty years ago, when she was born, it would have been called raffish. Because of the deep drinking in the small hours and the impulsive pairing off, with inevitable taunts and jealousies, there was an undercurrent of latent violence which dark-eyed and sturdy Dorothy seemed actively to foster and at the same time quell. Craddock admired this trick, as he once told her, because it was clearly good for business. She disliked the comment. He felt she also disliked him: he was lucky, in her view, to be a friend of Donald's. She suspected Craddock, which intrigued him. Perhaps he gave her the impression of being there to watch rather then join in; that his recklessness was really mimicry. She was undoubtedly shrewd enough to make that assessment. He half-agreed with it.

His telephone rang. He was at the dining table with his second mug of tea, having eaten a ritual breakfast of brown bread with honey and an unpeeled apple, and there were two unopened letters yet to read. One was from a book club, the other, he was almost sure, his monthly laundry bill. The 'phone's ring had an extra decibel or two because it was bounced back off the tiles of the fireplace, which was his reason for keeping the instrument there. But he didn't feel quite ready for incoming calls. He had yet to decide on the best way to make use of the day; this call could impose a complication. He decided to test the caller's persistence. He picked up his tea mug and walked steadily into the hall and up the stairs to his work room. He lifted the extension receiver.

'Hullo.'

'Oh, hullo. Is that Anthony Craddock?' It was a young man's voice, light and uncertainly pitched between eagerness and diffidence.

'Yes, speaking.'

'Oh, hullo. I hope I haven't disturbed you. I was told the morning was the best time because you work mostly in the afternoon.'

'Who told you that?'

'Liz Ellison.'

'Ah.'

'My name's Peter Franklin.' Craddock did not respond. He was immediately absorbed in deciding what reason he would give for avoiding meeting the young man. 'Hullo? Are you still there, Mr Craddock?'

An anxious deference in the tone – that 'Mister Craddock' had something of the sing-song of a school classroom – caught him off-balance. 'Yes. Sure. Sure. Go on.'

'Did she mention me to you?'

'Yesterday.'

'I hope you don't mind. I didn't ask her to. She insisted. It just dropped out in conversation that I was going to try to contact you, and she said you were old friends and she'd talk to you first. I said I wasn't sure you'd like that but Liz isn't easy to stop, is she? Once she's fixed her mind on something that's it, isn't it, with Liz?'

'Yes, mate, you're right.' Craddock found himself smiling.

'So she gave me your 'phone number and said I should call you in a couple of days.'

'Right, I see.'

'What she said was, if you couldn't see me, well, if you simply didn't *want* to, you'd say so straight out when I called and not just sort of put me off so that I wouldn't really know if I ought to hang on for you, on a kind of vague half-promise, or forget about you and go for somebody else. That's if Liz spoke to you first, I mean.' Craddock noted the growing confidence. There was more than a hint of toughness now the initial fluster had gone.

'All right. Tell me what you want.'

'Well, I work for *Voice* magazine. Do you know it?'

'Seldom miss an issue.'

'Oh well, you may have seen my name then.'

'To be honest, no. I buy it for the ads.'

'Yeah, well, that probably goes for a lot of our readers.' The accent had slightly changed, loosening as Franklin gathered conversational ease. Craddock guessed at a North Country background. Redbrick university? Degree in sociology? 'Let's face it, if you set out to publish the best entertainments guide in London it's stupid to complain that's what you sell on.'

'You also have your good dirty read at the back of the book. "Hirsute male, slim, seeks bald female, plump, for loving companionship", and equally extraordinary etcetera. That must pull a few in.' Craddock was sitting at his desk now.

'Right. Do you object?'

'Not at all. It's another window on the world.'

'Peepshow, I think.'

'That's what some people say about the television news. Roll up for spilled blood and guts.'

'Well, it's a fair point. Listen, did Liz tell you what I'm doing?' Franklin's tone now was totally relaxed. He could have been a friend for years, sitting in the same room. Craddock was stirred by an odd sense of danger. He answered flatly.

'Tell me.'

'Well, I cover politics for *Voice*. I don't mean parliamentary debates and that shit. It's a lot more particularised than that. I mean, to us politics is the law on conspiracy, squatters' rights, the powers of the Special Branch . . .'

Craddock overlapped him sharply. 'I know. I do at least read the headlines. What do you want from me?'

As Franklin talked Craddock was held far more by his delivery than by what he was saying. The verve of youth was almost bullying. But the vulnerability was always there in the vocal slightness. It was a disconcerting combination, and attractive. Craddock moved the receiver a few inches away from his ear. He needed no more than the gist. He had already decided he would meet Franklin.

They agreed the following morning would suit them both. There was a scruffy little coffee bar almost directly across the road from the tube station. 'I'll be the one who isn't wearing denim,' Craddock said.

'Oh, I know what you look like. There are photographs in the files.'

'If it isn't pissing down with rain or anything nasty I wouldn't mind stretching my legs. There's a bit of a park just round the corner.'

'Fine. Thanks.'

'Cheers.'

CHAPTER THREE

Craddock was right about Franklin's Northern upbringing but was displeased that he had not been more precise: Manchester, of course. But, as Franklin consoled him, the city was a conglomerate: urban sprawl epitomised. Its accent had been diffused to the point where its possessors appeared displaced, belonging nowhere.

'Exactly,' Craddock said. 'That's the distinguishing characteristic.' In other respects Craddock's deductions on Franklin were wholly inaccurate. He was not Redbrick, but Cambridge; not a sociologist, a mathematician. Nor, as Craddock had assumed, was he working class. His father was a chest surgeon, much attached to the rewards of private practice; his mother a sculptress whose special line was children's heads, and business was brisk.

'She's terrific on Jewish kids,' Franklin said.

'Oh, well then,' said Craddock, and into his mind came an image of a long table where the diners flashed with jewellery as if electrically operated: Manchester's rag trade and bookmakers eating frantically in aid of charity. Every chomping face was suddenly a clay child, the same child with the huge meek eyes of hunger beyond pain or reclaim. Newsreel eyes. But not only those. He had seen the reality as well; had held the bodies in his arms, an unforgettable fragility. They were nightmare children who never came to him in sleep. It took some random, disconnected reference such as Franklin had just provided to bring the living-dead children back into his life. Always when he was at his most alert, so that the memory had a relentness clarity. Children the colour of clay, and the texture of dust. That unforgettable fragility.

'She says it's because they're better behaved than other kids. Keep still longer. Better discipline in the home, it's called, poor little sods.'

It seemed often the excitement of pleasurable company, especially if new, that brought back the ghost children. A mysterious association. Probably it was not an association at all, and simply an illusion. It had happened once or twice before, and now again. That was all. Why should there be significance in it? Where the starving children were had also been young people, ardent and resourceful. New and exciting to him, as was Franklin. But the faces in his head were not those of the young volunteers, until he deliberately summoned them. Then they came vividly, glistening yellow with nauseous fatigue. The ghost children made their own way to him. This time with Mrs Franklin's boldly priced sculpture. As he turned his neck to look at Franklin his muscles juddered, only partly with the cold. But he spoke blandly.

'What was wrong with mathematics? Please don't say they didn't add up to anything.'

'Christ, I wasn't going to.'

'Sorry, I can do better than that if I really make an effort.' He saw that with this heavy-handed facetiousness he had unsettled Franklin for the first time. It was a boy's face he was studying, shut sullen with resentment at being patronised. He pursued the line mischievously. 'To be a good interviewer it isn't enough just to be quick-witted with clever people. You have to learn to be patient with the stupid ones as well.' Then he added, with a fractional delay, 'Peter.'

A flush of annoyance came to the face. The brown eyes which could hold an unnerving stillness – the first point Craddock had noted when Peter walked into the coffee bar and instantly fixed on his quarry – now darted at him and away again, irresolute. He did not have the experience to know for certain when pomposity was being feigned and when it was the genuine, repellent article. Nor could he contrive to tolerate it for his own purposes. He was twenty-four. The uncombed fair hair with its curling ends and the casual clothes, which seemed too thin for the weather, gave him the unkempt look of his generation; but it was natural to him, not studied. Both hands were dug into the pockets of his cotton parka so that it was pressed closely to him. Craddock, although not thickly built, felt bulky and ponderous beside him. He had an urge to put an arm round the stiffened shoulders, to reassure and to close the gap he had intentionally opened. He realised that Peter felt so much at a disadvantage in this dislocating silence he would be unable to break it except with an angry outburst, perhaps abandoning the meeting altogether. Craddock did not want that. They continued walking on the puddled gravel path skirting the bowling green where in summer earnest women in white competed rigorously; the green was dark like seaweed now. Craddock was not easily demonstrative. He jammed his fists across his chest and under his armpits, and began again.

'Presumably you could have exploited your degree.'

'The phrase was always "put it to proper use".'

'Your parents?'

'And Uncle This and Auntie That.'

'Sounds like a family conference out of Trollope. Any wordly old clerics wheeled in?'

'Agnostic household.' A shift of tone made Craddock look at him. Peter's shy grin had no connection with the subject of the conversation. He was welcoming the end of hostilities, and acknowledging their comicality since they had sprung from something so trivial. Oddly, he looked older when his face expressed amusement. Not so oddly, Craddock decided on immediate reflection; when amused Peter felt most assured. And it was plain he did not use smiles and laughter in order to charm as he could so effectively have done, with his open face and those remarkable eyes. Liz had called him 'very straight and nice'. He certainly was not devious and if 'nice' meant 'likeable' that was without question. But still, 'very straight and nice' was far from suitably descriptive. How well would Liz know him? She would have met him at some impromptu party, gone to bed with him, perhaps just once, and he had turned out as straight and nice as Liz could wish. Craddock wanted to know a great deal more about him.

They had passed the green hut with its verandah where the earnest white summer ladies drank tea and ate buttered scones, and were on a perimeter path around a triangle of muddy grass, with a bank of flower beds and a line of cypresses muffling the traffic noise from the road on the other side of the railings which ran in a dented curve towards a gate in the furthest corner. A few yards along the street from the gate was a pub. Warm sunshine could make this place a delight to Craddock: a jumble of footballers, infants, prancing dogs, lewd adolescents, elderly couples of a different world valiantly groomed as if to its memory. Today he and Peter had the park to themselves.

Craddock asked, 'Do you like football?'

Peter shook his head, and Craddock was disappointed as he always was when he encountered indifference to the game. 'I wrote about it for a while,' he said.

'Why?'

The question came from a born inquisitor, contradicting the earlier tongue-tied helplessness. The thin monosyllable was so neatly timed and flighted. Craddock was on the point of delivering a speech from the dock: football seen as the one true expression of working class culture; its perpetual struggle against entrepreneurial corruption; its capacity to accord joy or desolation in the humdrum . . . But he thought better of it and said instead, 'Haven't you ever been to a big match? Lovely thing to describe.'

'More than once?'

Craddock allowed a joke, and laughed. But Peter was wholly serious. They reached the gate before Craddock ended the reflective lull that fell, he thought, like a half-time interval. He led the way to the pub.

'They serve food here, after a fashion,' he said.

*

Peter drank tonic water. A severe bout of hepatitis had ended a long holiday he took when he finished at university. That was more than two years ago, but the condition had lingered, reactivating itself as it notoriously could, and alcohol had been indefinitely proscribed. 'It doesn't bother me,' he said. 'I never drank much before. It took up too much time.' Craddock, sipping a bottled light ale because he was afraid anything stronger could lead only to far too much of the same, nodded in agreement. Then he said that what he remembered most about his early years as a reporter was literally the wasting of time. The waiting; for reluctant or unsuspecting interviewees to come out of meetings, courtrooms, inquests, hospital wards, to the bad news and the jostling cameras. While one waited one drank, if possible. It was the custom. He was sure he had downed at least as much alcohol in the course of journalistic duty as he had in his own chosen leisure. 'You have a reputation for benders,' Peter said.

'Is that in the files?'

Peter shook his head. No smile.

'That's a relief.' Craddock was stern with mock-gravity.

'Would you care? If I mention it in the piece I write?'

Craddock checked his immediate response, which was to say truthfully he didn't care a damn. But true as that was he felt the same stirring of danger that had come to him in his first conversation with Peter on the 'phone. Again, he did not know what caused it. 'I think I'd want to know the context,' he said. 'Do you have some particular incident you want to recount? Or were you thinking of the casual aside, say like, "Craddock, whose enthusiasms include football and boozing night into day . . ." That sort of thing?'

The brown eyes had the concentration of a cat's. 'Our lawyer wouldn't pass it,' Peter said. 'I could only do it with a direct quote from you.'

'I *know*.' Craddock took refuge in his beer to avoid delivering an irritable reproof about his knowledge of the law on libel and Peter's refusal to accept a joke for what it was. Replacing the glass on the table and looking back at Peter again he found the eyes had never left him. More matter-of-fact, he said, 'Do you want a quote on the subject? Is it relevant? I thought you were specifically examining The Box on Politics, or in my case off it.'

'It's a question of candour. If I tape an interview I want to be able to use what's on it. I can't see any point in starting if you're going to keep saying, "This bit's off the record."'

'You think I might?'

'Well, that's why I brought up the benders.' The eyes relaxed at last, glancing lazily around the pub. The fingers of one hand stroked at the hair hanging down his forehead. The touch was feline. Repose followed so smoothly on attack. Peter obviously thought it unnecessary to spell out his reasoning any further. Craddock thought otherwise.

'If I'm willing to tell all about making a fool of myself I'm not likely to hold back on less sensitive matters, like my work. Have I got that right?'

'Yes, of course.' The manner was so studiously polite that

Craddock laughed outright at the condescension.

Peter looked perplexed.

Craddock said, 'But suppose I regard my work as a much more sensitive area than the way I piss about with my spare time?'

'Why should you? You write for public consumption.'

'But that's not what you want to dig into, is it, Peter? *You* want to get your claws into my sins of omission. Don't you think my reticence could be the thing I'm most likely to be reticent about?'

'So why did you agree to meet me?'

'I felt I ought to.'

'Because of Liz?'

'No.' Both found the pause awkward and tense. 'I thought it might be fruitful.'

'How?' The voice held suspicion, but not this time an interrogator's.

'I've got a book on the stocks. It's about politics. The first time I've written any fiction on politics. I'm only at the thinking stage so far. Doodling. I've got some research to do. I thought you might come under that heading.'

'Doodling or Research?'

Craddock recognised the style immediately as his own. His first thought was of parody. But the shy grin he got from Peter refuted that. He realised with a shock that Peter had copied him spontaneously, quite without motive unless subconsciously to please. The moment had established an intimacy that neither of them regretted.

'Look, Peter,' Craddock said, 'I think your questions could be very instructive for me, because I'm sure they'll come from a political slant I'm not too familiar with. As for what kind of answers you get, you'll just have to take your chance on that. I'm evasive by nature, so it seems. But we have an intriguing situation here. If I deflect your questions they're going to dry up, which is not to my advantage. It may be I'll get a lot more out of this than you will. But that's fair, isn't it? Look how much longer I've been in the game.'

He felt his smile to be much warmer than he could remember it for a long time. Peter gave him a curt, businesslike nod.

'Are these yours, squire?' The barman, too young for his

paunch, with a red T-shirt bearing the name of the brewery across the front, was standing over them holding a plate of roast chicken, mashed potatoes and peas in each hand. He banged them down on the table, and a trickle of peas bounced against Craddock's glass.

'Delicious,' said Craddock, 'Where's the gravy?'

The barman reached into a hip pocket of his grubby jeans and to Craddock's relief produced two knives and two forks, not a jug of gravy. From the other hip pocket came salt and pepper pots. 'On the way, squire,' he said. When he came back from the bar he delivered an oozing gravy boat and watched as Peter handled it gingerly and Craddock much less so. 'Plenty of work?' The barman repossessed the jug, scratching at his fatty shoulder-blades with his free hand.

'Knee deep, Giles,' Craddock said, and Giles beamed with pleasure for him.

The pub had red wallpaper and a black ceiling, strip lighting and red chairs of metal and plastic. It was busy now: salesmen in suits; building workers with ragged winter faces; lone old women sighing; lone old men watching. Unbroken taped music of the singing-strings kind infiltrated the chatter.

Peter said, 'Obviously you're known here.'

'I find it soothing,' Craddock said. 'Like this food – homely mush. It seems to put a poultice on the nerve ends.'

'I'm surprised how well you fit,' Peter said.

'It's home ground.'

'You mean nostalgia. You left this sort of thing behind years ago, didn't you? Chilled dry sherry and smoked salmon – that's Anthony Craddock. Everyone knows.'

'Now *you* know differently. Nostalgia isn't quite right. I've told you what the pull is – the warmth of coarse, conviviality. Therapeutic. A rub down with a barmaid's apron. A snooze in the sun on Mother Kelly's doorstep.'

Peter examined the room. 'But it isn't cosy.'

'Define cosiness.' Craddock finished his food as Peter considered. 'A thatched roof in the Cotswolds? Jocose old rustics yarning in the inglenook?' Craddock got a defeated shrug from Peter, but hammered his point home. '*This* is the heart of England. Formica and chips.'

'All right. What is there to like about it?'

'Reassurance. There's a stubborn tastelessness in British life that saves us from all kinds of dangerous excursions. People who are content to take their ease in a place like this are never going to fall in line behind the Workers' Revolutionary Party or the National Front or any other gang of lunatics. Look at it – it's a fortress. The walls of indifference are unbreachable. All over the country in places exactly like this, by the thousand, our islanders are gathered in total unity of purpose – not to give a fuck about anything. We shall not be moved.'

Peter needed time to answer. He produced cigarettes and matches from a pocket of his parka which he was still wearing, apparently unaffected by the stuffy heat of the pub. Craddock's sheepskin was hanging from the back of the chair; he ran a finger round his neck and throat, finding a film of sweat under the collar of his woollen shirt. He watched Peter inhaling the cigarette smoke, feeding himself greedily with it, whereas he had picked at his food reluctantly. It occurred to Craddock now that Peter was gaunt enough to be close to clinical undernourishment.

Eventually Peter said, 'Why are you so bitter against yourself? It's negative, isn't it?'

'That's jargon,' Craddock said sharply.

'Bitter?'

'Negative.'

Peter shrugged. 'Can you give me an answer, though?'

'I'm not admitting to bitterness of any kind.'

'To me it comes over very strongly. The jokes make it worse.'

'Why worse?' Craddock snapped out the question.

Peter held his ground, the voice remaining steady even though the pale face looked further blanched. 'It's as if you're ashamed,' he said.

'Of what?'

'Well, that's what I'm asking you.'

Craddock's back had stiffened with tension. He made a visible effort at relaxation, rolling his shoulders, stretching his neck deliberately to left, then right. Looking hard back at Peter, expecting to meet the troubling stare, he was surprised to find the eyes averted, looking at nothing as the mouth drew in deeply on the cigarette. As the hand withdrew from the mouth there was a tremor of the fingers and the lips. As in the park

Craddock's impulse was to reach out to touch him. He looked ill, or frightened. Craddock asked gently, 'Are you all right?'

'What? Of course.' Peter flicked at his hair again, brushing the question aside.

Craddock searched his face, and saw it regain its composure. But it was a conscious adjustment and needed a few seconds. Craddock nodded, and then said cheerfully, 'Do you have this tape-recorder concealed about your person somewhere? Is it a spy job, in your wrist-watch?'

Peter had turned up for the meeting carrying nothing. He grinned and shook his head, the hair sliding back across his forehead. 'I was pretty sure you wouldn't want to go straight into it.'

'In spite of your softening-up technique on the 'phone.' Peter responded blankly to this, showing no understanding that he was being accused of guile, even if it was done without complaint. 'So we need another day for the formal confrontation.'

'How soon can you make it?'

'Is *Voice* giving you plenty of time for all this?'

'Well, I've done most of the interviews now. We want to run the first piece the second week of next year. I'm writing over the holiday. No use trying to interview anyone then, is there? All gone to earth.'

'No festivities of your own?'

Peter gave an abrupt jerk of the head as he stubbed out the cigarette. 'The obligatory prodigal's return to the old folks at home. If I can get away on Boxing Day I ought to avoid most of the slobbering of in-laws. How do *you* handle Christmas? Perhaps you like it.'

'It's bigger than all of us, Peter. I don't fight it.'

Peter was lighting another cigarette, and Craddock again noticed the tremor in his fingers. The hands impressed him. They were thin, like the rest of the body, but the knuckles were thick knots on them: not delicate hands, but potentially very strong and indicating a general physical force not at the moment possessed. Lost, or never sought?

Craddock asked, 'Where did you get flattened by hepatitis? I can't see you on the hippy trail to Katmandu, but I suppose you might have felt the call of duty.'

Peter laughed, head and shoulders shaking and the eyes

alight with relish. It went on long enough for Craddock to feel the need to fill in the time. He caught Giles's eye as the barman carried a precarious mess of dirty plates and glasses towards the door marked 'Private', and waved the empty light ale bottle at him. Giles shouted, 'Will do, squire, seeing it's you.'

'I'm sorry, Tony.' It was the first time Peter had addressed Craddock that way. 'You're out by an entire generation. Katmandu! Christ, that was the Sixties.' A giggle hunched his shoulders again briefly. 'And what's this "felt the call of duty"? That's the pompous sort of joke my Uncle Bertram makes. He's an income tax inspector.'

Craddock held up both hands in a gesture of unconditional apology.

But the giggles had taken Peter over, as if he had been drinking. 'Felt the call of duty . . . call of duty. Christ almighty, Tony.' He drew on the cigarette, then squeezed his mouth tightly shut, hiccuping as the smoke suppressed the giggles. Craddock was already finding this behaviour tiresomely childish. He was relieved when Giles appeared with his bottle.

'Do you want another tonic water?' Craddock found himself talking with the effort-laden patience adults use on children when they are determined not to show exasperation. Peter instantly upstaged him by asking Giles with authoritative politeness, 'Do you serve coffee?'

Giles nodded, noisily scraping the few leftovers on Craddock's plate on top of the congealed meal on Peter's. He said breezily to Craddock, 'Funny mate for you, squire.' Then he waggled his drooping bottom with, 'He might like the upstairs room better – evenings only, ladies welcome Monday when we can do with the extra trade. *Very* quiet, Mondays.' He gave Peter a look of exaggerated haughtiness from above the lifted plates. 'No drag,' he said, and spun away with a flutter of eyelids. Craddock called after him, 'Coffee, Giles.'

Peter's voice had an edge of distaste. 'I like it black,' he said to Craddock.

'It'll come black with synthetic cream in a little plastic bag and a teaspoonful of sugar in another one. What else would you expect?' Peter was unresponsive, pressing his cigarette to the slit lips. Craddock was surprised at the effect Giles had produced; but then he was used to Giles. 'He's quite harmless,' he said. 'All he wants is a laugh. He thinks he might get one from a customer he hasn't seen before.'

Peter dismissed Giles and his needs with a quick lift of the shoulders. 'Boring,' he said. Then immediately after a pull at the cigarette: 'Italy. The hepatitis. Salerno was where it hit me, but it probably didn't originate there. I'd been on the move for a good three months then.'

'On your own?' Craddock did not know why that should be the first question to come to mind.

'Yes. I started off doing three weeks' tutoring in Lyons. Two kids who'd got lousy marks in their English exam. Daddy thought a crash course in the school holidays would do the trick, and it seemed a good way of getting a bit of extra loot to finance the grand tour. They were a nasty little pair. Still, they couldn't be expected to take much to *me*, since I was playing gaoler. I was supposed to do a month, but it all came to a dead stop when I smacked one of them in the mouth. Mummy was appalled.'

Craddock said, 'I bet. Did you draw blood?' He was looking at the hands, fascinated again by the prominent knuckles.

'A bit.'

Giles brought the coffee, with the sachets of cream and sugar, and gave a wriggle of the plump torso as he produced a plastic spoon from a hip pocket and placed it in the saucer, extending his little finger. This time Peter managed a tolerant smile. 'Well, at last,' said Giles. Craddock handed him a five-pound note and said, 'Take everything out of that and have a drink.' Giles said, 'Squire, you're so kind.'

'He's bad at it, that's the trouble,' Peter said.

'I know, but never mind. He believes in working for his tips – like calling himself Giles – part of the act.'

'Is there an upstairs bar?'

'Yes, Giles runs it. Puts his red velvet trousers on and plays Judy Garland tapes.'

'Jesus.'

'Were there any repercussions after you thumped this child? Lucky you weren't charged with assault.'

'Actually, I think his father thought I should have used a chair. No, we agreed mistakes had been made on all sides and I was let off with a caution.' He was lighting another cigarette. 'At least I'd found out I'd never make any kind of teacher.'

'Oh, I don't know,' Craddock said. 'In this country teachers are still licensed for violence.'

Peter shook his head in some agitation. 'I just don't have the patience. Hopeless.'

'Had you thought about it as a career?'

'At one stage. No great interest in it. I was just certain I didn't want the business world. Casting around for alternatives. I hate the word "career".'

'Class word. Miners, engine-drivers, bricklayers – they don't have careers, they just go to work.'

'That isn't my point. "Security of employment" is the working class version of "career". They both give me the creeps. They mean treadmill.'

'At the last count we had about a million and a half unemployed wanting to get on it.'

'Yes, sure.'

Giles brought Craddock's change. 'All the best to you, and yours,' he said and rolled back to the bar snapping his fingers castanet-style.

Craddock asked Peter, 'Were you very ill?'

'Death's door, it felt like. But I'm told it always does.'

'How did you get home?'

'Dad.'

'And you're sure you're okay now?'

'Of course. Don't I look it?'

'I think you can expect a lecture on food and nicotine when mum and dad see you.'

'Boring.' Again the irked lift of the shoulders.

The little exchange left Craddock feeling uneasily avuncular. He noted again that the distance of twenty-five years between their ages could close, gape and close in an instant, and not always at the summoning of either of them. His glass was still half-full, but he decided not to finish it. Peter was right about his liking for chilled dry sherry. Why was he punishing himself with warm light ale?

*

A light sleet gusted round them like showers of drawing-pins as they walked from the pub, quickening their pace inasmuch as Craddock was ever prepared to be hurried. His tendency in most kinds of unpleasantness was to cover up like a boxer backed into a corner and let the attack exhaust itself. So he plodded along huddled into his sheepskin up to his nose, while Peter loped with a stiff angularity shaking his wet hair as it persistently fringed his eyes. The sleet discouraged talk.

They went the short way, keeping to the main street. Arrived at the tube station they stood under cover to decide when they would next meet, and where.

'My house seems the best, doesn't it?' Craddock got one of Peter's curt nods, and with it a wet splatter in the face from the tangled hair. 'It's quiet. When's best for you?'

Peter said, 'The only complication for me is Lord Llewellyn. I'm waiting for him to give me an answer on when he'll see me. I hope there'll be a message at the office when I get back.'

'Royston Llewellyn?' Craddock wiped his wet face with the back of his hand.

'Is there more than one Lord Llewellyn? I mean the one at the Home Office.'

After a pause Craddock said, 'You'd better 'phone me in the morning. Say ten on the dot.' Another nod from Peter sprinkled him again.

CHAPTER FOUR

Nineteen forty-nine, and summer. A copper sunset, after a day of gold heat. A cornfield, with the fondling warmth of bed. Disjointed whimpering, and thrusting of loins. The uneven ground mitigated the difficulties of the novice.

Llewellyn had worn his subaltern's uniform because girls were susceptible to it, he said. Craddock wore his civvies because a corporal and a second-lieutenant couldn't have a night out together in khaki; and in any case Craddock took every opportunity to avoid wearing uniform, disliking the way it positioned him in the world without his agreement. In uniform he ceased to be himself and became this serge-covered functionary called 'Corporal'.

Llewellyn had been proved right. The village had yielded up treasure, one girl auburn and freckled, one blonde and fat-lipped, and both eager with summer. And curiosity. They had been sitting on the parapet of a humped-back bridge over a stream boiled to sediment, dandelion and dock rearing in it like miniature trees. Dirndl skirts and daring blouses, bright lipstick, creamy country limbs: 'There's the King's Head and the Wheatsheaf. But if you walk across the fields there's ever such a nice pub in Little Wickham. Isn't there, Rita?' Rita was the blonde, gleaming with smiles. This smile said that Beryl and she preferred Little Wickham because there was less chance of encountering most of the men and youths of their own village there. The King's Head and the Wheatsheaf presented every chance. Llewellyn asked in his assumed officer's voice if the girls would like to show him and his friend the way to Little Wickham. 'Oh well, we're waiting for our boyfriends really,' said Beryl. 'Aren't we, Rita?' And Rita's smile said perhaps they were and perhaps they weren't. 'But they're ever so late. Aren't they, Rita? That's the trouble with farm work. It's never finished. Somehow I don't think they'll be coming now. Do you, Rita?' Rita clearly thought it most unlikely on careful consultation with the lowering sun and the little heart-shaped pendant she toyed with at her throat. Llewellyn said that his friend and he would be terribly grateful if the girls would show them to Little Wickham because now he came to think of it he'd heard it was one of the prettiest villages in Worcestershire. 'Oh, it's a lovely walk. You don't have to go near a road, if you don't want to. Do you, Rita?' Rita let them know there was rural seclusion every step of the way. 'I think we've got time.' That was really jolly nice of them, said Llewellyn.

So now here they were, furrowing the harvest in two plunging embraces. Separated by a wedge of corn stalks the two couples were invisible to each other but audible, as if in adjoining rooms. The pairing had seemed natural: Llewellyn and the redhead, reciprocally provocative in their self-assertion; Craddock and the blonde denied option. For Craddock this first time was a bewildering confusion of alarm and desire, and he succeeded more by will than through pleasure. The girl recognised his ignorance from the first touch, and she was ingeniously tender. But he needed more help than she could give. He found it in a tangle of images: Llewellyn's sturdy legs pumping out those strange trilling gasps from Beryl; two soldiers, naked on adjacent beds, contesting the quicker ejaculation; Llewellyn's face, sunburnt and flopping with hair the colour of Rita's, suspended with a grin of triumph above his own as they wrestled when much younger; and merging with all these the puzzled but insistent smile of the girl pressed beneath him as their heads dipped and rose and twisted to, at last, a primal rhythm.

Afterwards as clothes were replaced and skin lost its flush Rita became talkative in a troubled mixture of kindness and resentment. She kept her voice low so that Llewellyn and Beryl, still entwined with sighs and soft laughter, would not overhear. 'If you didn't want to, you should have said. Just because your friend thinks he's God's gift to women that doesn't mean you've got to force yourself. You hurt me. And you meant to. I know you did when you knew you could. If you're bashful that's nothing. It's natural with some people. We're not all the same. I thought that was all it was at first, or else I wouldn't have let you. You're funny. Are you older than your friend?' He was not. Each was nineteen. He said he was sorry he'd hurt her, and she rounded on him. 'I can just hear you boasting about it.' It was a misunderstanding of his nature, the first she had shown. Although he did not speak she saw her first mistake in the withdrawn questioning in his face. 'You *are* funny. Are you very clever?' Walking back to the village with the girls he felt much more at ease with Rita. Overwhelmed by Beryl's bold chatter, as she entertained them with ribald comments on the life of the village – a chain of sexual impropriety without a missing link between vicar and idiot – Rita was mute with smiles again. But she was no longer a dumb blonde, and there was warmth in the goodnight kiss. 'Remember what I said. You just be yourself. I think you could be nice really.'

On their way back to the house outside the village where they were staying Llewellyn wrapped an arm round Craddock's shoulders, laughing as he begged for support and they zigzagged along the lane. Llewellyn pretended his knees had turned to jelly with exhaustion. 'Told you! Told you! Trust your Uncle Royston. You're got to let 'em know straight off you want it. That's half the battle. Oh, my aching prick.' Craddock did not resist the weight. He knew Llewellyn would soon tire of the game.

*

They were attending a week-long course on the subject of 'The Press and The Public', in a Victorian mansion which had been converted for use as a residential centre for adult studies. The two of them were the only National Servicemen among the score of students. The others were mostly much older: teachers; trade union shop stewards; unattached women who apparently spent all their holidays furthering their knowledge of the world at such courses; and a husband-and-wife pair of town councillors who fought with each other for the floor at discussion periods and thereby all but monopolised them in spite of piercing attempts at interruption from the unattached women. There were also two girls of about the same age as Craddock and Llewellyn, university students and close friends: so obviously too close, Llewellyn had quickly observed, to be worth a man's attention. Lecturers, half of them academics and half journalists, talked about the history of popular newspaper development, the influence of advertising, the role of the political commentator, the value (if any?) of literary and arts reviewing, and the slanting of reportage. The rooms were large, the furniture comfortable, the gardens sumptuous, the food substantial. The week was, as Llewellyn had promised Craddock in the language of army conscripts, 'a bloody good skive'.

They were stationed in different infantry training camps a hundred miles apart. Llewellyn had spotted the announcement of the course almost buried among a listing of more military affairs – such as a request for volunteers to be guinea pigs at a chemical warfare establishment – and had written to Craddock alerting him to the opportunity. It seemed that the army was required by meddling parliamentarians of the time to show more concern for the educational and cultural needs of its personnel. Unit commanders the length and breadth of the country were invited to send suitable men of any rank to a variety of courses organised by extramural departments of universities, local education authorities and philanthropic institutions. Furthurmore, as Llewellyn discovered and impressed upon Craddock with triple underlining in his letter, attending these courses would not be at the expense of the serviceman's entitlement to normal leave. Llewellyn had surmised correctly that commanding officers generally were unlikely to publicise these courses with much of a flourish; hence the obscurity of the notice on 'The Press and the Public', which amounted almost to concealment, as for that matter did the subdued appeal for men to be gassed, depletion of forces being unpopular whatever the reason. To his amazement Llewellyn found skives available on contemporary poets, ornithology, the poster as art, radio drama, the American war of independence, breeding cattle by artifical insemination, locust control . . . His company commander asked him icily to stop inciting his fellow-conscript platoon commanders to develop burning interests in one or other of these arcane issues. He reminded Llewellyn of the word 'suitable' in the reference to prospective students, and warned Llewellyn that any frivolous application might incur the penalty of extra nights as duty officer. Llewellyn, he added, might be the son of a prominent Labour Party rabble-rouser in his home town, and Second Lieutenant Llewellyn was no doubt the hero of sixth-form dissent at his grammer school; but none of that clever-clever nonsense had any place in the regiment on which, in the old days of a *proper* British army, no snivelling grammar school product would ever have been foisted at commissioned rank.

It was the company commander's error to deliver this diatribe in the officers' mess when the worse for drink and in the hearing of several brother officers both senior and junior to him. The company commander was not an imposing figure, being of slight build with drooping shoulders and thin sandy hair. He carried a walking stick too long for him. He was known to have had 'a bad war', which was to say he had seen action and been adversely affected by it without physical injury. The word 'nerves' was spoken with expressive avoidance of further explanation. Some other officers of his own age, and a few of Llewellyn's, undoubtedly shared his regret at the intrusion of the grammar school into their territory, but to talk about class was itself *déclassé* and as regrettable to them as Llewellyn's political father. In fact they resented this introduction of the senior Llewellyn into their midst, by the drunken company commander, far more than they did young Llewellyn who had so far had the decency to keep his mouth shut on the question of his erring parent's activities. Looking at Llewellyn, fair and scrubbed and wholesome, they felt he had overcome his unfortunate background admirably. 'Looks the part, young Llewellyn,' they agreed.

As much could not be said for his company commander, although this verdict had to be agreed silently. Llewellyn had withstood the assault with wordless dignity, so the mess observed. Had the onlookers been standing in the company commander's shoes they would have seen the contempt flickering in Llewellyn's face which had opportunistically turned an intended quiet reprimand, well merited, into a sick man's shrill rage.

Llewellyn followed the seizing of one chance with another. His company commander went officially sick three days later, surprising no one considering his intake of brandy. Llewellyn then contrived to slip into his in-tray, half-way down the pile of papers awaiting attention, his official application for permission to attend the course on 'The Press and The Public'. He dated his application five days previously. (It was, of course, unbreakable army procedure that such matters should initially be submitted to one's immediate superior and not directly to the unit commander.) The senior subaltern deputising for the stricken officer duly came to Llewellyn's letter. This was a great embarrassment to him, since its date was at the least damning evidence of the company commander's dilatoriness; worse, it possibly revealed the man's actual deceit. Llewellyn had put forward a thoroughly sound case for attending the course on the grounds that his chosen career, after completing National Service, was journalism. Further, he offered to supply letters from the editors of two provincial newspapers both promising sympathetic consideration regarding employment when he became available. There had been no hint of this in the company commander's near-hysterical outburst in the mess, or in any of his subsequent grumbling about Llewellyn's 'provocation'. Llewellyn's stoical silence throughout the incident showed an observance of regimental fealty that was deeply impressive. It now fell to the senior subaltern, a career soldier from public school and Sandhurst, to lay the facts before the commanding officer. And the facts were that a young subaltern from whom so little could be expected – day school townie, Bolshie father, the derided conscript officers' training unit – had behaved impeccably in the face of his superior's . . . neglect, vindictiveness? The senior subaltern, who was aged twenty-one and carried his years gravely, ceased to be embarrassed and became appalled. Llewellyn expected him to be. It was the first duty of men like himself, Llewellyn had often heard him say, to show 'these people', with which term he encompassed the lower orders from where all non-commissioned ranks and townie subalterns came, 'what's right'. Llewellyn had been wronged. The senior subaltern told Llewellyn that his application had now been submitted and thanked him for being 'so sporting' without elaborating on what. Llewellyn replied. 'Not at all, sir.' The senior subaltern, blushing in the company commander's chair, replied, 'Well done, Roy. Carry on.'

The commanding officer, meeting him in the mess that evening, said genially, 'Journalist, eh? Wouldn't surprise me if you change your mind about that. Army suits you. Well done, Roy. Carry on.'

*

Llewellyn had recounted the story of his victorious campaign as he and Craddock lazed in a succulent corner of the gardens on their first evening of the course.

Craddock said, 'Have you definitely decided to be a journalist? I thought you were still thinking about university first – the economics degree.'

'I am.'

'Which editors did you write to?'

'None. The letters don't exist. Pure invention.'

'Taking a bit of a risk, weren't you? Suppose you'd been asked to produce them?'

'Don't be absurd. I'm a gentleman. One of *their* gentlemen, now. We don't make things up like that. We don't have the brains, to begin with.'

'Haven't they even asked you about these fictitious newspapers, just in passing conversation?'

'Matey, they're not remotely interested. The civilian worlds' simply not part of their lives. That's the point – how I put one over on them. I'm *in*.'

Craddock nodded, looking up at the wispy blue sky. The moment he had met Llewellyn at lunch in the pannelled dining room that day he had noticed how much the voice had altered. It was not merely a case of a more polished accent; Llewellyn had never had more than a hint of the whining vowels of the Midlands town where both had been born and brought up. That had now gone without trace and the voice had taken on an overlay of command. It was the sound of English privilege, assumed but also convincingly assuming. The other students had clearly seen no counterfeit in it, and it did not change now that Craddock was alone with him. It was the new Llewellyn. But also, in his audacity and instant resource, it was plainly still the old one who had charmed teachers out of indignation and led the classroom teasing of another into tearful flight down the corridor. The man was a testy arthritic whose increasing pain eventually snared him in a muddle of self-repetition. Llewellyn had pounced with a dimpling smile. The reflex action of angry denial left the man at the mercy of the class. Of course, they gave him none. At the inquisition Llewellyn had been eloquent with concern, especially eloquent with reluctance to blow the gaff to the headmaster on a member of staff: 'We're all very upset about it, sir . . . We were trying to help . . . It had happened before and we were getting behind with our work and . . . We wondered whether we ought to say something to one of the other masters, but it didn't seem . . .' The arthritic teacher did not return.

Craddock was reminded of this epic contest as he pondered Llewellyn's humiliation of his company commander, who appeared to be another kind of half-cripple. This thought gave Craddock no pang of disapproval. Both sufferers were fair game, being oppressors of the young. Craddock had detested school once he had entered adolesence, mostly because, being compulsory, its life was necessarily ruled by rules. The army had now imposed the same form of imprisonment on him two years after he had escaped from the first. For Llewellyn, who had stayed at school until eighteen, the army was obviously less irksome. He had made a sideways step from one hierarchy to another and into much the same position. As a subaltern he had roughly the status and function of a senior school prefect. By requirement, and consent, he was still playing the role of promising boy. Paradoxically, though, he had acquired this command of a worldly man. Craddock had been earning his living for two years as a junior reporter, yet felt his immaturity beside Llewellyn. He had accepted it as a schoolboy. Now it was troubling. He wanted to smudge the other's gloss, repair an imbalance.

He said, 'This company commander, Roy . . .'

'Gillies, Captain Stanley Gillies. He'll never make Major.'

The remark momentarily disconcerted Craddock. It had such a ring of soldier-to-soldier that it removed Llewellyn from him. Craddock was entirely indifferent to anyone's prospects for military promotion, and the nearest he ever got to a discussion of the subject was when he overheard one among other N.C.O.s. Usually they were Regulars or National Servicemen thinking of signing on for more. Craddock's friends were not of that kind.

'Is he stupid?' Craddock asked.

'Weak. Quite out of his depth.'

'What? As a company commander in a basic training camp? A scoutmaster could do it.' Craddock was incredulous. He was the clerk in a basic training company and knew its wearying routines all too well.

'Gillies is one of life's mice.'

That was more like the Llewellyn Craddock knew, the malice so lightly delivered it sliced the victim without leaving a mark. Craddock said, 'If you'd put your application in to Gillies, quite straightforwardly in the first place, what would have happened?'

'I'm sure he'd have sent it up to the C.O. without any argument. But I couldn't resist the chance of a bit of fun. Half the junior officers queuing up for these daft courses – throwing the place into confusion. Smashing idea. Gillies called it subversive. Very silly of him.'

'Not a military man's word, "subversive".'

'Quite. Can't have that sort of talk. Sounds as if the chap reads books.'

'Did any of the other subalterns actually put in applications?'

'No. They were still arguing about who should claim what. That's how Gillies got to know about it. He's always creeping about, listening in – sure sign of basic insecurity. He hadn't got the sense to realise it would never get past the jolly jape stage, as far as the others were concerned.'

'Didn't *you* realise it?'

'Do I detect a note of suspicion?' Llewellyn sat up, comfortably cross-legged, his tone full of mock-hurt. 'Are you doubting the truth of my story?'

Craddock stayed put, feeling he was gaining ground. He said, 'If you expected the others to back out you must have known you were sabotaging your own plans by spreading the word.'

'And *there*, matey, is the difference between you and me.' Llewellyn was irresistible in his tolerance. 'I wanted a lark. I knew I was bound to stir up *something*. That was the only plan there was.'

In the pause that followed, Craddock's memory found Llewellyn as a child leaping into a snowdrift in a farm ditch just to see how deep it was. The soft snow had closed over his head.

Between laughs Craddock said, 'Well done, Roy. Carry on.'

Llewellyn stiffened his features and saluted. As his hand dropped Craddock asked him quietly, 'Did *you* tell this Gillies man about your father and all that stuff about school?'

'He had me round for Sunday lunch a couple of times. *En famille*. Scraggy wife and two little girls who kept bursting into tears. One would expect Gillies' issue to behave like that, I suppose.'

Craddock found this new information more intriguing than he cared to show for the moment. Casually he said, 'Twice?'

'I think he regarded me as an interesting specimen. He's the sort of man who goes through your documents very carefully. Peculiar, that. Furtive. *Not* regimental. Does your company commander read up Personnel Selection files?'

'Never been known. He comes and asks me, if he needs to know anything.'

Llewellyn nodded vehemently. 'Gillies snoops. He'd obviously seen the bit about "Father's Occupation" and given it a lot of thought. So I gave him the full works. Yes, the old man lectured in politics and economics at Birmingham and did a lot of extra hours for the Workers' Educational Association, *and* he was the local ward chairman for the Labour Party. Yes, he *had* been brought up in some squalid row of terrace houses without a bath and the shit house in the back yard, and yes he had *improved himself* but no he had *not* therefore changed his views to agree with all straight-thinking men that life was a question of the survival of the fittest. I ask you, from a pathetic little runt like Gillies – the survival of the fittest! I nearly puked trying not to laugh.'

'Presumably he wanted to know if you're following in father's footsteps.'

'Of course. I told him I'd made a modest start by recruiting for the Young Socialists at school. He was thrilled to bits. Yelled out to his wife – she was draining the cabbage or something and he obviously felt he needed someone to share the fun. "Mabel, come and listen to this. We've got an agitator in the house!" You made a big mistake, Tony – you should have had a real go at getting a commission. It's a laugh a minute.'

'They don't take working men. Schoolboys only.' Craddock could not resist the jibe, but he continued quickly not wanting to disturb Llewellyn's mood. 'Was it like that both times you went to lunch?'

Llewellyn's mood changed in spite of Craddock's precaution. 'No. Second time he was . . .' He stood up, stretching his arms high and yawning.

'What?'

'Oh, he got a bit creepy. Put on a lot of old gramophone records. Jazz from before the war.' Llewellyn was looking about him, restless.

'Sounds friendly.'

'Yes, he was playing at being one of the boys. Talking about when *he* was at school, and some master he got on man-to-man terms with, and how an older chap could be a useful friend if a *younger* chap found the going a bit rough. It was like one of those sickly novels of public school life. I really thought he was going to give me a squeeze on the knee. *Very* creepy.'

'Was his wife there then?'

'Oh yes. In and out of the kitchen, where she'd top herself up with port and lemon. The kids were out playing somewhere by this stage and he kept shouting after her, "Tarts drink that." Then we'd wink at me and say, "Thinks we don't know, old boy." He was falling about with brandy, of course.' Llewellyn's voice had taken on a rasp. Now he affected a different hardness, mimicking the rough accent of home. 'Bourgeois degeneracy, lad. The seeds of their own destruction.'

They heard the sound of the supper gong coming from the house and set off towards it, their movements activating the heavy scents of the shrubs. After a year of the barracks, where sights and sounds were aggressively harsh in order to intimidate, Craddock found it difficult to adjust to all this drowsy boskage. In the barracks he had secured an animal wariness, keeping in the shadows of what he had recognised on first view as a hostile world. And in that way he had come to terms with it, suffering surprisingly little damage. He had even discovered a surreptitious resource – had been called 'a cunning bastard' and felt gratified – that won him a certain degree of power. But here, where he wanted a different alertness, he was having to fight to clear his head. One particular question nagged muzzilly and had to be answered.

'Hey, listen, Roy.' Llewellyn was walking ten yards in front, at ease in the balm. He turned and waited for Craddock to catch up, standing with his hands stuffed deep in his trouser pockets and his head lifted with a tilt to one side. It was a characteristic stance, mixing challenge with caprice.

'Yes, matey. You sound anxious.'

'No. Just want to clear a point. Getting on the course – you wouldn't have cared if you'd had to drop it. It was only because Gillies went sick . . .'

Llewellyn shrugged. 'Yes, like I said.'

'But you'd already written to me, saying let's meet up.'

Llewellyn's grin was not an adequate answer.

'It was your idea, Roy. Had you forgotten that?'

'Of course I hadn't. I always hoped I'd make it. But I knew you'd jump at the chance of a week like this. You didn't need *me* here.' He turned and started again towards the house unhurriedly. As Craddock's head thrummed with objections Llewellyn changed the course of the exchange without showing he realised he had. 'How did you swing it, by the way?'

Craddock found himself answering mechanically with the conscript's boast. 'Dead easy.' Then he explained with acid glee, 'My company sergeant major's barely literate. Among the duties I've acquired is a highly-charged correspondence between him and his mistress. I type his love letters for him and then he copies them out in his own fat hand. Let's say it's understood I deserve the odd favour for keeping quiet about exactly where, when and how he gets his leg over without the wife finding out.'

Llewellyn's laughter bellowed among the blooms. Craddock recognised exaggeration in it – a gesture from Llewellyn towards making amends. The guffaws expended, Llewellyn's thinking took a natural direction. 'On the "leg over" front, matey,' he said with a deepening tone, 'we ought to find something juicy in the village.'

And they did.

CHAPTER FIVE

Craddock's office was the lightest room in the house. Normally it would have been the front bedroom. He had replaced the original sash windows with double-glazed ones, the most expensive improvement he had made to the house. Books, piles of his play scripts and more of old magazines filled the tall shelving against most of the wall space and helped to muffle external noise. His desk was in fact an oak table four feet square with no drawers to get in his way when he wanted to stretch his legs. There were two armchairs on either side of a smaller table which was always heaped with scribbling pads and more old scripts whose backs he also used as note-pads. Some of these notes referred to work he had finished as much as three years before. He retained an old reporter's habit of hoarding notes, and in one corner of the room there was a stack of four cardboard boxes crammed with yet more pads and books carrying the hurried shorthand and cryptic half-sentences of ancient interviews. Mrs Readhead dusted round all this stuff without disturbing it. She opened up the boxes from time to time for inspection because vermin liked old papers, she said, 'And you never know, they say even in Buckingham Palace . . .'

Peter was sitting in one of the armchairs when he fainted.

He was hunched forward on the edge of the seat, elbows on his knees, waiting for Craddock to answer a question when a flinch gripped his face and held it. Craddock was immediately reminded of the look of sickness or fear he had noticed four days earlier in the pub. This time there was no point in asking whether Peter was all right. He half-slid, half-fell of the chair to a crouching position on the floor.

Weakly he said, 'Oh, Christ.'

Craddock was sitting at his desk. He got up, aware that he was not surprised by what had happened. He lifted Peter under the armpits and put him in the chair so that his head rested against the back. There were tears blurring his eyes as he looked at Craddock. Then he passed out cold.

Or rather hot, as Craddock found when he put his hands to Peter's face, cupping it while he considered what to do next.

His mind flickered with half-remembered instructions on first aid. The patient should not be moved. Make the patient comfortable. The patient's head should be placed on one side in case of vomiting. On no account try to force the patient to take liquids . . . All of this seemed to refer irrelevantly to street accidents or sea rescues. Dial 999? Again, a hurtling ambulance, a stretcher teetering down the stairs, hospital, drip tubes . . . He could connect none of that with the figure in the armchair in his office.

He knelt beside Peter, keeping one hand on the damp face to support it, and studied him. He saw a feverish child and acted accordingly.

*

'Chadbon,' said the doctor, striding in with the irrefutable black briefcase, the moment Craddock opened the front door. 'Upstairs? Which room? Awake?'

'First right. Door's ajar. Wasn't a minute ago.' Craddock caught the doctor's tone unwittingly, which is the effect of doctors on those unused to them. He followed up the stairs and hovered by the bedroom door now wide open.

'Been sick?'

'No.'

'Come in. Your house.'

It was also Craddock's bedroom. Peter lay in the double bed undressed down to his briefs but wearing Craddock's dressing gown. He was lying flat on his back, dressing gown and bedclothes parted so that Dr Chadbon could go over his chest and stomach with hands and stethoscope. Peter was awake but groggily dismayed and uncommunicative, as he had been off and on throughout the five hours he had lain there.

Dr Chadbon grunted repeatedly – going up and down the scale. 'Mmm, mmm, mmm-mmm, mmm-mmm-mmm.' Then he said, 'Skin and bone, this boy. What d'you feed him on? Bird seed?'

Craddock tried to summon a succinct answer. But of course

there wasn't one. To begin with, the question was rhetorical and explicated a whole bundle of assumptions on the doctor's part. These were entirely reasonable, but correcting them was a daunting task given the circumstances and the telegraphic language required.

Craddock had 'phoned his doctor's surgery as soon as he had put Peter into bed. He had carried him, which confirmed his suspicion that the boy was seriously underweight. The bared figure was short of flesh to the point of emaciation. This distressed Craddock but also justified to him the initial mildness of his anxiety. He was not fool enough to pretend any medical expertise, but he had seen Peter's condition in other places and other times. Craddock seldom saw his doctor, who was a man in his seventies called Fazackerley. 'My name's Craddock, twenty-seven Parton Street. I've got quite a worrying problem here. Could the doctor call . . .?' He was stopped sharply by a woman's voice which said, 'Requests for doctor's home visits should be made before ten a.m.' In the accelerating give-and-take that followed, Craddock suggested it couldn't be the first time Dr Fazackerley had been asked to call on someone inconveniently taken ill *after* ten a.m. He was told he ought to know Dr Fazackerley *always* took a month's holiday during the Christmas period – and who earned it more in this whole wide world than *he* did? The implication seemed to Craddock to be that anyone without that knowledge of the doctor's habits deserved to stew in their own endangered juices. On the contrary, he was advised, the practice was in the best possible hands of Dr Fazackerley's locum who was rushed off his feet with all this 'flu about . . . And so on, absurdly, but somehow the conversation established the fact of sudden sickness in the Craddock household and the assurance that medical duty would be done.

So here was Dr Chadbon, short and stocky with grey curls and the fists of a navvy, who appeared rushed off his feet by his own momentum whether or not by calls for help. Two strangers were at cross purposes which Craddock could see no point in straightening, if it meant diverting the other from his job.

Peter was now face down. One red-rimmed eye peered unfocussed through the tumble of hair.

'Eighteen? Nineteen?'

'Twenty-four.'
'Mmm. Mmm-mmm. Just keel over?'
'About quarter-past-eleven.'
'Stay right out? Long?'
'Comes and goes.'
'Notice coming on? Last few days?'
'Very tired. Suddenly.'
'Then shake if off? No fuss, me fine?'
'Yes'
'Mmm-mmm-mmm.'

The doctor turned Peter over on his back again. His fingers explored neck, armpits and groin. It was the second time, Craddock noted. Then the doctor resettled the dressing gown and bedclothes around him and stood with his fists on his hips staring down at the dejected face. Peter's lips parted in a trembling attempt at a grin. There had been several during the afternoon but this was the first since the doctor's appearance. Craddock thought this one contained more apology than the others which had mostly reiterated fear. Craddock smiled back, but Peter's eyes had already closed again.

'Wash my hands?'
'Facing top of stairs.'

*

The doctor's staccato, as he stood at the front door with one hand on the Yale, did not prevent him from getting across a good deal of useful information with a minimum cross-examining of Craddock. It was his experience that severe hepatitis scared some people so much that they developed an aversion to food. This was neurotic or, if a less sympathetic term was preferred, bloody silly. But then some people were terrified of crossing footbridges over railway lines. Human ailment was of limitless variety. Phobic fear was in most cases intermittent. It looked as if this unhappy young man had lately been struggling through a tough patch of it. Anyone who refused food long enough would fall down in due course, as his common sense would tell him. Since he knew he was courting danger he was likely to be highly strung-up, which would make him less able to act sensibly. Empty stomach, plus cold winter's day, plus rising anxiety . . . Timber! As to the moment of collapse, it could occur simply when the body decided enough was enough or it might be precipitated by some immediate emotional alarm. The possible complication upstairs was an attack of glandular fever, whose favourite targets were youngsters, principal effect exhaustion and most tell-tale symptoms high temperature and swelling at the points Craddock had noticed Dr Chadbon testing with exemplary care.

'But don't think so,' the doctor said. 'No lumps, Time yet, though . . .'

As Craddock walked back to the stairs he reflected that Dr Chadbon would almost certainly reward closer acquaintance for professional purposes: Craddock's. The doctor suggested itinerant years in distant rough places. Sea-going? Oil fields? Gold mines? Something of the sort. It showed in the skin colouring, a mottled rust suburban England had yet to remove and might never. And that peremptory manner was not eccentric. It surely had more to do with an enforced habit of reducing language to its most simplified forms. Several languages, probably. Yes, interesting man. Another couple of pages of notes would presently be added to the pile on the smaller table in Craddock's office.

The most worrying question in Craddock's mind was why Peter had been unable, or unwilling, to speak since the collapse even though he was conscious from time to time.

Dr Chadbon had replied, 'You ever fainted?'

'No.'

'Shock. Humiliating. Too much for some. Big boys don't cry. Same thing. Needs a hug. Kiss it better. Mother? Girlfriend?'

'Not here.'

'You then. Your boy.'

Craddock knew he ought to have explained the truth of the circumstances at that stage. But the prospect seemed even more daunting than before, proceedings having advanced so naturally. By supplying all the answers Dr Chadbon needed he had reinforced an innocent misrepresentation. Retracting it would inevitably lead to questions he could *not* answer: he had no idea where Peter lived and did not even have a telephone number. Did Peter have a doctor? If so Chadbon would need to refer the case. They would have to go back to Peter and try to elicit . . . It really did not seem to matter. And even as these thoughts rushed through Craddock's mind Dr Chadbon was talking about glandular fever which clearly mattered very much.

So now Craddock stood beside the prone figure in his bed, waiting for the eyes to reopen. When they did he said loudly, with an edge of anger that came without bidding, 'What you've done is literally to frighten yourself sick.'

Then he sat down on the bed. He moved the sheet and blankets so that he could get his arms fully round Peter's body and lifted him, not gently because they were too awkwardly placed for that. He was aware that if Peter had not made an effort to help the embrace would not have been possible. The bony body shook with its sobs. Among them Peter's voice raged, and was abject. 'Sorry . . . Oh, fuck it . . . Sorry . . .'

The living-dead children with huge stupefied eyes came crowding into Craddock's head, and this time there was no mystery in their arrival.

CHAPTER SIX

Craddock's alarm clock woke him, at seven-thirty the next morning. Normally he got up a full hour later, but he had Peter to think about. When he had gone to sleep he had been asking himself over and over what should be done. The only reply that made any sense was, wait and see.

He was in the spare bedroom, so small it was almost filled by the single bed. When he had carried Peter from his office he had gone first to this tiny room, where Mrs Readhead maintained a spotless reception for any visitor who might turn up: linen without a wrinkle; a towel neatly folded at the foot of the bed; the glass of the pine-framed wall mirror without a blemish. But unoccupied for several weeks – Donald Bennett had last slumbered here, stunned in the small hours on Craddock's brandy – the room had the frostiness of a cell. So Peter went into Craddock's bed and Craddock remembered to turn on the radiator in the spare room soon after Dr Chadbon left.

It was cosy now. He could reach open the curtains at the narrow window without needing to sit upright. There was a grey unpromising light, which gave him a spasm of disappointment followed by an irritable reminder to himself that nothing else could be expected at seven-thirty a.m. in Parton Street on December the twentieth. He switched on the reading lamp which stood on top of a miniature chest of drawers under the window and got out of bed. Always sluggish at the start of a day he struggled to recall to mind exactly what it was had nagged at him most specifically the night before, after he had decided Peter was going to sleep peacefully until morning. It came to him as he plodded to the bathroom in slippers and dressing gown – the rayon one he kept for travelling because it could be compressed to wallet-size. It was the phrase 'precipitated by some immediate emotional alarm' which had come from Dr Chadbon talking about Peter's collapse. That was to say it *derived* from the doctor, Craddock acknowledged as he relieved himself, staring into the murk of gaunt tree-tops and chimney-pots visible through the angled slats of the venetian blinds. The phrase was an elaboration of the doctor's own, which was spare to the point of pidgin. Now Craddock racked his brain for Dr Chadbon's words. But without the man's physical presence they lost their form, although the essence endured. 'Big upset.' Had he said that? It sounded too commonplace for the importance Craddock felt sure it had. But then, linquistically the doctor was entirely commonplace, common understanding being his aim with this dislocated utterance.

Still pondering, Craddock looked in on Peter. The boy had grown adult again. The pale jaw needed a shave. He was asleep on his right side, his breathing steady. The flopped hair curtained most of his face, but Craddock could see there was no flush or tremor. Craddock felt more moved by this safely sleeping figure than he had at any time the day and night before when he was compelled to be nurse and comforter. Events had been disturbing. But even holding the shuddering body to his own had been an impersonal act compared with this moment of watching Peter sleep. The weeping had persisted until Peter's misery of shame was at last expelled. Afterwards there was no embarrassment between them. Craddock asked, 'Is there anyone you want me to call? Anyone you want me to send for?' Peter shook his head firmly, then gave a weak laugh before shutting his eyes in dismissal of a deeply unpleasant day.

Craddock had moved restlessly about the house, drinking tea and munching biscuits as he stood like a ruminant in the white kitchen; then wandering back upstairs to peer at Peter; then into his office to get down some description and speculation under the heading: 'Nomadic Doctor – Chadbon (real name).' Then he took another look at Peter and was troubled to note the renewed uneasiness of his sleep – a nervous twitching and the face unnaturally reddened as if it had been struck. Craddock considered hunting through Peter's clothes to see if they might yield names and telephone numbers of family or friends he could contact, in spite of Peter's objection. He found the idea distasteful and rejected it. He sat at his desk again trying to persuade himself to 'phone the *Voice* office, but could not deny that vehement shaking of Peter's head. Then he was back downstairs for some sherry and bread and cheese. And as he was once more halfway up the stairs Peter appeared from the bedroom supporting himself with one hand against the wall. 'Could I have a drink of something, Tony?' His voice was matter-of-fact and Craddock said, 'Sure. Were you thinking of walking downstairs?' When Peter nodded Craddock said, 'Well, I don't think that's a good idea. Get back into bed and I'll bring you up an old English remedy.' He squeezed the juice of a lemon into a mug of hot water and then stirred in two teaspoonful of honey (and did not add the whisky he would have laced the mixture with, had it been his own cure-all). Peter drank it with the couple of aspirin Dr Chadbon had advised could do no harm should the patient be prepared to take nourishment of any kind. 'Rich fare,' Peter said, and then settled himself for sleep with a certainty of movement Craddock found encouraging: so encouraging that he mixed a repeat-prescription and took it up to the spare room, the earliest night-cap he'd had since he could not remember when.

Now, in the unpredictable morning, he smiled faintly at the realisation that he was awaiting Peter's instructions. He went off to prepare for them, starting with a pot of tea and then a bath . . .

★

It seemed to Craddock essential that he should give Peter the most detailed exposition of Dr Chadbon's comments he could muster. He got an attentive hearing, although it was clear enough to Craddock that Peter was being told nothing, or at best very little, he did not already know. Now and again Peter would nod or say, 'Yeah, right.' Or else, 'Yeah, he's got it.'

They were sitting in the two armchairs in the office, Peter having taken the one he had not occupied the day before, laughing as he said, 'Let's not press our luck.' He had washed but not shaved, because he normally used an electric razor and Craddock did not have one; and he was dressed in his jeans and sweater. He had asked for another mug of 'the elixir' and had eaten two pieces of toast. Craddock had watched in wonder and Peter had made a joke about feeding time in the monkey house. 'Well, then, why the hell . . .?' Craddock's exasperated question was interrupted by a shrug which Peter followed with,

'That's how it is. I'll be all right now.' But Craddock was not accepting that. 'Preposterous' was the word he used. Hence the review of events.

'That doctor's obviously a bright bloke,' Peter said when Craddock had finished; or almost – he was keeping something back for the moment.

Craddock said, 'So this isn't the first time.'

'In one sense it is. I've never actually passed out before.'

'But you've refused to eat.'

'You don't *refuse*, exactly. You just don't fancy it. That goes on a bit and then, as I said, everything's all right again.'

'Except this time.'

'Yeah. I just couldn't seem to pull out of it. Still, it's over now.'

Craddock could not be party to this show of unconcern. He said, 'Now, look. When was the last time you cried like that?'

There was a pause before Peter said flatly, 'It's out of character.'

'Of course it is. So it matters.'

'I hardly knew what was happening. I couldn't tell you what that quack looked like. Tall? Fat? Black? I don't know.'

'Well, you could find out by paying him a visit when you're ready.'

'What for?'

'There's this glandular fever thing. He needs a blood test to know for sure.'

Peter shrugged the whole matter aside. Craddock persisted. 'Actually you ought to go and see your own doctor and tell him about *all* this. Have you got one?'

'No.'

'For God's sake . . .'

'Listen, it won't happen again. I won't let it get that far. Let's call it a chastening and salutary experience.'

At this point Craddock raised the nagging aspect he had deliberately withheld. He found it easier to adopt something of Dr Chadbon's style. It made him feel less as if he were prying. 'Emotional stress,' he said. 'Yesterday. Something upset you. Big, wasn't it?'

Peter's hands were on the arms of the chair. He took a firmer grip as if about to lever himself to his feet. But he stayed put, staring beyond his knees to the floor. Then his hands met across his middle and the fingers twined. The perkiness had left him. He looked up at Craddock who saw in the face the hurt he had expected but also an aggression, and he was unprepared for that.

Craddock asked, 'Was it something to do with me?'

'Yes!' Peter shouted the word, jutting his head forward, the eyes brilliant. Then the head and shoulders dropped and the hands were limp again on the arms of the chair.

A pop group came whining along the street, penetrating the double glazing with one of those songs that consisted of a single line repeated for as long as its androgynous performers could bear the monotony. Most pop music sounded like that to Craddock whose own tolerance to the monotony was low. He stood up to look out of the window and found a girl of around twenty passing his house wheeling a pram. The transistor radio dangled at its side. The group stuck steadfastly to the production line. Craddock was alarmed to see the girl halt and start dabbing and poking at the baby's coverings. Perhaps she was preparing to leave pram, baby and pop group right there outside his sitting room window and go about other business, leaving the group to drone on and on and on and on . . . But she straightened at last, took a grasp of the pram handle and pushed the droning away. But in his tension he was unable to speak until the last vestige of whine had released its hold on him.

'You're obviously still pretty weak,' he said to Peter. 'Understandably enough. You can stay here as long as you like.'

Peter said, 'Legs are a bit wobbly. I could get a cab home.'

'Why don't you leave it for a few hours? Then see how you feel.'

'All right. Anyway, I've got to explain to you. About you and Lord Llewellyn.'

CHAPTER SEVEN

When Peter returned to the *Voice* office after his first meeting with Craddock the message he was hoping for from Lord Llewellyn had not been received. He put in yet another 'phone call to the press department of the Home Office. Once again he was told his request for an interview had been passed on, but his Lordship had not yet agreed or refused. Peter reminded the official, a young woman, that he had now been waiting nearly two weeks for an answer. The official reminded him she had suggested in the first place he might do better to put his questions in writing. Peter replied that exchanging letters was unlikely to give him the kind of thing he could expect from the minister's lively tongue, and might prove a complete waste of time. The young woman said she didn't feel she ought to comment on that, either way. Peter said he was now getting close to his deadline and the young woman said that having been a reporter on an evening paper she knew the feeling. Not for the first time, when dealing with press officials of government offices, Peter was conscious that an unfavourable comparison was being made between the exacting requirements of orthodox papers and the whimsical attitudes of upstart publications such as his. He said he hoped his request was not going to be lost in the Christmas torpor. She said she had no information to hand concerning the minister's festive arrangements . . .

Peter reported to his news editor. They agreed Llewellyn was deliberately avoiding them. This might be because he was indifferent to *Voice* or because he suspected they had questions he preferred not to answer.

The news editor and his young staff were well used to rebuff from officialdom. By and large they expected to be unwelcome wherever power dwelt. Their bread-and-butter interests were black adolescents alleging harassment by local policemen, collectives of one-parent families threatened with eviction, groups of homosexuals denied a meeting place . . . It was the standard *Voice* approach that such disadvantaged people were in the right unless this police spokesman or that director of housing could show they were not. This was seldom the case however detailed an official statement might be. To *Voice* an accusation of callousness, for example, was not invalidated by proof of non-payment of rent or of hazard to health in the form of overflowing lavatories caused by vandalism. So even with its accompanying reply from authority a *Voice* news story was by nature one of victimisation. This is not to say these accounts of official malfeasance were the magazine's main editorial content. Four bold pages of them were the usual weekly dollop. *Voice* was an entertainment, not a crusade. At greater length it discussed the offerings of stage, screen, art gallery, bookshop, concert hall, and the offerers, and did it aggressively. *Voice* took pride in its aggressiveness.

How, then, were they to pin down the unwilling Lord Llewellyn? The chairman of a local council could be pounced upon outside the town hall or 'phoned at home late at night, to provoke the 'No comment' *Voice* often found entirely satisfactory. A junior minister they wished to cultivate rather than offend was a different proposition. Did they know anyone who knew Llewellyn well enough to effect an informal approach on their behalf? They did not. They could name a handful of Members of Parliament, perhaps two handfuls, whom they would regard as friendly enough to help in particular areas. One made a speciality of brutish behaviour by immigration officers. Another was a champion of the underpaid in the hotels and restaurants industry. A couple more were sympathetic to the legalising of smoking cannabis. All could be placed in the category of the 'actively concerned with civil liberties'. None was imaginably a confidant of Lord Llewellyn. But surely there was *somebody* to assist them . . .

Peter mentioned idly that Anthony Craddock had given the impression he knew Llewellyn: not that he'd said so, but there was something in the way he had responded to the name. Perhaps it was mere inquisitiveness. On the other hand, now Peter came to think about it, Craddock had used Llewellyn's first name in a certain manner. Lord Llewellyn was always referred to as 'Lord Llewellyn'. One had to make a conscious effort of memory to pluck the christian name from the potted biography. But Craddock had asked, 'Royston Llewellyn . . . ?' The tone of voice, the set of the face, the little delay that imposed itself as if . . . well, as if Craddock's mind was reaching back over the years. The news editor thought Peter should see what he could dig out on any past connection before he next saw Craddock. One or other of the friendly M.P.s might be of use after all. At least he'd know something *about* Llewellyn.

*

Peter said to Craddock, 'I found in the files you'd been at the same school. Same time. I hadn't been looking for that sort of thing before. Didn't mean much, of course – for all I knew you could have hated each other's guts, or just never had anything to do with each other. But then I made a few 'phone calls, and I got lucky with Bill Bradfield. You know Bradfield.'

Craddock nodded, his head teeming with memories. 'Yes, I know Brother Bill. Llewellyn once referred to him at a Labour Party Conference as "The Member for Envy". Did Bill no harm at all – got his face all over the papers. That's the sort of thing that made Llewellyn's career in the House of Commons so short.'

'He seems to have been well looked after,' Peter said.

Craddock let the subject of Llewellyn's progress lie for the moment.

Peter continued after a few seconds. 'Well, Bradfield told me you and Llewellyn have been close mates for ever. "They live in each other's pockets." That's how he put it.'

Craddock said quietly, 'He's out of date.'

Peter had acquired a curious dogged insistence, the lightness gone from his voice and language. His tiredness would have much to do with this toiling delivery, Craddock told himself.

'Well, that's what he said. According to Bradfield you and Llewellyn were never out of each other's sight as kids, and when you grew up you went on holiday a lot together, and because he'd been an officer in National Service and you hadn't there was a standing joke that you went as his batman.'

'I think Brother Bill actually put that one round himself,' Craddock said.

'Another joke was that Llewellyn thought he was God Almighty and you worshipped him.'

'This is all going back to before you were born, Peter. There's nothing unusual in that kind of backbiting in a small town. Llewellyn and Bully Boy Bill were natural rivals. They both thought they were the perfect choice for the home-town constituency once the venerable sitting tenant handed in the keys. Neither of them got it in the end, precisely because they couldn't keep their hands off each other's throats. The local party didn't need that kind of splitting of the ranks.' He paused, frowning. 'It's very juvenile of Bill Bradfield to be still trotting out those old jibes at this stage of the game. He found his niche eventually, just as Llewellyn did.'

'You quoted "The Member for Envy".'

'Who wouldn't? It was much more recent for one thing.' Then he remembered again Peter's youth. 'Not in the *Voice* files?' Peter shook his head. 'All right, that also belongs back in the mists of time. It *was* one of the gems of the year, though.'

'Doesn't Llewellyn still put the boot in? I mean with Bradfield.'

'I wouldn't know.'

'Don't you see him at all?'

'Not lately.'

Peter brooded. Craddock's head produced a rapid series of overlapping snapshots, as if a thumb were streaming the pages of an album: loudspeaker vans; Llewellyn at a microphone on a platform; men's hard faces framed in the prison-like bars of factory gates . . . He said, 'I always rather liked that joke about being Llewellyn's batman. Bradfield never knew how near the truth it was.' As he spoke other pictures skimmed behind his eyes: a mound of rucksacks on the Dover-Calais ferry; thronged tables on a Montmartre pavement . . .

'It was a hell of a surprise,' Peter said, 'when Bradfield told me he came from the same town as you. M.P.s are automatically associated with their constituencies – I mean if you think in terms of where they're from. Actually with Bill Bradfield the immediate association in my mind is the poverty trap. He really is good on social security benefits and that whole area.'

Clearly Peter was treading water. He was merely keeping the conversation afloat as he gathered strength to strike out of his indecision. Craddock thought it best to wait passively. The silence forced Craddock's concentration back on to Peter, as if he was in a train and its stopping had jolted him out of a reverie. He watched the now-familiar combing of the hair with those stiff fingers. The eyelids had a faint, spasmodic flicker, uncharacteristic and indicating a rewinding tension: more that, Craddock thought, than the debilitation of the last few days. How did he feel about Peter now? More troubled, certainly. *For* him, or *by* him? Equally certainly, both. He knew that further involvement was inevitable, and it would be complex. The sexual attraction that had been so potent on first meeting had diminished unsurprisingly. There were many precedents for the process. Did Peter feel drawn to *him* sexually? He had not considered this possibility until now. 'Emotional stress . . . Something to do with me?' He had asked the question instinctually: a shot in the dark, no more. This entangled silence was perturbing but magnetic. Craddock could only wait and see.

When Peter spoke at last he had shed some of the diffidence; but as if he had settled objectively on a means of advance, not dismissed his anxiety. 'These old barbs of Bill Bradfield's – they seem directed more at you than Llewellyn. What did you do to him?'

'It's an illusion,' Craddock said. 'You asked him how Llewellyn and I related – how closely. It was always Brother Bill's line in the old days that Llewellyn was the kind of self-regarding glory hunter who needed yes-men around him. Obviously it's *still* his line. To prove his point he has to identify these comtemptible people. You gave him the nod in my direction and he said, "Dead right, son, he's First Idolator." I haven't spoken to Bill Bradfield for at least ten years, maybe fifteen. Or about him, for that matter. Don't forget how busy I've been not writing about politics.'

Craddock leaned forward in his chair to tap the switched-off tape-recorder on the table between them. 'You've still got that to deal with. We didn't get very far yesterday.'

'I know,' Peter said.

'Shouldn't you ring your office?'

'Some time, yeah.'

It was not lost on Craddock that *Voice*'s interest in him, as a subject for critical examination in his own right, was now markedly subordinate to whatever else Peter was trying so painfully to get at.

'According to Bradfield,' Peter hesitated but forced himself on, 'Llewellyn owes you a few favours.'

'Then Brother Bill's an impertinent sod. What kind?'

'He said you've covered up for him. Kept things out of the papers.'

'Again, what kind?'

'He said you'd know what he meant.'

'Didn't you press him any further? He seems a willing enough informant.'

'He said, considering the kind of things Llewellyn used to get up to, he needed friends on the papers.'

'And he means me? I'm supposed to have multiplied myself into a dozen different reporters in some magical way.'

Knowing he was making ground Peter was able to affect patience. 'No, obviously what he's saying is that you used to square things with the others.'

'Oh, I see. A conspiracy of silence. On what?'

'Bradfield said only right-wingers could get that sort of soft treatment from a capitalist press.'

'Llewellyn *wasn't* on the right of the party at that time. He was to the right of Bill, but so would Karl Marx have been.'

Craddock would have been disappointed if Peter had missed the opening offered to him. 'So you do know what Bradfield was talking about?' Peter said lightly.

Craddock was brusque. 'Women. So what? Why the hell should you and *Voice* be interested in Llewellyn's old screws? Or new ones. I've no doubt he's still hard at it.'

'Well, we're not, of course. Not directly – for publication, I mean.'

'Why at all?'

'Well, we're trying to put together a dossier . . .'

There was a pause as Peter caught the shift in Craddock's attitude. Craddock had folded his arms across his chest, the right hand jammed tightly under the left shoulder. His head was lifted so that he was studying Peter with hooded eyes, not unlike a palace guardsman staring from under his bearskin.

'. . . In which case whatever names cropped up might have some relevance, mightn't they? It would depend where they led.' He gave a quick grin. 'If it's just a case of "Lord Llewellyn Slept Here", well no, we don't give a damn about that.'

Two things came to Craddock's mind. The first was Liz's commendation of Peter as 'very straight and nice'. The second was his recollection of shrugging off a vague sense of danger during his first conversation with Peter when he answered a 'phone call against his inclination. Perhaps this memory explained why he should now repeat exactly the words he spoke then. He said, 'What do you want from me?'

Peter's voice, he registered, was not the engaging mixture of eagerness and uncertainty he had first heard. Now it expressed a different conflict: determination and apology. 'I want you to get me a meeting with Llewellyn,' he said. 'And I also want you to tell me all you know about his private life. What interests us most is where his money comes from.'

Another recollection came to Craddock's mind. He had begun the day gently amused at the thought that he was awaiting Peter's orders.

CHAPTER EIGHT

There was a particular brand of tinned chicken soup by which Craddock's late mother had set great store as a nutrient.

Craddock's late father always said she was merely over-impressed by its price, which was higher than that of other brands, to which Mrs Craddock replied that the extra cost proved her judgement conclusively. The tin presented unarguably a more dignified appearance than others, having a label in shades of quiet brown as against the more garish reds and yellows of cheaper brands. Craddock had come to respect his father's intelligence greatly in the last few years of the older man's life, when communication between them had eased with the maturing of the younger and the dropping of pretence that came with it. Once he had stopped trying to hide his fondness for drink and young male company, Craddock found his teetotal, chapel-elder father unappalled and much relieved that the barriers of courteous taciturnity were down.

Craddock senior had been a close reader of the more serious newspapers and a grateful listener to the B.B.C's radio discourses on subjects and from places, as he pointed out, otherwise lamentably inaccessible to him. He was surprised so few other people took advantage of this remarkable flow of information on political jockeying in the West Indies, the disturbingly high birthrate in Mexico, low productivity in Chinese industry, the menacing reappearance of malaria . . . Craddock found an acuteness and broad human understanding which surprised him in a man he had previously seen as grey and confined, like the job he did in the despatch department of a factory making screwdrivers and wrenches and the like. The worst disservice a man could do himself, his father told Craddock shortly before he died at eight-one, was ever to let the world frighten him out of speaking his own mind. That was why he was opposed to all forms of censorship and said so with emphatic, untutored eloquence when a breezy woman of national fame came in a flourish of sanctity to a meeting at his church. She wanted recruits to her organisation, which was dedicated to the cleansing of the country's television screens and bookshelves, daily growing more corrupting and obscene, so she said. Old Mr Craddock warned the company against the adoration of false gods, such as propriety, which induced a torrent of wrath from the famous woman unaccustomed to the defence of pornography by octogenarians in holy places. Now that was just the kind of distorting of argument of which he had observed the misguided lady to be guilty more than once on television, the old man riposted, and he wagged a mischievous finger . . . Craddock recalled with pleasure his father's cackle of laughter when recounting this contest.

But if Craddock senior at least divided the day with the formidable famous woman he never managed to dissuade Mrs Craddock from paying over the odds for the brown-labelled tins of cream-of-chicken soup. Their son always felt that a woman's opinion carried the greater weight in such a controversy. Faiths implanted in childhood are variously enduring. Craddock had long forsaken the God of Sunday school and harvest festival. But at this moment, with a glass of sherry in his left hand, he was stirring with a wooden spoon held in the right the simmering contents of a saucepan smelling so evocatively of the only true chicken soup. He proposed feeding it to Peter, and after it some scrambled eggs with grated cheddar cheese. Peter had approved the menu before he went to lie down for an hour or so, on Craddock's prompting. Resistance to this advice was abandoned when Craddock said if Peter passed out on him again it would be 'a bloody ambulance job'.

Craddock now found nothing unexplained in Peter's collapse the previous day. Stringing along an interviewee, waiting for the moment to change course and embark on a line of questioning that could reap reward or disaster, was a nerve-testing business; he had good reason to know. A form of severe stage-fright could afflict reporters just as it could, for example, footballers before a match. He could name international players who were all but disabled by nausea; and newspapermen with big reputations as foot-in-the-door investigators who suppressed their fear with drink all through their careers. Given Peter's inexperience, and that he was in poor physical shape and already overwrought because of it, there was no wonder he should fall victim (literally) to his own duplicity. The shame, being twofold, was equally understandable in its intensity.

Craddock tasted the soup and adjudged it was time to add the lemon juice; his mother, he suspected, would have regarded such an additive as constituting 'fancy cooking', but might have conceded its medicinal value. He went into the hall and shouted for Peter to come downstairs.

★

It could not strictly be said that Detective Sergeant Gavin Whittle made an approach to *Voice*. Nor was the reverse true. What happened was more in the nature of a throwing together which each made haste to exploit.

The detective liked rock music. Especially he liked the 'heaviest' kind played by bands which went under names with an industrial flavour: *Trip-hammer, Forklift, Blowlamp, Waggon Shed* . . . Immersed in the discordant frenzy of these bands, in their ragged dungarees and string vests, Sergeant Whittle found the release he sought from the bitter tensions of his work.

Voice took a solemn interest in these musicians, sending reviewers to the clubs and pubs and public halls where the performances raged late at night. The tone of the reviews was combative, as *Voice*-readers would expect. A band might be praised as 'genuinely anarchic' or 'free of cant'. But it might offend by sounding 'insidiously doctrinaire' or 'politically neutral'.

Among the freelance contributors the magazine employed to make judgments of this kind was a girl called Fran. She was fearlessly insulting to any band she found wanting. First and foremost she wanted 'commitment'. If her ears could not discern 'commitment' Fran's review would smite the performers without mercy.

Fran was as uninhibited in conversation as in print, and because rock bands had their devotees, whose loyalty might not be weakened by her contumely, she was often caught up in angry argument at concerts she took against. This was how Fran and Detective Sergeant Gavin Whittle met. One such dispute, which centred on Fran's use of the phrase 'cock-sucker music' about a band called *Gridiron*, became heated enough to develop into a scuffle. The detective, in denim like most people present, found himself shouting in Fran's support and then using his professional skill to drag her clear of the flailing arms. Off-duty he would normally do his best to avoid involvement in any such incident. But he had felt much in need of a dose of rock that would numb his brain; *Gridiron* had failed him, so he vented his disappointment on their supporters, first verbally but soon with hand and foot.

Fran's rescue was an excuse for this violent outburst, as he told her with sour candour over a drink afterwards. He was seldom physically violent, although there were people around he would willingly strangle. That was half his trouble, he said: having to suppress anger. He had the right kind of abilities for his job, but not, it seemed, the required temperament. He envied the men in other departments who were expected to throw a few punches in the common run of events. That was to say, he envied them that particular indulgence and not their duties in general. If he was going to remain in the force he would stay with the fraud squad, where there was a chance of getting to grips with the worst of all evils afflicting society, which was the massive theft from the ordinary man and woman in the street by unscrupulous, hypocritical bastards in positions of trust and privilege. Yes, he'd like to lay his knuckles along a few of those well-connected cheeks. But that wasn't the style in the fraud squad, unfortunately.

Fran's only previous contacts with policemen had been when she was searched unsuccessfully for drugs (three times) and when she joined demonstrations (many times), the most recent of which was against Sexual Oppression in Education. Then she had carried a placard declaring, 'Teach Sex, Not Sexism'. In due course she told her friends at *Voice* she was sleeping with a policeman who had some dark but elliptical things to say about villainy in the corridors of power. It was not her field, and he was a strange guy. But she had the firm impression he wanted her to confront him with a news reporter, and then he might be much more specific. This was how Peter and the detective sergeant met.

Whittle directed Peter's attention to a report published three weeks before – in the week Whittle and Fran came together –

of an inquiry by the Department of Trade into the affairs of the Felden Property Corporation. This was a company of impressive size, its worth approaching the resounding round-figure of a hundred million pounds. Its founder and chairman had been the late Sir Benjamin Felden, the very model of the self-made tycoon, the son of a gents' clothier in North London. His company bought, sold, built, developed and redeveloped in a whirlwind of acumen, attracting share-buyers like wasps to a picnic. The same could be said of Sir Benjamin as an attracter of friends. They swarmed to his perpetual feast of generosity. His nickname of Big Ben was due to the extravagance of his gifts and style of life, not to his physique which was unextraordinary. This delight in spending money would almost certainly have landed him in prison by now because, as the report stated, very little of the money was his to spend. It belonged to his shareholders. The inspectors who had toiled for several months over the complications of Big Ben's personal and business finances were not satisfied that they could put an accurate figure to the total misappropriation of the company's funds. Therefore they gave what examples they could of his improper munificence, letting it be understood that much more might well have passed undetected. Even so, with his endearing habits of paying for other people's holidays in the Caribbean, and putting on lavish luncheon and dinner parties, and sending crates of champagne by the vanload to wedding receptions and birthday binges, and installing tenants rent-free in company owned houses and apartments . . . It seemed Big Ben had handed out the best part of half a million he did not have. A heart attack ended his life at the meagre age of fifty-three. Whether bankruptcy proceedings would have begun before his appearance in a criminal court was a matter of newspaper speculation.

That coronary, Sergeant Whittle told Peter, was a lucky let-off for some. If the police had been given the opportunity to question Big Ben at length he would have delivered up some names which also belonged on the manifest of one of Her Majesty's prisons. The fraud squad was preparing its own investigation when death intervened. That was a big catch lost, and the fact gnawed at his guts.

Peter objected that the report had, in fact, named some very well-known public figures among the recipients of Big Ben's largesse. They included politicians, both Labour and Conservative: two of them were ex-Cabinet ministers indeed. The newspapers had belaboured these embarrassed men for days.

Whittle asked Peter if he could think of a more effective smokescreen. Peter, of course, wanted to know what Whittle meant by that. Whittle said that when august figures caught with their pants down, so to speak, were able to talk freely about being foolish, naive and decieved, this distracted attention from more damaging possibilities: such as their complicity, or if not that then their turning of a blind eye. If the source of their embarrassment was now a corpse there was further distraction in picking over the bones. The dead could not be libelled; nor could they argue, rebut or point fingers accusingly in other directions. So public interest had naturally been turned on the dark corners that could be lit with impunity, if Peter got his drift. Whittle was not saying that the politicians named were necessarily felons. He *was* saying they would have had to face much more searching examination if Big Ben had been brought to court. There was, to begin with, the matter of the uncounted *unknowns* among his beneficiaries. Did the well-known innocents – giving them the benefit of the doubt, regarding their own gifts – know *these* people? What had they been given? Why? For services rendered, perhaps? Whittle found it 'intriguing', to say the least, that Big Ben had courted politicians so assiduously. Those named, apparently, had given him nothing beyond their friendly company in return for his overwhelming kindness. Had no one at all ever done him a favour? He was involved in the property business; property involved government departments, national and local; there were rules and regulations; planning permission and the awarding of contracts . . . Big Ben's business was a large and complex operation, with various subsidiaries and associates. He was not just a wheeler-dealer, like a super-estate agent; in more recent years he had built houses, office blocks, shopping precincts . . .

Peter could see Whittle's drift now, quite clearly. But had he anything more to offer than suspicion of persons unknown? Whittle said Peter had to understand what a long and frustrating job investigating corruption was. It was not a question of dusting for fingerprints or doing the rounds of villians' drinking haunts to see who was spending unwisely. Peter imagined not.

Whittle said it was a sore point that fraud squad men were often not given the time they needed to complete an investigation satisfactorily: to satisfy *themselves*, he meant. The work load was such that if a line of enquiry proved slow going an impatient superior might redirect an officer, or a team, to something that looked more promising. Peter thought he could understand that: establishing whether there *had been* fraud in some instance of commercial or governmental life was by its nature exploratory, unlike a hunt for a murderer which presented a clear objective, a quarry. Whittle was glad his problems were recognised. One of the effects of what might be called having to leave stones unturned, he said, with *him* anyway, was that his brain crawled with half-glimpsed bits of possible evidence, dropped names that produced long-delayed echoes; in short, he was plagued by a sense of unfinished business. Colleagues told him he would go off his chump if he let the job mangle him like that – hence the trips into oblivion with the screaming rock bands; but that was the way he was made. He simply could not, would not, forget. Now, take the Big Ben affair. He was a member of the team which had opened preliminary enquiries before Big Ben died, and then been replaced by the inspectors from Whitehall. A particular name cropped up. It had set the ants marching and counter-marching in his head, because it belonged to unfinished business of a couple of years ago up in the North. He found, in chit-chat with fellow officers, the same name had been dropped here and there in other explorations – he liked that word, he told Peter – which had not produced results. He read the report on Big Ben's breathtaking effronteries, and was surprised by little of its content. Lord Llewellyn, whose name the ants had been trundling like a bramble inside his skull, was not mentioned.

The omission, Whittle was convinced, was more important than any of the report's revelations.

CHAPTER NINE

Craddock asked Peter, 'You don't think you and *Voice* might find yourselves out of your depth with this, do you? I mean over your heads by a fathom or two?'

He was sitting at his desk, legs stretched out and crossed at the ankles, meeting Peter's fixed gaze from the armchair. Craddock's ease was a pretence, and he knew Peter was fully aware of that. He needed a little time to cover the stress he felt churning inside him. It was a strange feeling, and when he identified it he was surprised enough to give a little smile: it was exactly the mixture of fear and expectation he used to experience ages ago when he first took off in aeroplanes for other continents and unpredictable events. Since the smile had introduced itself he thought he might as well make use of it, if unpleasantly. He said, 'You don't think perhaps you'd be safer having another go at the barbarities of the Chilean régime? That's always a good angry read.'

Peter said softly, 'Christ, Tony . . .' He stood up, making slowly for the door. Catching the questioning turn of Craddock's head, he muttered, 'Cigarettes.'

Craddock's first thought was that the last time he had seen Peter smoking was immediately before he fainted, which was worrying. His second was that if Peter wanted to smoke now it was probably a good sign of his return to normality. Another sign was that lazy, cat's exit, whose manner was now repeated in Peter's return from the bedroom. He was carrying his parka by the collar, replacing cigarettes and matches in one of its pockets as he sucked on the cigarette. He dropped the parka on the floor beside his chair before he sat down again, settling one bony knee over the other and letting one hand cradle the edge of the chair-arm. Craddock marvelled at the self-containment, coming so swiftly after the wounding tension. He had noted this facet of Peter's nature at their first meeting. Observing it again – indeed, studying it – Craddock realised Peter must appreciate the compelling effect it had on others. Yet Craddock was sure it was not a deliberate playing for attention: probably he had had too much of that for his own liking – the over-petted child and striking youth from whom so much was expected? It could account for the impression he often gave of a cold self-isolation, as if fending off a world he found offensively importunate. Craddock had sensed that chill of distaste several times during Peter's account of his exchanges with Fran, Whittle and Bradfield: being suspicious of his informants made him all the more persuasive. Now, he sat untroubled by Craddock's scrutiny, trustful enough not to look up and examine it in return.

'Forgetting the bad jokes,' Craddock said, levering himself upright and giving his head a couple of abrupt little shakes as if releasing a crick in the neck, 'do you really think you can handle it?'

Peter said, 'I'm not frightened of people like Llewellyn.' Tone and gaze were both quick with combat.

Craddock repeated the words slowly. ' "People like Llewellyn". Tell me what you think Llewellyn's like.'

'Obviously he's no fool.'

'I agree, that *is* obvious.'

'All right, I imagine he's pretty tough, resourceful, wily . . .'

Craddock waited. Peter shrugged.

Craddock asked, 'This series of yours – I'm assuming you intend doing it, as they say, for *real*?'

'Of course.' Peter's look was genuinely puzzled. 'Why do you ask that? I've talked to a lot of people; got some quite good stuff.'

'Was Llewellyn always on your list of interviewees?'

'Oh, I see . . .' Peter concentrated for a few seconds on tapping his cigarette in the ashtray, seemingly held by the need to find the exact centre of the receptacle. Then he said briskly, 'You mean it wouldn't surprise you at all if I'd given you a whole pack of lies about the politics-on-the-box thing – just an elaborate front for getting at Llewellyn?'

'Not quite,' Craddock said evenly. 'If that were the case it would mean you set *me* up from the beginning, as well. And plainly that's not so.' He paused. 'Not from the beginning, anyway.'

'Yeah, I really botched that, didn't I?'

Quickly Craddock said, 'Llewellyn. *When?*'

'After I met the fraud squad man. You know Llewellyn's job at the Home Office – special responsibility for the police, prisons, borstals, kids' remand centres . . .'

'Lord Screw. Give Bill Bradfield that one next time you have one of your little chats with him. He'll love it. Sorry, Peter. If you want my help you'll have to put up with my misplaced frivolity. I know it irritates you.'

'*Are* you going to help?'

'Llewellyn. More.'

'Originally my series was going to be confined to politics in its narrower sense – party propaganda; the way anyone who goes on strike always has to *defend* it against television interrogation; the way racial discrimination is played down; middle-class conditioning in children's programmes . . .'

'I can see it all.'

'There didn't seem any reason why we shouldn't deal with law and order – for example, there was a play about borstal which was banned this year. Okay, let's get the Minister for Incarceration to tell us how much he had to do with *that* piece of censorship. Or, if he preferred it, he could take the opportunity we're delighted to offer him to explain how ignorant he is of any interference in broadcasting of that kind. So now we'd got a specific reason for wanting to interview him . . .'

Craddock interrupted, shaking his head. 'He'd never do it. No minister would – except off-the-record, and even then he'd only talk to one of the parliamentary boys.'

'Or someone he knew well?'

Craddock let the suggestion slide by. He said, 'You people at *Voice* must know it just isn't on to nobble a minister like that.'

'We know it isn't the way things are normally done. But *we're* not expected to behave like that, are we? Anyway, we had to get the ball rolling somehow, so why shouldn't we play the innocent and simply ask? His own curiosity, or vanity, or generosity, or *something*, might get the better of him, and he might just say, "Yes, pop round for a natter". It's interesting, isn't it, that he hasn't actually said "No" yet?'

Craddock reflected on how interesting that might or might not be, and admitted to himself it was highly significant.

Peter was saying, 'So you can see how I got the job.'
'They're overloading you.'
Peter dismissed the comment with an impatient flick at his hair. The vigour of the gesture was another encouraging sign of his improved condition, Craddock noted.

'I take it,' Craddock said, 'that this hastily drummed up inquiry into the banning of controversial telly plays explains why you came to me so late in the day.' He got one of Peter's cat-like stares. 'You would need a comparison between what's kept off the screen and the anodyne drivel that gets on it. Like mine. Is that what you had in mind? Roughly?'

'Your plays aren't drivel. They're quite perceptive in some areas.'

'That's very kind of you. But it is my *acceptability* as a dramatist that you proposed to maul. Yes? With a few well-chosen quotes out of my own mouth? Well-chosen by you, I mean. In that way you'd have a reasonably entertaining piece to print, in typically contemptuous *Voice* style, even if you'd got little, even *nothing*, out of Llewellyn. So your time would not have been wasted, and you could still fish for Llewellyn in his murky waters without having raised his suspicion. Yes? Roughly? That was the plan?'

'I hadn't met you then.' Peter's mumbled regret – it fell defiantly short of apology – prickled Craddock's nerve ends. It magnified the distracting ambiguities in his relationship with Peter. At the same time it seemed to embody the whole muddle of elements in what was now lodged immovably in his head as The Llewellyn Operation: the cynicism and gaucherie Peter brought with him from *Voice*, the enormity of the accusation and its almost playful levelling . . . He knew he was already forced into the role of investigator. Forced *back* to it, and it had never been his strong suit. Could *he* handle it?

Craddock tested a few more inches of ground. 'If you ever get to Llewellyn, how do you propose asking him if he's a crook?'

'It wouldn't be my first question.'

'I'm glad to hear that.'

'Don't you have any faith in my competence at all?' Craddock lifted his hands briefly, palms outwards, taking the rebuke. Peter went on, 'It's a matter of getting him to talk as widely as possible, isn't it? If the focus of the conversation is the televising of tricky subjects, and let's say I specify prisons and the police, that could lead on quite naturally to corruption in public life, couldn't it? I'm not fool enough to try to confront him with anything. I want the flavour of the man; his attitudes. Is he a tightrope walker? Or does he play it all close to his chest? All that's going to be invaluable to us when the story breaks.'

'You mean *if* it breaks. If it *exists*.'

Peter's demonstrative shake of the head indicated he did not mean that.

After a pause Craddock tugged towards him the portable typewriter that sat at one corner of the desk. He said, 'I think we ought to write this unflattering little piece about me. Four hundred words?'

Book Two

CHAPTER TEN

Llewellyn was twenty-seven when he was adopted as the Labour parliamentary candidate for Dodburn. A year later he won the seat at a by-election, following the death of the sitting Conservative Member in a car crash on a blustery, wet night, driving hurriedly away from the town over the Pennine moorland surrounding it.

Dodburn's Labour party workers divided fairly evenly on who was the more fortunate: they, in acquiring such an obvious vote-catcher in the person of this handsome, exuberant young economist with so warm a nature; or Llewellyn, in getting the chance to reach Westminster so young.

Llewellyn's early view was that he could well have been more lucky with his constituency. It had an unstable air at close quarters which was at variance with the solid, enduring appearance its stone houses, stone factories and stone chapels presented to an observer on the peaty skyline. These factories were changing hands too hastily, and so were their functions: carpets today, pyjamas tomorrow . . . He suspected an electorate made fitful by uncertainty. He was proved right. Seven months after his victory, which brought him a great deal of publicity, he lost the seat at the 1959 general election. The prevailing verdict among the party workers was that politicians can sometimes be too young and glamorous to retain voters' confidence. And too clever. Dodburn did not ask him back again. Nor did Llewellyn find another seat in the Commons, although he fought one other election. Unforgettably.

*

It was early summer, 1962. The boarding houses of Brinsley Bay were reopening for business, their landladies thrilling to the yearly ritual of exchanging misinformation with one another concerning bookings from holidaymakers. Set their figures too high, and they risked jealousy now and humiliation later, should the triumphant 'No Vacancies' sign never hang in their front windows. Declare pessimism, and the wounding gossip would conjure impending doom due to last year's soggy lettuce and lack of lavatory paper and other forms of dereliction of duty – because, with summer visitors, *the word soon got around* . . .

It was a huddled little town. It huddled for protection from the slashing wind that came off the North Sea. It huddled in cliques. It had a smart end, where there were imitation ships' wheels for garden gates – middle management land, housing young families with outsiders' accents. The smart end breadwinners drove twelve miles to work in the offices of industrial estates on the outskirts of the city up the river. It was a great asset – agreed? – that their jobs enabled these young men to bring up their children on the bracing, unspoilt North East coast. The old town huddled against them; and against the weekend yachtsmen who had their own club. It had been winter when Llewellyn first saw Brinsley Bay, invited to meet the local party's executive committee, and the place had a still-life chill. In the silence and rime of its streets at dusk he renamed the constituency Dead-Alive-on-Sea.

Brinsley Bay's M.P. at that time was a fat Tory knight who had represented local interests for seventeen years. It had once been asked in the Commons whether he thought, in fact, he represented Johannesburg, since he spoke of little else but South Africa's moral splendour. But that was not the kind of joke Brinsley Bay enjoyed, on the whole, and the celebrated bulbous nose was not in the least out of joint, or unwelcome, the next time it appeared at the Conservative Club. Yet he had lost ground at the last election, for some reason: was it simply that people felt he was a bit past it? When he suffered a stroke and had to resign his seat the Labour party already had their candidate for the by-election and were eager for combat. They felt Llewellyn was just the man to reduce that diminished majority to next-to-nothing, or even . . .

'You know we don't have a hope in hell,' Llewellyn had said to Dick Goddard. That was right at the beginning, when

Goddard first suggested Llewellyn should offer himself to the constituency on the understanding that discreet recommendations would be passed to Brinsley Bay from the leadership in London. Goddard had waved the objection aside and reminded Llewellyn of his need to establish more *service to the party*. After his first visit, on that steel-grey winter weekend, he told Goddard, 'They're deluding themselves. Three or four earnest young couples from the trendy end have volunteered for duty and the old guard think they're seeing the dawn of the brave new world at last. They're talking about social revolution and the fruits of the welfare state.'

'Don't discourage them,' said Goddard. 'Pull out all the stops. Enjoy yourself.'

They were talking in the study of Goddard's house in Hampstead: the room in which, the first day he entered it with some speech notes for Goddard, Llewellyn felt he had *arrived*. Leather and mahogany furnished it: a don's room, a club room, when Goddard wished it. But more. Here Goddard was historian, biographer, polemicist and party cardinal. And it was that last role which most interested Llewellyn, as it did Goddard himself. It was both sanctum and operations room. A sense of the secret hung in it. This was where Goddard sifted his privileged intelligence, made his special 'phone calls, steered the quiet meetings with three or four like-motivated men, advised – or instructed – his protégés. There were other cardinals in the party. But Goddard, Fabian-bred (wealthily) Oxford double first and decorated commando, was English élite. And he was Llewellyn's cardinal . . .

Goddard had placed him under tutelage during Llewellyn's short but obtrusive appearance in the Commons. He liked the young man's irreverence, which was clearly inbuilt and not a style deliberately acquired: it embraced people and shibboleths to be found in the senior ranks of his own side, as well as across the floor of the House, and Goddard was refreshed by that. Not that there was any shortage of members eager to fly at the throats of colleagues in order to save the party's soul. But Llewellyn's concern was not with doctrine, Goddard noted. It was with power. Goddard had seen many ambitious young politicians; but *ambition* was not what gave this one his drive. What sustained him so ebulliently was less definable. It was not self-satisfaction; he was plainly impatient to progress. He seemed not to court limelight, applause, even private congratulation, although they came his way. His craving, Goddard saw, was for influence. He wanted the most elusive of political achievements: to effect change.

Goddard recognised the longing; it was also his own. But Llewellyn's seemingly unflagging exuberance was inconsistent with this yearning. Where was the nagging frustration? The anxious reappraisal? The release sought in cursing hostile fortune? He could be lacerating in his ridicule, particularly of colleagues slow to be persuaded out of lifelong attitudes – 'mental lockjaw' was his diagnosis in the case of one obdurate stalwart – but whether attacking or attacked he remained blithe. It was borne in on Goddard that Llewellyn was assuming the imminence of power – personal power. The expectation was inbuilt, with his mischievousness. The audacity was in the bone. Llewellyn was certain to offend – Goddard wryly admitted *he* had to work far more assiduously at the art than did his new protégé. Quite so. He needed the services of that formidable insouciance . . .

Goddard's target was the deputy leadership of the party, at the time held by John Lowndes, whose bouts of heavy drinking produced occasional press pictures of an embarrassing stumble into a policeman's arms – once, to the photographers' immense gratitude, into the arms of a police*woman* – or of a grinning cossack dance in bow tie and drooping braces, or of . . . 'Johnny's little anti-party acts', a Tory columnist called them, asking for more. But Lowndes' boisterous indiscretions were counter-balanced in the public mind, so it appeared, by the unequivocating line he would follow in any political comment. He was most eloquent in passages which allowed him to talk in capital letters: *Our Children's Future . . . The Country I, For One, Am Not Afraid To Say I Hold So Dear . . . We Are, Each One Of Us, Our Brother's Keeper . . .* This pulpit oratory struck a nostalgic note, rekindling for many the myth of happier days when people, in some unspecified way, were simply better – that is to say, more like dear old Brother John Lowndes. Goddard did not dislike him, although he was bored by his company. He endorsed the usefulness of an unashamed sentimentalist: no other cardinal could blur the issues of an internal party conflict as effectively as Brother Lowndes, with one of his hymns to the crusade. Goddard's objection was that the man was too highly placed. He was in Goddard's way.

The problem was to devalue Lowndes. Not to discredit him in any moral sense, but to re-position him in the eyes of the party in a lower category. He was to be shown as a hero of the long years of opposition who, sadly, was not of the stuff of which a Deputy Prime Minister, a Foreign Secretary or a Chancellor of the Exchequer was made.

'Why isn't it obvious?' Llewellyn asked.

'Because it isn't true,' Goddard said. 'He's just as able as plenty of other senior Cabinet Ministers, past and present. Terrifying, isn't it?'

Goddard, of course, could not be seen publicly hacking away at the earth around Lowndes' feet. Llewellyn did the spade work.

The strategy was to concentrate attention not on Brother Lowndes' faults but on his talents, on the basis that the former might be endearing but the latter more important. Identified and quantified, these assets were shown to be flimsy material on which a man could expect to build a life as a major politician. A shop steward in a foundry when barely seventeen. Local party secretary at nineteen. Town councillor at twenty-two. Precocious indeed. And his knowledge of pre-war poverty, pre-war industry, pre-war local government was consequently unsurpassed in terms of first-hand acquaintance. And then there was his diligence as a constituency M.P., even if that had understandably waned of late under the demands of Shadow Cabinet and party national executive work. What were his strengths in these larger fields? His vigour, sincerity, his common touch . . . Yes, it was remarkable that a man of little education, of localised experience, should carry so much support for his claim to high office. But that sincerity, that winning common touch –
it would be a pity if the best of the man were wasted, as it surely would be once he was yoked to the toil of government.

'Listen to me, young man,' Lowndes said to Llewellyn one night in the Members' Bar, which was as well-attended as ever, 'you're tripping the light fantastic where angels fear to tread.' He had downed his second large whisky after two pints of beer, and the voice bore the unmistakable mark of developing combativeness. The delivery of each sentence would rise in a steepening curve to hit the last syllable with an almost falsetto shriek, when he was in full flow. 'What's a nice lad like you doing playing bumboy for a snake like Dick Goddard?' Llewellyn gave him a smile of deferential bewilderment. 'He'll ruin your chances, son. Done it before – hasn't he, brothers?' He stood on the balls of his feet, remaining a small man with a pot belly, and glanced around his little group of regular drinking pals. They were known as Lowndes' Lushes, without complaint. 'Like his style, do you? Hitched your wagon to a star – that what you think? He's a loser, lad. Want a drink?'

'Well, thanks a lot, but I've got a meeting,' Llewellyn said.

'Off you go then. Give Tricky Dicky my love. He doesn't get much of that – does he, brothers?'

The brothers laughed. Llewellyn went away to report to Goddard, who sighed and said, 'Poor Johnny. He takes everything so personally. That's his weakness. Simply incapable of objectivity.'

When Lowndes was proposed as chairman of the campaign committee for the general election Goddard was emphatic with his support. Such a role was exactly suited to the man's special qualities, he insisted when doubts were raised. The opposition came from cautious men who wondered whether Lowndes might overplay the cheerleader and vulgarise the cause. Goddard argued patiently that the nature of the cause mattered less than that of the electorate. In other words, Lowndes was the horse for the *course*.

He believed it, and was wrong. Or so he bemoaned over the dire results as, in the sour early hours, it was made plain that the Tories had not only held on to power but added a handful of seats to their majority. (Llewellyn's was a loss Goddard especially regretted. He would have to find some other means of retaining his aide; he was determined not to lose him.) Later, Goddard reconsidered without the distraction of bile and decided he understood.

'It really wasn't that we were too crude, Roy,' he said to Llewellyn as they hunched among the sodden laurels and rhododendrons of the Hampstead rear gardens, as if prisoners in an exercise yard. 'It was the *way* we were crude. I don't blame Lowndes for talking too much, or for dragooning everyone else into too much *yack*. That's quite the silliest complaint that's been made against him in my view. The public expect politicians to talk their heads off. His mistake, and far too many of us followed his lead, including myself, was to flail at the other side too much. We all thought we were hogging the headlines. So we did a lot of the time. And what was the first word in most of those headlines? 'Tory . . .' 'Tory cock-up,' says Fiery Fanny. 'Tory kidology,' says Tiny Tim. *Their* name was the one on our lips day after day. We should have been talking about ourselves – about what *we* want the country to be like.' He winced as raindrops slid between neck and collar and dribbled halfway down his backbone. 'God, it hardly got a mention.'

Llewellyn said, 'How would you describe the country we want?'

'Where it's fun to be alive,' muttered Goddard, squelching wearily towards the house.

Llewellyn grinned at the dejected figure, and said, 'I like the evangelical ring to that. Amen, brother.' But Goddard was fumbling irritably with the wobbly handle to the kitchen door, and made no response.

The inquest was the ferment of recrimination the political commentators unanimously predicted. The Leader, whose nature was forensic rather than dynamic, could hardly be faulted as a coroner. He busied himself unsparingly in asking questions of every faction, so that he avoided answering all but a scattering of grievances levelled at himself. Lowndes did not. Attacked from three or four directions, he saw himself as the friendless scapegoat and impetuously denounced the party as mindless ingrates, one and all. He got very drunk several times during this trying time. Shrill, stammering, swearing, tearful, he was the self-made defendant and eventually defenceless. He quit the field for a while to sulk and dry out. He would recover shortly, it was generally agreed. That defiant strut would carry him around the Westminster corridors again, the yellow and grey bangs of hair bouncing off his ears as he gave a blessing here and an admonishment there. But the reputation had been damaged where it most mattered: at the heart of the party. Such brittleness under pressure had not been suspected. Allowing for the entanglement of desolation and rage, it was still surprising to see how readily his composure had collapsed. He was no longer in Goddard's way. It was a displeasing irony to Goddard that, in the end, he had removed the obstacle unwittingly. Not he alone, of course; but no one had pushed harder to place Lowndes in that exposed position. Politics, Goddard reflected, had a habit of manipulating the practitioners.

Goddard had to play his part in the collective self-inquisition, as befitted a cardinal who knew he had erred and led others astray. But he saw no point in dwelling on error. Both in public comment and party enclosure he extended the theme he had begun during that bedraggled hour of penance he and Llewellyn had performed in the glum rain of his garden. The party had to think of government, even obsessively. The electorate should be shown – 'conditioned into believing' was the phrase he sometimes used in private – that the party was brimming with new ideas. Bold innovation must abound in every sphere. Once in government the party would not merely reform but *transform*. The public should be persuaded – 'made', he often said, but again only in private – to expect it. This changing of popular attitude towards the party would, of course, take time. And empty rhetoric would not achieve it. It was necessary for the brightest minds in the party to put together a series of policy documents for general use in public re-education. These papers should not bookishly philosophise but should be terse and explicit, based on the plain man's line of *what this country needs is* . . . 'The kind of stuff even some of *our* dimwits can't make a bollocks of,' he told his intimates. He wanted a steady flow of this material so that the party troops could rely on it – 'don't find themselves forever stuck for an answer,' as he put it to the inner circle.

The Leader approved of this workmanlike approach and invited its proposer to turn thought into deed. He recognised that Goddard was promoting himself; but he had chosen a dangerous path. In a party of such tempestuous contradiction as theirs Goddard was certain to affront left wing and right simply by claiming there was an agreed view on anything at all. By offering to spell one out on all manner of things he was challenging the dissenters before even his team was picked. By asking some of them to join the team he added quandary to their vexation. If they refused to serve they would be on weak ground if they complained their opinions were not represented. If they accepted, would more than polite lip service be paid to their contribution? In that case were they not both frustrated and compromised? The Leader saw Goddard's mind at work and admired its clarity. He was prepared to draw the aim of the enemy while forcing them, for the moment, to withhold their fire. And in politics the moment was the only measurement of time to be seriously considered, as every leader should know.

Goddard's team duly suffered no disruption from those he called 'the wild, wild wingers'. They chose to concede his little coup, finding the moment best employed in discussing the production of their own, rival policy statements. These discussions spumed with rancour; integrity was preserved; no agreements were reached. The Leader said at a parliamentary party meeting how grateful he was that all sections were now applying their minds so positively to the future.

Extra research staff was needed to devil and draft for Goddard's working party, and Llewellyn's credentials were sound. Llewellyn's wife suggested he might find the work 'a bit menial after being an M.P.' Llewellyn explained to her that it would enable him to stay in London and 'in contact'. When she asked what that meant he was at first so dumbfounded by her stupidity he could only repeat, *'in contact'*. Then he added, 'with everything – where people stand, what's happening'.

His wife said presumably that meant he wouldn't be spending any more time with her and the baby than he had as an M.P., and Llewellyn said she seemed determined not to understand that politics wasn't a nine-till-five job. She shouted at him that if she knew nothing else about politics she knew that! Then the baby began to cry and she said *her* job wasn't nine-till-five either, and started crying herself as she went to see to the child. She and Llewellyn had been married for a little less than two years.

The truth was that Valerie Llewellyn was glad when her husband lost his place in the Commons. She hoped he would never get another. He had told her he might not. She had not bargained for this new work he had been given. Hardly understanding its nature, and not caring, she had perceived almost as soon as he began to talk about it how deeply the job excited him. And she also saw, if vaguely, that this excitement didn't come from the job itself but from what he thought he could make of it.

Researcher? A kind of secretary? It mystified her. It *was* menial. Also, it came to her momentarily as a ray of hope, wasn't it clearly temporary? Well, the job itself might be, but again the job was not the point. He was staying at Westminster, with those people, in that little world; *that* was the point. But there was more to it than just relief. He seemed to find his new job an advance from being a backbencher. He had enjoyed being an M.P. – had never treated it seriously enough, she'd thought, for all the hours it had kept him away from her. But he wasn't being flippant about this thing Goddard had dreamed up.

Goddard. Valerie hated Goddard; had hated him from their first meeting, when she'd been invited to tea on the terrace of the House. With Goddard it *would* be that, wouldn't it? She had never been invited to the place at Hampstead. She hated Goddard's way of staring into her eyes with that same kind of ever-so-understanding look he used whenever he was on television – and which he never used when he was talking to Roy. He didn't use it when he talked to his wife or to women politicians, either, Valerie had noticed: just with Valerie and waitresses and people like that – the great unknown and never-will-know, which was how Goddard wanted to keep them: at a respectful distance while he dedicated his life to them for a few minutes a year with his I-am-the-Light look.

She hated him, as well, because he had held the gaze on that first meeting long enough for her to become flustered. Valerie liked men to pay her attention. She liked to see in their eyes that they were admiring a pretty girl. But she wanted this from men of her own generation: young, trim, spruce men with faces of balanced contours and easy with smiles. She understood their interest in her. It was natural. But when men of Goddard's age inspected her in that way she felt a disgust. Men old enough to be her father had no right to think of her sexually. Goddard had. She'd sensed it. And when he'd sensed her recoil, her fear, he'd been pleased with himself. At every subsequent meeting he had treated her the same way: the condescension which changed subtly to lust. She said nothing of this to her husband. When Llewellyn asked what she thought of Goddard, on first impression, she said he was the sort of man who always looked as if he needed a shave. Llewellyn said he should have known he'd get a ladies' powder room answer, and didn't she realise she was talking about one of the cleverest political brains available? Obviously they put a lot of make-up on him when he went on television, said Valerie.

Llewellyn had met her when he went to work in the economic intelligence department of the oil company where she was a secretary. It was a happy time in Valerie's life. She sat high up in an air-conditioned office behind big windows looking out over the Thames and the London skyline. It was a clean office: chrome and glass, white telephones, venetian blinds. It was a rich company. Her boss and her friends' bosses journeyed abroad, came back from lunch smoking cigars, sipped iced water with slices of lemon during the afternoons. There were clean-cut young men about the building, with confident voices, white shirts and cuff-links. At weekends there was a club to go to fifteen miles down river, with springy lawns, tennis courts, private moorings for sailing dinghies. The young men's sports cars were at her beck and call. Valerie had smooth skin, grey-green eyes of a child's delicacy; she liked the touch of her hair on her neck as she walked with a stab on high heels. Her father drove a double-decker bus, which she never denied but tried to avoid mentioning at work and at the club. She was surprised, and disappointed, when one or another of the clean-cut young men was found to be the son of a machine tool fitter or an electrician, although she wouldn't say so. At twenty-two she was still a virgin when she met Llewellyn; she was not when she married him.

He had been teaching economics at a technical college, in his home town, a job he did with a determined mixture of patience and zest for eighteen months until he felt its constrictions weighing on him. (Education, he argued with his father, might make political converts but it led with the most laborious uncertainty to action.) He moved abruptly to London and to the heart of big business, which used him eagerly and where, equally eager, he learned a lot very quickly. Valerie was excited by the impetus of the man as much as by the blond handsomeness. She had no interest in politics, but she saw in Royston Llewellyn the coming charmed life of the V.I.P. lounge, the waiting limousine, the account at Harrods.

None of this connected with anything she knew of the Labour party, which was mostly a disagreeable recollection of thinly attended dances in the local community hall, where clumsy youths had disarranged her taffeta dress in her middle teens. Otherwise 'Labour' meant a hazy muddle of epithets such as 'pig-ignorant' and 'smarmy', which encompassed her father's views on the party luminaries. He voted Conservative.

Llewellyn had gloss, and a future. What else mattered? The first time they had sex she astonished herself by her own avidity. She had intended something she thought of vaguely as romantic – caresses and the brushing of lips dominating the proceedings, with the act of penetration as gentle as a sigh at the end. She found that was not at all what she wanted. The neat, smooth body met him with an urgent strength. And she surprised Llewellyn, who had expected mere compliance, submission. She had never felt less submissive in her life.

When she became pregnant there was no hesitation about their marrying. They wanted each other. And it was no handicap for Llewellyn to take a pregnant wife with him to smile blissfully at Dodburn when asked to present himself for preliminary inspection. Just as luckily he was the father of a becoming baby girl, much photographed, when he contested the election.

There was little about Dodburn for Valerie to enjoy, except for the fuss made of her and little Victoria. But she was not expected to live there, and her boredom with all the political chatter she had to endure – trivial local arguments involving road improvements and extensions to old people's homes and the like – was alleviated by knowing a new life was waiting for her in London.

The reality was a let-down. Looking after Victoria kept her to the flat. She had no income of her own. A backbencher's pay was less than Llewellyn had been earning in private industry, although he added to it by intermittent freelance work – 'advisory assessments', he told her when she asked its nature, and she was no wiser and had no wish to be. He knew that, as she well understood. What concerned her, creating a knot of resentment she at times felt like a physical pain, was her husband's virtual desertion. It had taken so little time, a matter of only a few weeks, before she realised she was dismissed from his life for days on end. He would come home in the early hours of the morning, parrying questions with the reminder that she was indifferent to his political activities. It was the catch-all answer. She was the more slighted because she felt no less attracted to him. He was clearly thriving. He had a sheen of relish. *His life entertained him.* But Valerie found she had to make an effort to keep her hair the way she liked it. She caught herself slumped in the living room, still in her dressing gown at noon, her face unwashed, sometimes with her right elbow resting on the left arm hugging her middle as the fingers of her right hand tapped abstractedly at her mouth. It was the abiding image she had of her mother. She shuddered at it before hurrying to the bathroom and the dense-packed shelf of lotions and creams. The mirror would reassure her. And on the nights – much better the afternoons! – when she and Llewellyn made love she could lose herself in a frantic pleasure that didn't diminish. But she was his tart, his bit of stuff, not his wife: she saw that now. Wasn't that what she'd offered him? Wasn't it also what she liked being? She accepted it as long as it was private to them. She was humiliated when she saw it recognised in the faces of Goddard and his kind. So, in due course she chose to avoid them.

*

'Is Valerie coming up?'

'She might sort of pop her head in at some stage. Maybe,' Llewellyn said. He was walking with Craddock along the sands below Brinsley Bay's half-mile of esplanade. There was a pale sun and the familiar aggressive wind. Neither of them was wearing a topcoat, which they regretted. They held their jacket collars closed over their throats with one hand, the other clenched in a protecting pocket. Every few yards the hands swapped places. A woman in wellington boots and a duffel coat threw a stick into the sea for two big brown dogs to chase. Otherwise they were alone on the beach. It would be a month yet before the Scottish holidaymakers would take their places on it; family groups making camp with canvas windshields, grandparents lashed down in their deckchairs with tartan blankets, staunchly claiming their money's worth of fresh air. The by-election would be decided before then.

'What does she think of the place?'

'As a matter of fact she's never seen it,' Llewellyn answered.

'Really? Never?' Craddock checked his step in surprise.

'Well, she's pretty busy. She's working again. Does half-days for some chap in the rag trade. Importer. One-man show. Needed a smart girl to keep things neat and tidy for him. Made quite a difference.'

'How?'

'Pays well, for one thing.' Llewellyn gave him a quick grin. 'Neither of us likes having to watch our pennies.' Craddock nodded. 'She looks good. Gets her clothes cheap, of course – being around the business.'

Craddock said, 'What about the baby?'

'Smashing. Fine. Old enough for day nursery now, you see. Valerie picks her up when she's finished with Rosenpants, or whatever his name is. Oh sure, Vicky's fine.' He paused and then said, 'It really has made a difference. All the new friends, I mean. The world of politics didn't seem to make Valerie feel at home.'

'She doesn't know you're here, does she?' Craddock's mock-solemn delivery was intended to take some of the sting out of the barb, as Llewellyn understood.

'Christ, Tony, it isn't as bad as that. I just don't expect her to play the *ever-loving*, ever-present, that's all.'

Craddock said, 'Aren't the local worthies a bit put out? They're bound to think there must be a few votes in having that little cracker on your arm – I'm thinking aloud for *them*, when I word it like that, of course.'

Llewellyn said quickly, 'As it happens, we've got one or two little crackers doing the rounds with the leaflets and the loudspeaker van. I've got a very decorative team, Tony. This blighted bloody outpost actually has one very randy corner. We shall not go short, old son.'

'Hadn't you better behave yourself?' Craddock dabbed at the wet end of his nose with his handkerchief.

'Look, Tony,' Llewellyn spun round to put his back to the wind and faced Craddock, the two of them standing still with trousers flapping and hair flicking. Llewellyn had always been amused by Craddock's spasms of earnestness, and he saw one now in the furrows around the mouth and eyes. He wanted to grab Craddock, bear-hug him, make him scuffle, as he would have done when they were children; but not since a failed attempt in adolescence – Craddock rigid with embarrassment – had he tried to break these moods with horseplay. He smiled and shook his head in a show of despair. '*Look*. What do you think I'm doing here?'

'Wasting your time.'

'Wrong. I've just told you.' Llewellyn put on a comic rustic voice, 'Theer be crumpet.'

Craddock was obstinately patient. 'I mean professionally. Politically.'

'God, you're a solemn old sod when you put your mind to it,' Llewellyn told him. 'If I'm wasting my time trying to win this seat – and you're right, of *course* I can't win it – what the hell does it matter . . . ?'

Craddock walked on again. 'Fair enough. Just asking,' he said.

'Well, it's got *some* value. Of course it has.' Llewellyn had to raise his voice as he hurried to catch up. The sand was more powdery here, where a curved set of stone steps met the beach from the esplanade. Craddock started up them. 'I make a fight of it. Narrow the gap. The doughty warrior. Party before self. It's an investment. Hang on, man – *I'm* supposed to be the big show-off around here.' Craddock had run up the last dozen steps. He stood with his hands on his hips, taking deep gulps of the morning air. Llewellyn took the steps two at a time, and when he reached the top he continued running along the pavement. Then he added a few jabs of shadow boxing.

Craddock called to him, 'Save it for the photographers.'

They had agreed on this pre-breakfast walk the night before. Craddock had arrived in time to watch the Tory candidate in action at a public meeting – an attendance of seventeen; no questions from the floor – and then he had joined old Hector Brunskill for a drink and an Indian curry. That is, while Craddock had drunk lager Hector stuck to water; he had remained teetotal since being treated for alcoholism 'in the fancy-that farm', as he called it, a year or so before. Also, he was not strictly speaking old, being in his early forties. But he walked with a stick because he was a chronic bronchitic, and Craddock had always known him with grey in his thin hair and straggly moustache. They had worked on the same evening paper ten miles along the coast for a while as Craddock followed his treasure hunt to London. Now old Hector was chief reporter on the weekly *Brinsley Bay Chronicle*. He was wearing a new brown suit with a red waistcoat. He told Craddock he'd already bought four of these sporty waistcoats, in different colours, and wondered whether that amounted to an addiction. He also told him about the time in hospital, shrugging away any unpleasant memories and providing a wealth of circumstantial detail on a ceremonial inspection by the hospital management committee. Hector knew several of the members, as a local reporter would, and so the medical superintendent roped him in to help show them round. The prospect amused Hector greatly – *fancy that, if it isn't Mr Brunskill!* – and the event did not disappoint. In the recreation room the woman chairman sat down beside some gaunt unfortunate staring blankly at a pack of cards, and found the seat wobbling under her weight. It was one of the tubular framed stacking-chairs to be found all over the hospital. The diligent woman set about testing chairs 'like a berserk little Red Riding Hood', as Hector put it. Eventually she announced her findings: *wonky screws*. 'Well, madam,' said Hector reasonably, 'where else would you expect to find a screw or two loose if not here?' Some laughed, some didn't. Among the latter was the chairman who thought jokes about the sick were in bad taste. Hector found this so funny he went dizzy with breathlessness, and the inspection concluded without him. As he laughed about it now over the curry he wheezed and spluttered enough to alarm Craddock. 'Don't fuss, Tony,' Hector said between gasps, 'do you think I want to live forever?'

'Quaint old bird, that,' Llewellyn said when Craddock phoned him from the Royal Hotel after leaving Hector at the door of Mrs McMahon's boarding house where he occupied a bed-sitter. 'That's you in ten years' time if you don't get a good woman and some property behind you.'

'Nobody's mother could express it better,' said Craddock.

Llewellyn had rented a small flat for the duration of the campaign. It was more private than the Royal, where he had stayed overnight before in cheerless company: old salesmen who sighed a lot, young ones with big signet rings who guffawed. 'I've got some preparation to do for tomorrow,' he said when Craddock suggested a nightcap.

'If you feel you need it,' said Craddock when Llewellyn proposed the morning stroll beside the seaside.

It had proved far too cold for the relaxed old-mates chat they had in mind. But a day later Llewellyn was back on the sands at the same bold early hour, this time in slacks and a sweater and tennis shoes. The photographers caught him shadow boxing. They were cheerful, out-of-the-ordinary pictures to come from a by-election and appeared in most of the national dailies, as well as the locals. The captions referred to a *left hook*, or *jab*, or *swing*; one, not quite so predictably, to *the man in the red corner*. Llewellyn laughed appreciatively when he read Craddock's comment in his paper – *from our own correspondent* – that 'the politics of the engaging young Labour candidate lack the punch of his personal publicity'.

*

The punch Brendon Cope threw at Llewellyn two nights prior to the poll would have disarranged the candidate's face greatly, had the blow landed. It was a free-style lunge with the right arm, delivered on the run. But for the run Llewellyn would probably not have seen what was coming. Brendon Cope, however, was too angry for stealth or deliberation. He ran at the handsome face so hard that his impetus, when Llewellyn stepped back and ducked under the fist, carried him on in a whirling stumble until he tripped over his own ankles and fell. He knocked over two wooden chairs before coming to rest, and this delay reduced the impact of the back of his head against the bare floorboards. It was still enough to leave him dazed. He had to be helped up. There was no blood to be seen, but his eyes bore the blank aimlessness of the concussed. He was helped to a chair.

All this bewildering activity occurred in only a few seconds, and no one present had yet had time to ask its cause or suggest what should be done next. There was now another unexpected entry. Two men and a woman came hurrying into the room. The woman was Brendon Cope's wife, Eileen, known to everyone present. The men were strangers, although one was immediately recognisable as a newspaper photographer because he had a camera at the ready as he made straight for the half-stunned attacker. In a voice that was half a sob and half a shriek Eileen uttered the first word spoken since her husband had come running from the swing doors. 'Brendon' was all she said. She crouched beside him, her face creased tight in anxiety. The photographer moved in closely on the couple. His companion, looking round the faces, caught Llewellyn's eye for a moment before Llewellyn threw up an arm as if to ward off another flying fist, at the same time turning his back to the company. The reporter – as it was clear he was – began, 'Mr Llewellyn, can I ask you . . . ?'

He got no further. A thickly built man in his late fifties bellowed, 'Get out of here, the pair of you. Take one more bloody snap and I'll break that bloody thing over your head!' Councillor Gilbert Hobbs, the leader of the Brinsley Bay Labour group and Llewellyn's agent for the election, advanced on the photographer with both burly arms reaching out. The photographer hesitated, then lowered the camera.

'Listen, we're from the . . .' But again the reporter's voice was overwhelmed by Councillor Hobbs. 'Out, out, get out! Bursting in here! You're on private property . . .'

The reporter, in his middle twenties with neat hair and a closely-cut suit, was not intimidated. 'We're from . . .' he tried again.

'Out, little man!'

Now the rest of the company came to life, crowding on the two intruders and urging them out through the swing doors. Llewellyn heard the reporter's voice and Councillor Hobbs crushing it:

'I want to ask him . . .'

'Out, out!'

A door slammed and a bolt banged. Llewellyn looked at Brendon and Eileen Cope. She looked back, biting on her lower lip. Brendon also looked at him, or vaguely in his direction, and declared with an oddly bored-sounding sigh, 'Bastard.'

Councillor Hobbs led his helpers back through the swing doors. 'This is handy. Very handy, this,' he said, lifting his thick jaw at Llewellyn. Then he studied Brendon. 'What's *his* condition? Fighting fit? I hope no one laughs at that.' No one laughed.

Eileen's voice was milky with love. 'Come on, pet. I'll take you home.'

'Bitch,' said Brendon.

'Oh, pet.' Tears welled in Eileen's eyes.

Councillor Hobbs said to her, 'Is that his shooting-brake outside – the Ford?' She nodded. 'Do you want someone to go with you?' She shook her head, and took the keys from Brendon's left jacket pocket before she stood up.

'Bren, pet, come on,' she said, putting an arm across his shoulders.

'Bitch,' Brendon muttered as he got up. He was six feet tall, with glistening black shoes and a golf club tie. Her arm slid down to settle round the small of his back as he rose, and it was clearly customary. He held her head in the crook of his arm and they made unsteadily for the door. It was not the first time one or two of those present had seen the Copes set course for home in just this way, although under different circumstances: usually from licensed premises on a Saturday night, Brendon giggling drunk with Irish whisky.

'Those two press lads are waiting outside,' said Councillor Hobbs. 'We can't stop them taking pictures in the street. Just have a care what you say to them.' He held open the swing doors.

'What's there to say? Shan't say anything,' Eileen said, her voice muffled as Brendon forced her face tightly against his chest.

Llewellyn lit a cigarette as he heard the bolt bang open, the door slam and the bolt bang shut. Back came Councillor Hobbs. 'Right then, Roy,' he said, 'what's to do with this little lot?'

In the past minute or so Llewellyn had become sharply aware of how dismal his surroundings were. He was in the Trades and Labour Hall. It was a rectangle with a raised platform at one end. The walls had lately been papered in zig-zag lines, alternating green and black. It was the kind of pattern known as 'contemporary', and he had seen it in snack-bars, and at least one factory canteen in recent weeks. It suited Dead-Alive-on-Sea like livery. Beyond the swing doors was a corridor to the outer door with the banging bolt, and off the corridor were the two dank lavatories with bars at the broken windows and the dank office with dull brown cupboards and a floor of red linoleum. Such were his campaign committee rooms. It was mid-evening. The dim old hall was beginning to feel the cold.

Llewellyn could not remember a deeper sense of futility.

He looked flatly at Councillor Hobbs and asked, 'What do *you* think it was all about, Gilbert?'

The councillor opened his mouth but did not immediately speak. He glanced round the little group of helpers, who variously examined the floor, the distant corners of the ceiling, their finger-nails, their wrist-watches. Then he said to Llewellyn, 'Well, to start with, let's say it was a personal matter. D'you agree with *that*? Very, very *personal*.' His eyes bulged with exasperation as Llewellyn gave thought to the matter. The councillor shouted, 'Roy, bloody hell!'

'I'd call it private,' Llewellyn said at last.

Councillor Hobbs gulped as he again looked round the group and again found evasion. He pointed at the swing doors. 'That's the *Sunday Star* sitting waiting for you out there. How many more husbands . . . ? The group emitted a form of collective exclamation, suppressed. A nose sniffed, a throat coughed, hands became busy with coat buttons, a handbag was opened and snapped shut. Except for Llewellyn and the councillor all present were women.

'What does the *Sunday Star* matter?' asked one of them. 'Polling day's on Thursday. It'll be all over then.' She was plump, with a great mound of black hair. Llewellyn gave her a smile. She was one of the first of the score of young women to be recruited as canvassers; Llewellyn's Chorus Line, they had been dubbed in some of the papers after he was photographed performing a rather ragged high-kick routine with a bunch of them on the esplanade.

'Matter? All over?' Councillor Hobbs was breathless. He raised both arms out to shoulder level and let his hands fall noisily against his thighs. He glared round the company. 'Mud sticks where it lands,' he said.

Llewellyn started for the swing doors. Briskly he said, 'Let's not forget the night shift with the loudspeaker van. I just want to make a 'phone call from the office and then we'll be off. Right, girls?'

As the doors squeaked behind him the half-dozen young women produced lipsticks and compacts and re-touched their warpaint.

*

Eileen Cope would be able to handle Brendon; there was no need for any further worry on that score, Craddock assured Llewellyn. The man was still a bit groggy when Craddock arrived at the couple's house soon after talking to Llewellyn on the 'phone, but his wife had already begun to repair his injured pride and adjust his understanding of what the *Sunday Star* had told him. She was a strong and persuasive woman, very hard to resist on her home ground, Craddock imagined. Brendon would come to believe her innocent because she wanted him to, and disbelieving was too painful for him.

Brendon was known as a 'technical sales rep'. He worked for a company that supplied central heating installations to factories and office blocks. He liked to emphasise the incautious broth-of-a-boy element in his character, having a grandmother from County Cork; and if the *Sunday Star* knew that, it was a good reason for opening inquiries with Brendon rather than with any of the other husbands they might have gone to. And might visit yet, of course, Craddock added.

It seemed they had been waiting for Brendon to get back from work, staying in their car until he drove up to the new house in Windermere Close and allowing him a few minutes of domestic chatter before ringing the ding-dong front doorbell and asking Eileen if her husband was at home. She was dressed ready to go out. In fact she was already overdue at the Trades and Labour Hall. There had been a short-tempered exchange with Brendon about his being late home and her needing the car. Brendon had said work was work, and how did she think she'd pay for all these new hair-dos and babysitters if he didn't flog his guts out for her? She said there was beer on his breath. Ever likely there was, said Brendon, when he knew he was coming home to another bloody ham salad and she was off round the town playing at politics which she didn't know from hoola-hooping, if truth be told. So Eileen was for a moment glad that two men should come asking to speak to her husband, presumably about central heating. It was not until she had taken them into the open-plan living room, and Brendon was straightening his tie to receive company, that the *Sunday Star* reporter said, 'Actually, we want to talk to you *both*. We're from the *Sunday Star* and we're making inquiries about Royston Llewellyn's election campaign. Is it true he's been threatened with violence for getting too friendly with his women canvassers?'

The reporter was a bright lad, Craddock said. If he'd got tired of waiting for Brendon, and put the question to Eileen on her own, she would have had the presence of mind to brazen the whole thing out with cold indignation. Instead, her quick mind worked to her disadvantage. Her eyes shot to Brandon, to see whether the reporter's implication had registered, and the look made all plain to him. It was a close marriage.

Eileen knew her husband was about to strike her. But the photographer chose now to produce the camera concealed under his raincoat. This distracted Brendon. The camera – as is often the case when people are under stress, Craddock commented – was suddenly the most offensive presence, and Brendon gave it his full attention. The photographer recognised the glower as of the kind best left unrecorded, and the camera went back under the raincoat. Brendon's mind was now cleared of obstructions. He saw the primary target, and without a word he rushed at it.

His estate car was out of Windermere Close before the *Sunday Star* men had their own vehicle on the move. Eileen, in the back seat, directed them to the Trades and Labour Hall.

Llewellyn asked, 'Do you think they'll do a story?'

Craddock said, '*Has* anyone threatened to beat you up?'

'No.'

'Warned you off?'

'No.'

'Any of the girls talked about being worried? About their husbands knowing what's been going on, I mean.'

'Not a word.'

'Apart from Eileen Cope, how many more of these women have you actually had your leg over?'

After a short pause Llewellyn said, 'Three.'

'How long has Gilbert Hobbs known about it?'

'I think it all came as an amazing revelation to him tonight.' Llewellyn gave a short laugh. 'He's said to me once or twice I'm the first candidate he's known to lay on girls for the visiting reporters. He thought he was making a big joke.' Llewellyn imitated the councillor's voice, 'Very enterprising piece of press relations, Roy . . . chuckle, chuckle.' He reverted to his own voice. 'It would never occur to that fossil you *can* actually mix sex and politics. Not a gamesome kind of man, our Gilbert.'

Craddock lifted the whisky bottle, and when Llewellyn shook his head poured a couple of inches into his own glass and carried it to the wash basin for a splash of cold water. They were in Craddock's hotel room. The night porter had brought them cheese sandwiches and a pot of coffee. Craddock had acquired the whisky from an off-licence after his call on the Copes, anticipating a long night and mindful of the mark-up on hotel bar prices.

'You bash that stuff pretty hard these days, Tony,' Llewellyn said. He was on the single bed, propped against the headboard. The sandwich tray was on the floor within reach of his right hand. He felt sleepy. What alarm there had been earlier had been dispelled by the simple passing of time.

'How much do you care?' Craddock sat in the only chair, of moulded plastic with a gap at kidney level in its curved back. It belonged in a cafeteria, not a bedroom. The Royal was that kind of hotel.

'Drink what you like, old son.' Llewellyn bit into a sandwich and closed his eyes as he chewed.

'What?' Craddock sounded puzzled, then immediately irritated. 'I didn't mean that. I like a drop at night. I hardly touch the stuff in the daytime. Not the hard stuff, anyway.'

Llewellyn opened his eyes and waved the half-eaten sandwich, acknowledging he was a tired man who had misunderstood.

Craddock went on quietly, 'I mean how much do you care if the *Star* run their story?'

'Depends what's in it.' Llewellyn was exhausted by the sandwich. He settled lower against the headboard, a padded panel fixed to the wall, and closed his eyes again.

'Christ, man, we know that.' Craddock's irritation surfaced again. 'They'll give the readers a giggle with a nice old-fashioned piece of Sunday paper innuendo. Lots of quotes about chasing the women's vote, and charming the ladies, and taking a personal interest, and it'll add up to the juicy implications that you *solicited* for votes with your cock in your hand.'

'Nasty,' said Llewellyn, yawning.

'Their one problem is finding a peg to hang it all on. That's what they hoped to get from Brendon. If they'd arrived on the scene in time to get a picture of him taking a swing at you . . .'

Llewellyn's eyes opened and he sat up. 'All they've got is a picture of a chap sitting on a chair looking a bit unwell. Means nothing at all.'

'If someone tells the *Star* what happened . . .' Craddock was absorbed in working out the professional problem posed. 'You see, if they *know* he tried to thump you and then went arse over tip they're home and dry. They don't have to name their informant in the story, if he or she won't let them. They just have to give the name to the news desk to keep the lawyer happy. But if they've got that information all they have to do is ask you if it's true. Or ask Hobbs. Or any of the lovelies who were there.'

Llewellyn said, 'So it's no comment, piss off. Like we said it tonight.'

Craddock said, 'It would go something like, er, 'Roy Llewellyn, the pin-up boy politician, refused to comment on reports that he was involved in a scuffle with the husband of one of his pretty women canvassers . . .' Or it might go, 'Labour party officials have drawn a blanket of secrecy over an incident involving pin-up boy politician Roy Llewellyn and the husband of one of his team of women canvassers. Burly Brendon Cope had to be helped home suffering from concussion following . . .' Do you see what I mean?'

Llewellyn nodded gravely.

Craddock continued, 'There's the comment from the local copshop – 'No complaint has been made, blah, blah'. Then there's good-looking, ash-blonde Eileen Cope tight-lipped behind closed doors in her executive-style home. And of course the party officials who expressed surprise that Mr Llewellyn's pretty young wife Valerie did not accompany him . . .'

'You're enjoying this, you bastard,' Llewellyn said.

Craddock was on his way back to the wash basin with his whisky. 'I'm a bit rusty. It's three years since I last shovelled shit for the nation's leading tabloid. The little matter of a transvestite cat-burglar was my parting contribution to the *Daily Heave*. You definitely don't want this story in print, do you?'

'No. It'll look very squalid. And it hasn't been like that. Some people have found some pleasure in unlikely circumstances.'

There was impatience in Craddock's manner as he drank and then went back to the chair. 'What's wrong with that?'

Craddock shrugged. 'You make yourself sound like some kind of sexual missionary. They've been copulating here for years.'

Llewellyn heard something in Craddock's tone he regretted. He could not identify it. He knew he regretted it for Craddock's sake. He said, 'Look, I'm talking about pleasure. What are *you* talking about?'

After a pause Craddock said, as if he had not heard the question, 'It's surprising what people will tell newspapers. The *Star* are bound to make the rounds of these women. I think you ought to assume one of them's going to talk. Jealousy. Self-importance. Ten quid. You can take your pick of reasons.'

Llewellyn asked flatly, 'How can I kill this story?'

Craddock replied, 'Why don't you try putting out the authorised version?'

★

It took them a good hour to draft the short statement, picking their way carefully to reach the note somewhere between contempt and saddened indignation which they agreed was the right one.

Llewellyn took it with him when he drove himself the few hundred yards back to his flat. Waiting outside the block when he arrived were the *Sunday Star* reporter and photographer. As Craddock had predicted they had kept away from the Royal to avoid meeting the other journalists who had gathered for the last few days of the by-election. The pair got hastily out of their car, with its steamed windows.

'Mr Llewellyn, Roy, can we have a word . . . ?' The reporter smiled: amiable, intimate. He put out his right arm. It could have been an attempt to bar Llewellyn's way or merely an offer of a handshake.

Llewellyn walked steadily past and up the short flight of concrete steps to the front door. 'I'm having my usual press conference in the morning. Nine-forty-five. Goodnight.'

Fifteen minutes later he was sound asleep.

Craddock was not. He was in the residents' lounge at the Royal, where he was softly telling a hunched group of five other daily newspaper men that the *Sunday Star* were around, up to no good at all as far as present company was concerned. They were after an exclusive, and if they got it there would be some awkward questions, come Sunday morning, about the story that got away right under other people's noses. What they were trying to do was blow the gaff about the Chorus Line dropping their knickers.

The bastards! Llewellyn's lovelies had been accommodating to several representatives of the fourth estate.

Llewellyn appreciated that, said Craddock. He could, of course, stonewall the *Star* and wait to see what they served up. As far as he was concerned it might be a matter for legal action, or complaint to the Press Council, or personal protest to the editor, or it might be he could afford to write if off to experience. But he wasn't the only one involved. If the *Star* carried their piece follow-up enquiries by the dailies would be inevitable. And then who knew what names might get bandied about? Wasn't there an unwritten law against causing your mates to get dropped in the mire like that?

Too fucking true there was!

Normally, of course, nobody's news editor cared a spit if one of his lads found himself a bit of spare. Good luck to him. But if it got in the way of his work, compromised him on a story, he was in deep trouble, wasn't he?

Abso-bleeding-lutely!

Craddock thought it might be wise if they all had a word with their offices now. Let them know the *Star* were creeping around trying to make some dirt about Llewellyn stand up. Show their offices they were already on to it. Llewellyn was saying nothing tonight, but he was promising to cut up pretty rough tomorrow. That way, nobody could accuse them of being caught on the hop.

Good thinking, Tony. Same again?

*

Llewellyn delivered his statement next morning in the Trades and Labour hall. His dictation speed was measured for the reporters without shorthand:

'With great distaste I have to report that the activities of a national Sunday newspaper have caused much distress to members of my election campaign team.

'I discovered yesterday evening that representatives of this newspaper were responsible for certain rumours implying impropriety between myself and a lady canvasser, or canvassers. As a result of these rumours one canvasser and her husband came to see me during the evening at my committee rooms in a state of considerable agitation.

'I understand that several more of my campaign helpers were interviewed at their homes during the night. In view of this, and the nature of the questions put to them, I feel I have no option but to make this statement. I would prefer to ignore this gossip-mongering or deal with it privately. But I am forced to make public my disgust, and my protest, on behalf of others who may be callously hurt.

'I do this in the hope that the newspaper concerned will discontinue its offensive activities immediately. It has already caused deep unpleasantness, quite unnecessarily, in a small and harmonious community.'

Llewellyn declined to name any of his distressed or agitated helpers, as everyone present knew he would although the question was dutifully put. He declined to name the offending Sunday newspaper – although he surmised most of those present knew its identity. If the paper chose to identify itself by publishing its gossip pickings it was at liberty to do so. No doubt its lawyers would give appropriate advice.

Craddock asked him whether on reflection he thought he might have overplayed the publicity gimmick of Llewellyn's Lovelies, even if it had brightened an otherwise rather listless election. Llewellyn replied tartly that his loyal, hardworking helpers were not to be slighted as a gimmick. He didn't see why canvassing couldn't be cheerful, especially at the seaside.

Hector Brunskill asked if Llewellyn proposed to make any political comment of any kind today, which gave everyone a laugh – which, in turn, served as an answer. The press conference broke up. The young man from the *Sunday Star* left without speaking. He went directly to a telephone box.

*

By and large local newspapers welcome the opportunity to quote derogatory references to national newspapers. For the three evening publications in the region – Brinsley Bay itself had only its weekly – Llewellyn's words were front-page material. There was, for one thing, the sense of closing ranks against meddlesome outsiders. With phrases such as 'certain rumours implying impropriety' and 'small and harmonious community' Llewellyn had simultaneously provided evidence of others' prurience and justification for printing it. Several of the women canvassers, unnamed, were credited with being 'bitter' or 'shocked' or 'dumbfounded'. One said, tearfully according to the reporter, that she felt 'as if I've been branded'. Another, said to be a youth club leader, described the rumours as 'sheer wickedness – a sign of the times we live in'.

National newspapers commonly avoid acknowledging the existence of other national newspapers if at all possible. So the following morning the dailies' coverage was largely a matter of bold headlines and timid text. *Would-be M.P. In 'Impropriety' Storm* promised well. An opening sentence declaring 'a by-election town rocked by rumours' carried energy. But thereafter, with no villain, not even an unidentified newspaper, the story seemed more on the defensive than the people in it. The dailies all handled it much the same way. No one was embarrassed by another's unexpected interviewee. Craddock, whose paper was a 'heavy', which meant it permitted its reporters to mix opinion with descriptive reportage, wasted no more than two paragraphs on the story in the middle of a thousand-word forecast of Tory success. 'A candidate who promenades through a campaign with a different girl on each arm daily is a provocative figure in "a small and harmonious community",' he wrote. 'In a town like Brinsley Bay even the seagulls go tut-tut.'

Gilbert Hobbs had refused comment to the papers, beyond a formal endorsement of Llewellyn's statement. He had little more to say to Llewellyn, giving him a long shake of the head on the candidate's arrival at the committee rooms and telling him within the hearing of a dozen campaign workers, 'We'll stick to our own kind in future.'

Llewellyn, who had been stimulated by his breakfast reading – he had woken Craddock with a 'phone call, relishing discussion, and been rebuffed for intruding on a hangover – felt depression settle on him like fog at this bleat of rebuke. Once again he was abruptly weighted with that feeling of futility: a futility of place, of being somewhere which would never matter because it was determined not to.

He shook off this instant misery for the sake of personal reputation, making a joke of his agent's hostility. 'Quite right, Gilbert,' he said, 'over-optimism can lead to disappointment.'

Soon after midnight the Conservative candidate was declared elected. His majority was slightly increased. In his victory speech from the balcony of the town hall he noted that more of the electorate had turned out to vote than was generally expected at by-elections. And he thought he must thank Royston Llewellyn for doing so much to keep the election in the public eye. There was some laughter at this among the crowd of about a hundred people. During it Llewellyn shook hands with the victor and murmured, 'Rather you than me, old son.'

CHAPTER ELEVEN

Llewellyn did not hasten back to London. He would have done, had Dick Goddard not wanted some inquiries made in the city up the river. 'Life can't be all play,' he said when he explained his requirements to Llewellyn on the 'phone. That had been a week ago, part of what Goddard called 'clearing the pending tray' before he set off to America for ten days to discuss the world's ailments with a variety of diagnosticians. It was part of the preparation for Government. So was Llewellyn's diverted journey, even if it seemed to him an unequal comparison.

Goddard's primary interest was the nature of one Councillor George Birtles. Llewellyn felt he'd had his fill of local eminents. Goddard said this one was being represented to him as very much out of the ordinary. Llewellyn said he knew the man ruled the roost in his native acres, but wasn't it a law of life that every town had someone of the kind? If that was all he was Goddard would not be sending Llewellyn on this inspection, came the answer.

'What am I looking for?'

'Whatever there is,' Goddard said.

Llewellyn consulted Hector Brunskill.

'Birtles? Clear case of arrested childhood. He always wanted the biggest box of toy building bricks in the world. Well, it's taken about thirty-five years and now he's the happiest little lad you ever did see.' Hector's cough left his head trembling.

Less fancifully Hector supplied the bare bones of Birtles' life. He was a slum boy. By trade he was a motor mechanic. He became a Labour city councillor nine years ago, when Labour were a disorganised opposition overstocked with deaf grandfathers. In that time he had become the Labour leader and put his party back in firm control, with himself calling the tune on pretty well everything from the composition of the gravy on school dinners to the design of the proposed new civic sports centre complete with Olympic-size swimming pool.

Llewellyn soon saw Hector's point about the building bricks. He had, of course, passed through or round the city a number of times on his way to and from Brinsley Bay, but he had never stopped to look at it before in his eagerness to be back in London. Now he realised the whole place was being re-made. Its centre seemed to be populated almost entirely by men in protective helmets. It shook to the noise of pneumatic drills and pile-drivers as if under heavy shell-fire. The huge craters reinforced the illusion. So did the sight of the surviving clusters of shops and offices: mud-spattered remnants, some of them propped up by angled timber supports, defying the bombardment. The traffic followed a maze of half-streets, ordered left and right by makeshift barriers beyond which the holes gaped and the dust rolled in waves.

The new city would be a hallelujah to concrete. The framework already grew from the judder and murk of the craters. And around these soaring lattices the men in helmets clambered, dwarfed by their creation like infants on a gigantic climbing frame: George Birtles' playmates given the freedom of his toys – with all the overtime pay they cared to earn.

This imagery of the childish was not destroyed by Llewellyn's meeting with Birtles, the very important person. Llewellyn like him immediately. He liked the atmosphere of glee the man carried with him. Just as old Hector had said, 'the happiest little lad . . .' Except that Birtles was nearing forty, against Llewellyn's thirty-one; and he had a bald dome from where straggly yellow hair fell around his temples and his ear lobes – they were big, pronounced ears, standing out from his head as if permanently cupped; and the shoulders and forearms were thick under the jacket of his grey check suit – rather a good suit, not from one of the multiple tailors, Llewellyn observed. But Birtles had eyes of positively *baby* blue. He had an exuberant way of jerking his arms and shoulders to emphasise a point when he talked – and he talked much of the time in emphases. When he walked he bounced with excess of energy.

He walked Llewellyn round his vast playground. They both wore helmets, Birtles' yellow spikes of hair protruding as if he had a prize chrysanthemum lining his. He sustained a monologue at the headlong pace of a small boy telling a friend how he beat up the entire Corporation Street gang single-handed.

'. . . First and foremost it's a question of self-respect, Roy. That's what all this is for. The self-respect of the people of this city, this region, this country. And when I say the people of this country I mean the *real* people, the *common* people so-called, the ones who do the toil and earn the soft life and the three-hour lunches for the few. *My* people. If you want me to put it that way I will. Ten years ago I never gave a thought to politics. I'll tell you what happened. I used to live in Meadow Street – *Meadow* Street, my God, you should have seen the state of that; early Victorian *midden*, that's what Meadow Street was – and we'd got slates off the roof and rats in the lofts and walls so damp you could make holes in them with your *fingers*. And there was a private landlord, and he wouldn't do a *thing*. And the council was deaf, blind and dumb, and let him get away with it, so I said *right, it's a rent strike*. And you know, Roy, the people in Meadow Street – most of them old, I grant that but it's no proper explanation – they were frightened to do it. They thought they'd be put out on the street with no one to turn to. And *that* did it. From then on I was in politics. And I knew why, and I knew what I wanted. These people were *broken*, Roy. The Twenties, the Thirties, no work, starvation level – they'd never got their heads up since. And that's when I saw what had to be done. Make do and mend? Remember that from the war? Perhaps you're too young. No? Right, you remember. But wrong! Won't do. Not on your life! Only one answer. Start afresh! Break the hold of the *past*. Roy. *That's* what we do. *Our* streets. We *build* our own future – that's an intentional pun. Hullo there, good morning, yes and all the best to you, good morning, thank you . . .'

They had emerged from one of the craters and encountered a little knot of his fellow citizens, without helmets, waiting at a temporary bus stop. They were mostly middle-aged women and when they saw Birtles there was a flurry of hand-waving, smiles and warm encouragement. *Hullo, Mr Birtles. It's looking fine. Well done, pet.*

'Do you get the *feeling* in the place, Roy? Exciting, isn't it? Something's *happening. That's* the point . . .'

The comic and the dynamic were entwined in Birtles like two

crossed fingers. He had much the same effect on the army of building workers as on the old dears at the bus stop. Grimed faces scarred by the weather broke into grins as he sped among them. There was even laughter – open and approving, the kind that says, *Here's someone who doesn't give a damn, and good luck to him.* Birtles responded with uninhibited delight, whirling his right arm in the air as if with a soccer fan's rattle, even clenching both fists above his head in a fighter's salute. More laughter. Some of the men beat out a greeting with spanners on the metal scaffolding. Birtles was a star turn. Llewellyn could not call to mind anyone else he had known who so winningly affected to flout authority while exercising it. Unquestionably he was in charge. Work resumed in his wake with a quickened pace.

Llewellyn was led up ladders and along cat-walks and delivered to a vantage point where he gripped a rail with tremulous white hands. The backs of his knees felt weak. Birtles was balanced legs apart, like a naval skipper on his bridge. On went the monologue. He ticked off the embryonic wonders of his new city with his right hand thrust with a flourish from the shoulder.

'. . . Eight sixteen-storey blocks radiating from a common circular recreation area – lawns, children's playground, trees. Visualise it, Roy. A vertical village within a city. It'll be one of the sights of Europe. I tell you, Roy, the town planners on the continent are going to *flock* here. We'll *amaze* them . . . The new shopping precinct – on *three levels* not counting the underground car park. Escalators without steps – can't get a baby pram up steps. There'll be coffee bars and restaurants in that precinct. Keeping up the sense of *community*. The family that shops together stays together – it's an American slogan but it fits the bill . . . The new leisure centre. We'll have a civic theatre in there that'll have London green with envy . . . What's the matter, Roy? A bit off colour?'

'It's heady stuff,' said Llewellyn with a smile through pale lips.

For the first time Birtles noticed Llewellyn's anxious gripping of the rail. 'I'm sorry,' he said 'I get carried away. I love it up here. Let's get you back on terra firma.' He patted Llewellyn on the shoulder. 'Just keep moving steadily.'

They were halfway down one of the ladders when Birtles stopped and flung out that semaphoring right hand again. 'I've got to point out *that*. New civic administration centre. Hate that name *town hall*. Victorian. The Dark Ages. It won't be a hall, it'll be a *tower*. Built on a natural hill right in the middle of the park. It'll dominate the city. We'll floodlight it at night. I *love* floodlighting. Like candles on a birthday cake, isn't it?'

Llewellyn's attack of vertigo had left him. He was far more in danger of being shaken off the ladder by laughing. Yes, without doubt, the happiest little lad . . .

*

Harrison, the Leader, was getting close to paranoia in his mistrust of the civil service, according to Goddard. 'The conspiracy to obstruct. I don't see it myself. But then, Harrison's always been hostile to servants of any kind. Notice how he roughens his accent when he's dealing with a head waiter, for example. It's supposed to be a warning that he knows all the tricks – 'I worked my way up through a rougher school than you'. That sort of thing. The press think he does it to ingratiate himself with the working class. Not at all. It's aggression. Suspicion. Head waiters and senior civil servants are the same breed in Harrison's mind. They're here to trip him up, catch him out, doctor the figures. I hoped he'd grow out of it. It's a pity he never got into uniform during the war. He might have learned to give orders. It saves so much time.'

Llewellyn commented that the Leader usually got his own way.

'Eventually,' said Goddard with some irritation. 'But he will persist with this maddening business of planting his own ideas in other people's minds and then pretending they've convinced *him*. He actually believes no one's ever tumbled to it. He worries me. There simply won't be the elbow room for all that fandango when we're in office.'

When we're in office . . . The phrase peppered all Goddard's conversation now. The present government had a big enough majority to see it through its full term, which had the best part of two years to run. But Goddard's certainty of change was so strong it gave that change imminence.

Llewellyn had never known him more stimulating. The American trip had been a whirl of breakfast meetings, private air flights, campus lectures, interviews on television and radio.

He was not susceptible to the flattery of this kind of attention, but he much enjoyed its sheer busyness. America liked his elegant spontaneity, surprised and entertained that so English an Englishman with the sound of gentry in his voice and military valour in his past, should argue unabashed socialism. He had lost some weight, Llewellyn noted; his step was quicker.

And Llewellyn had not known him so outspoken about the Leader's failings before, however cutting he might have been on some others.

Harrison's dark misgivings about an unco-operative civil service had been the reason for Llewellyn's inspection of George Birtles, it was now explained. Harrison intended gathering together a form of 'alternative advisory service', in his own words. It would draw from industry, education, the law, the unions, the City . . . 'The main qualification,' said Goddard, 'is innocence of any previous connection with central government.'

Llewellyn said, 'Presumably these chaps are also expected to be able to read and write and do simple arithmetic?'

'They're expected to be brilliant as a matter of course,' Goddard answered without a smile.

'It's hardly going to be the first time a government's called in help from outside,' said Llewellyn.

Goddard wagged his head sharply. 'Different altogether. Harrison wants one or a brace of these watch-dogs – or a whole pack if it's thought necessary – *guarding* every ministry. What they're supposed to do is sniff out the booby traps set by the Whitehall saboteurs.'

'Does he really think like that? Honestly? Sounds more like one of his pigswill performances.' (Llewellyn was referring to the Leader's style when seeking to reinforce his popularity with the party backbenchers.)

'I told you – he worries me.' Goddard spoke very quietly. 'When we're in office we'll be sitting ducks if we antagonise the Permanent Secretaries. They simply won't put up with some kind of Inquisition. Who would? They'll resign and say why. What a gift to the opposition!'

But the Leader usually got his own way.

'Because usually he's an excellent judge of what can be made acceptable. With this he's horribly off-beam.' Goddard raised a hand to still the comment on Llewellyn's lips. 'Yes, there may be some true-blue old brick-heads among these Whitehall chieftains. But if a minister's dissatisfied it's for him to bang the table and impose his will.'

Goddard's voice had expanded and he added force to this statement by letting his raised hand fall with a smack on his desk. 'Two or three of us have volunteered to recruit this corps of advisers. If *we* don't someone else will, and then Harrison might get just the people he wants – and that would never do.'

Llewellyn had always been impressed by Goddard's capacity for instant acceleration. From a mood of troubled reflection he had now gone straight into urgent practicality.

'We want people with ideas. People looking ahead. Out and out star-gazers. Let's have some visions of the future. What's going to be possible? What's going to be forced on us? Twenty years from now will every postman have an arts degree? Will it be that kind of society? Or do we start building barbed wire camps for the hordes of marauding unemployed? Or what? Bold, highly individual opinion with plenty of data to back it up. I'd welcome that.'

'It isn't what Harrison's talking about,' objected Llewellyn.

'He'll gorge himself when he sees it. "Lo, my people, harken unto me, your prophet . . ." Can't you just see him? And the Whitehall chieftains are bound to urge caution: pour scorn here and there. So then he can say, "*That's* given the buggers something to think about." No doubt it will too. But the point is they won't feel their toes are being trodden on by a gang of presumptuous outsiders.'

'Soothsaying not being a civil service function.'

'Quite, Roy. Tell me about your friend George Birtles. We've got to have some voices from the grass roots. Are the natives restless? Do they know what they want from us? Birtles has a very low opinion of the effectualness of his local M.P.s, I know that.'

Llewellyn said, 'He thinks local government should work its own bellows – he uses phrases like that.'

'Can you translate, please?'

'He means fend for itself. Go hunting for investors. He likes to draw an analogy between underprivileged parts of the country like his and the Third World. So he talks about "the grudging dribble of aid from Whitehall". Making "bilateral agreements with private consortia". It excites the populace up there no end.'

Goddard nodded gently, as if to say he supposed it would. He looked disappointed.

Llewellyn grinned. 'Don't be misled by the jargon. Bits creep in if he likes the sound it makes. He's a genuine political primitive. He's building Jerusalem up there – with night-clubs.'

Goddard thought for a few moments, right elbow on his desk, tapping his chin with his forefinger. 'All right. I'll put him on the list of possibles.'

Llewellyn said, 'No harm in asking. He could probably be persuaded to make the odd flying visit in his chariot of fire.'

CHAPTER TWELVE

When we're in office . . .

Such was the excitement at success even Harrison's celebrated equanimity while under public scrutiny wavered enough for the phrase to slip out when he intended to say, '*Now* we are in office . . .'

Occurring during his first speech in the Commons as Prime Minister it permitted the recently displaced Opposition a burst of catcalls and laughter to relieve their own despondency appreciably. This in turn discomfited Harrison more than many members on his own side thought it ought, considering the triviality of the incident. His supporters, unused to lapses of such a kind by this most wary of men, were a little slow to set up their shield of counter-jeers. So for a moment or two Harrison suffered abuse unprotected and groping desperately for a riposte. There were those, Goddard among them, who seriously wondered if he would manage it. But the covering fire of verbal disorder all around him gave Harrison just enough breathing space, and he produced in the end a characteristic smack in the collective bared teeth opposite him. 'What a pity for the honourable members that an enlightened electorate will never allow them to make my mistake themselves,' he said, using his most deliberate enunciation. It was a light blow, of the right weight for the occasion. It sufficed.

But there were winks and raised eyebrows afterwards. 'Just for an instant I really thought the ice was going to melt,' was Goddard's comment.

And Harrison was in tetchy mood for the rest of the working day.

The next morning his mood was blacker. The parliamentary columnists in the national dailies latched on to his gaffe and consequent unease with a good deal of merriment. The general nature of the joke was that modesty in a prime minister might be commendable but patent amnesia was something else. A heavier variant said the style of Harrison's tenure had been clearly established: whatever happened he would be the last to know.

Harrison had grown used to what is called 'a good press'. The political journalists liked him in Opposition for his highly quotable insults and interventions in the House, so studiously prepared; and his off-the-record briefings usually gave them some awkward questions to level at someone else. Now, almost overnight, he was their butt. He was enraged by this ingratitude.

Senior colleagues and members of his staff agreed that such over-reaction was not likely to be repeated. He would quickly learn to ride the punches. The daily knock-about, superficial hostility he could expect from the parliamentary diarists – the press having a Tory bias – he would soon overlook, in company with so many of the newspapers' readers. Once he was immersed in the business of government he would simply not have time to dwell on trifling personal slights.

Matters developed differently.

On an evening in early July, 1968, Goddard settled himself into an armchair by an open window of his study, put his feet up on a worn leather stool and composed his thoughts before he began talking into his tape-recorder. Or rather, he tried to compose them and found the task unusually difficult.

It was a hot evening, after a hot day; but he could not blame drowsiness. He liked the rich garden smells. Usually he much enjoyed these occasional dictation sessions – the ones which were quite different from those which sent streams of memoranda to this junior minister or that in the many-headed economics and industry department over which he presided. (He was also Deputy Prime Minister.) These special bouts of dictation were typed by his wife, not exactly as they were spoken; she would clarify with punctuation, insert names or titles or functions of people mentioned where Goddard's memory was insecure, check and correct dates; she would use her own discretion in setting down his use of swear words – the emphatic she included, the merely lazy she expunged.

This material was very dear to Goddard. He was undecided how much of it, if any, he would ever reproduce should he publish memoirs one day. He recorded it mostly because he wished to establish his immediate view of certain events which either troubled or gratified or puzzled him. Distance would alter the view. It was also a kind of therapy. Speaking his thoughts aloud into this tireless ear soothed some of his tensions, and sometimes actually rearranged major problems so that he could see a plain line of approach to them. He and his wife, in fact, spoke about the transcripts of these sessions as 'the couch file'. He might talk briskly for ten minutes; he might ramble haltingly for an hour. This evening he began:

'This is going to be a sticky one. Where the fuck do I start? Everything seems such a fucking mess. Shall I have a drink? No. I'll do it cold. My head's tangled enough as it is.'

Silence. Goddard took his feet off the stool, then wriggled himself more upright in his chair. It did not help. He slid down again and recrossed his ankles on their comforting perch. He resumed talking, more quietly:

'I hope I'll become more coherent as I go along. To start with I shall just, as the frightful modish phrase goes, let it all hang out. That really is ugly, isn't it? Fits my humour, sorry to say. Here goes, then . . .

'Four years in government now, or very near it. A few things done. Quite decent things. Mostly under the heading of 'humanitarian'. Not really political. Most families have their own bathrooms. More youngsters get to university. Queer consenting adults can do it in private, legally. People generally seem more lively. All these kids taking to the road all over the world. There really *is* a sense of free movement, isn't there? Physical, social. It's *something* . . .

'But we're grinding to a halt. I mean *we* are, the government. We're tying ourselves up in knots. Suspicion. Secrecy. Cliques. The atmosphere's foul. It's been building up for so long we accept it as normal. Slow cancer. Don't notice till it's too late. But that isn't true, is it? Of *course* you notice. But you don't *do* anything. It's happened with *us*. We're finished as a government. Probably have been for a year. All we do is fight among ourselves. We're so busy at it we hardly know what's going on anywhere else. We tell each other lies. Got to. Because we know everyone's leaking stuff to the papers. That's one of our favourite weapons of war. The plant. Watch where it pops up.

Shoot it down, together with the unprincipled bastard you entrusted it to, who happens to be an old and previously valued colleague. We're a sorry crew . . .

'Harrison's done this to us. What a humiliating admission. We *let* him do it. We wanted office. Individually. *I wanted office*. If there's one thing he understands it's the driving force of political ambition. If you've got it God knows what you'll put up with to pursue it. We always knew about Harrison. Some of us, anyway. He wanted to be top dog. That was *all*. There was nothing he wanted to do when he got there. Except stay. Just that. But the force that drove him! We needed that. It would take us with him. An extraordinary performance. He created a personality. That sense of concern he could communicate. Total invention. The mask never slipped. I suppose we thought we could manipulate him. Idiotic notion . . .

'He's surrounded himself with fixers. He's surrounded *us* with them. Downing Street, the Lobby, Whitehall – it's an infestation. The special advisers have their special advisers who have their special assistants.

'Hell, I was so naive. With my little teams of prophets. Of course he welcomed them with open arms. "Yes, Dick. You've got it. Keep them well clear of the Whitehall mandarins. They work on their own. They're floaters." That was what he said. But it wasn't what he meant. He left out an important word. He meant, "They'll be *my* floaters." And so they are. They're his private army, complete with recruiting officers. There were a few prophets to begin with. But the fixers took over long ago . . .

'His hatred of the press, of the media in general. In *total*. That's where the rot set in. The media had to be fixed. Press officers and P.R. people seemed to multiply by the herd. They were supposed to "correct our image in the public mind", apparently. It scarcely mattered what came up for discussion with Harrison, one question preoccupied him – "How will it affect our image . . .?"

'Fix the media. Fix the unions. Fix the City. Fix the captains of industry. Fix the backbenchers. Fix the party. And so the army grew. By "fix" he means deflecting all these people from laying any blame for any governmental failing on *him*. It's all P.R. The great plague . . .

'I don't know what can be done about it. Probably nothing. We're stuck with what we wanted – office. The opposition are not strong enough to force us out. But I'm sure we'll be defeated at the next election. The country will punish us for sheer inactivity. I won't complain. That funny little pixie Roy Llewellyn's got so thick with, Birtles the pocket bulldozer, now I once heard him put our situation in a nutshell – it's a case of crap or get off the pot. Quite.'

Goddard clasped his hands in front of his chest and let his chin rest on his extended thumbs. He held this tensed position, an habitual aid to thought, for nearly a full minute. An observer would have thought he was praying. A sudden breeze, strong enough to flutter the curtain and even make it billow slightly at the open window, raised goose pimples on his bare forearms and in the well of his throat where his shirt was unbuttoned. He took his feet off the stool and sat up straight.

He began again:

'The one area where we do seem to keep forging ahead is in redeveloping some of our more blighted regions. Some of them, anyway, where there's a Birtles by another name to crank the handle . . .

'Llewellyn's found a proper role for himself here. Keeping the channels open between the local authorities and the building industry and the ministries – that's very tricky navigation. Now if half the fixers were half as useful as Roy . . .'

He stopped. He felt chilled again, although the curtain remained still. He rolled his shirt sleeves down. The pause was the longest since he started the session.

'I'll leave it there. Actually I think we should scrub out that last stuff, about Llewellyn. Just small talk. Right, finished. Thanks.'

He found himself more clumsy then ever nowadays with things like doors, cupboards, briefcases, keys. Yet he was surprised by how much noise his jerky actions made, closing the window.

CHAPTER THIRTEEN

She was billed as Della. Her real name was Gillian, and she came from Dover which was a long way from the working-men's club circuit of the North. The money was the best there was for strippers of her class. She had answered Craddock's questions in a tone declaring pride in achievement when he talked to her before she went on stage. She could probably make more if she worked Soho, but that was sweated labour: as many as six shows a day, moving among three different clubs, and getting pawed by drunken customers, half of them foreigners not above exposing themselves. A stripper got better treatment in the North: a proper stage, to keep her the distance an artist should have from the audience. She was expected to give value for money, of course. She defied anyone to say she didn't. She looked after her body, and at the end of the act everything came off. If any man in the audience missed anything it was his own fault for not paying close enough attention. She was reckoned to have one of the cleverest pairs of hands in the business, she said, making Craddock think instantly of boxers. He saw what she meant when he watched her twist and turn, dip her shoulders and elbows and use her long hands like fans, opening and closing around the groin to tantalise in peek-a-boo style. The audience liked Della. She was a big girl with a long stride, and the firm flesh shone under the lights as she worked up a vigorous judder of breasts and bottom. Craddock liked Gillian too. She had been cheerfully frank as she changed out of her street clothes during the interview, conducted in a corner of the club secretary's office curtained off on a right-angled rail. She had talked about her audiences with a note of sympathy coming close to compassion. 'I mean it's to do with sex but it's a good laugh as well. You watch their faces. They're all smiles. It isn't like Soho, that nasty sort of dribbling old men feeling you always get, even if it's young business-men – they're the worst, actually. I couldn't stick it. Up here it's different. I suppose it's because they live here. Do you see what I mean? They've got their wives and girlfriends just up the road. They don't look at me like that. Well, I expect some of them do. But for most of them I think they like to see someone being a bit cheeky about it for a change. You know. It can get a bit heavy, just you and the wife, can't it? I think a lot of men wish they didn't have to take sex so serious. I like to give them a nice relaxed feeling. Not that I'm tame. No one can say that. But I'm clean, aren't I, Dave?' Dave nodded vehemently.

Dave was her boyfriend-cum-manager, who looked anything but clean to Craddock. Dave had a puffy pale face and puffy eyes and a puffy midriff; gone to seed at thirty. Dave drove the car and handled the money. Dave lived off Gillian. Why was it so common, Craddock asked himself, for generous women to saddle themselves with sponging men? Immediately he was annoyed at the silliness of the question. Generosity is natural prey. There was no mystery.

Craddock now watched Della strip. He also watched the audience watch her. It consisted entirely of men: about three hundred. He was experiencing the phenomenon of the Monday lunchtime stag-show. He sat with Hector Brunskill at a round table near the stage. They were back in the industrial coastal town, that rough-edged neighbour of Brinsley Bay, where they had once worked together. The club was barely a year old, set in the middle of a council housing estate where as yet the only shop was a bookmaker's. It was next door to the club. The traditional first claims on the local pocket money had been preserved.

The faces Craddock looked at were mottled: metallic ship-yard grey, dawn grey, winter grey. Here and there among the predominant grey of middle-age – it overtook men early here – the texture of youth delayed his examination. These few faces, with their pastel subtleties still lingering from childhood, moved him deeply. They had been sentenced. One of the youths met Craddock's eyes halfway between an excited grin at Della and the lifting of his beer glass. It was a face that had been little shaved. Thick auburn hair hung forward in curls across his forehead. He was confused to find Craddock's gaze on him and stared back as if trying to remember the man who obviously knew him. The innocence in the response made him appear even younger. Craddock wanted to break the spell of sadness he felt creeping over him. But he could not force his mind away from his beautiful face and its decreed destruction. Then the face grinned and the grin fastened on the pint glass and the round eyes turned a little inwards towards each other, and Craddock realised the youth was drunk. Hector's coughing laughter at his elbow rather than the sudden burst of noise from the rest of the tables brought his mind back to Della. She was executing a series of hand movements in front of her crotch as she teased in and out of a spotlight. Craddock found himself laughing.

He was back in the North-East on behalf of a magazine which wanted to portray the Britain of the last year of the Sixties. 'A whole issue,' the editor had said, awed by his own inspiration. 'Like a lovingly collected scrapbook. Something the readers will want to keep by them. A sort of Britain Revisited.' Other writers would look at London's exotica and underworld; the new Glasgow, the new Birmingham, the new Manchester – the assumption being that this newness was readily definable. There would be portraits of pop singers, actors, film directors, clothes designers, interior decorators, playwrights, feminists . . . the luminaries of the Swinging Sixties, as the decade had come to be called by one headliner writer after another.

Craddock had spent most of the last five years abroad. Turned freelance he had at last become the endlessly roving reporter he had longed to be as a small boy. He had observed military dictatorship in South America, famine in India, primordial tribalism in Africa, exquisite landscapes here, panoramic bleakness there; and everywhere the obscenity of being poor at a level of degradation he had never before imagined. He had written at length about this poverty.

Back in England he was surprised by how adrift he felt. Not that he wanted to hurry abroad again. On the contrary he sensed he was over-travelled and needed to immerse himself in Englishness. Of course, he told himself, the place could not have changed greatly in his absence. It was simply that he had missed the arrival of a few superficial matters like new television shows, catchphrases, pop stars – familiarity with the small coinage of life without which a man feels displaced.

So he welcomed the invitation to 'do' an old stamping

ground. Now he was there he realised how much he needed the re-education.

Hector had not told him what to expect at the Moortown club. He had said simply, 'I've got something to show you. It's highly significant.'

Craddock agreed it was. He had seen strippers before; and clubs with carpets; and men drinking in large numbers at midday on Mondays. He was not prepared to find it all on this housing estate.

'It's the revolution,' Hector said. He gestured at the drinkers as the chatter grew louder in the wake of Della's proud stride off the stage. 'In all its glory. The day of freedom has dawned.'

Craddock smiled. 'Nothing new in blokes sneaking a day off after a heavy weekend.'

Hector raised his right forefinger aloft – his mock-orator style. 'But they've institutionalised it. Note the defiance in this weekly demonstration. Because that's what it is. How more provocative can the labouring class be? Give them full employment, fat pay packets and a fortnight's holiday a year, and are they satisfied? No. They want a strip-show to ease the pain of starting another week's work. Could there be anything more calculated to affront the decent, hard-working middle clases, otherwise known – to themselves – as The Country!' His voice dropped to normal conversational tone. 'I'm serious, as a matter of fact. I think it really is a way of saying, "Get stuffed!"'

'Subconsciously, you mean?' Craddock said, his eyes wandering among the faces absorbed in talk and drink. 'Aren't they just having a good time when they can?'

'Of course they are. What's subconscious about that?' Hector's vehemence set up one of his bouts of coughing.

Craddock found the auburn-haired boy again, now with his face squashed on his fists and his eyes shut dangerously close to the pint glass.

Hector went on, 'I've been here for the best part of twenty years. People who live on estates like this know one thing for certain, because of what happened before the war – nobody else gives a damn about them. The kids learn that piece of social history at the breast. They know how *The Country* sees them – just draught power, to be made use of and laid off as required.

'When these men hear phrases like "the wages explosion" and "the expanding economy" they just shrug it all off as London propaganda. All that matters is that most of them have got jobs at the moment. They don't know how long that'll last. They *do* know they'll have very little say in it. So it's "Get stuffed" and Della's arse to 'em all.'

Craddock said, 'May I quote you, sir!'

'Well, I can't get away with language like that in my own paper.'

'Can I use your name?'

'Good God, man, whatever for? That won't do your reputation any good. Reduced to interviewing old geezers on the local rag . . .' Hector sucked wheezily through his teeth, exaggerating disapproval. 'Invent somebody. How about "a local trade unionist boasting twenty years of militant idleness"? It even has the exceptional merit of being true.'

Craddock said flatly, 'I've been working on that.'

Hector nodded and was serious again. He looked suddenly too tired to carry on the banter. 'I know. You've done some good stuff. It was the best thing for you, setting up on your own. But don't get too solemn about it. Don't forget you're in the entertainment business, just like Della. Any editor who tells you differently is either barmy or lying.'

Craddock's face showed he was uneasy. He remembered Hector in his drinking days lecturing with comic contempt on the commercialism and adjustable scruples of the press. Sober, Hector's judgment on the only work he had ever known had a resigned dismissiveness which was much more affecting.

'Look, Tony . . .' Hector was interrupted by the sound of breaking glass and accompanying thuds and raised voices. The auburn curls lay in a puddle of beer and blood. The boy's head had slipped between his fists to smash the pint pot. The older men at his table lifted him gently under the arms. Craddock watched, appalled and fascinated, to see what jagged damage had been done to the young face. There was a long curved cut stretching from the left cheekbone almost to the jaw. A smaller cut under the curls sent more blood coursing down the other side of his face. His eyes had not been damaged, and Craddock turned to nod with emphatic relief at a man at a nearby table who commented loudly on his lucky escape. There was an atmosphere of deep interest, more than alarm. Men came to kneel at the boy's feet, inspecting his torn face with keenly narrowed looks. So far the youth had remained silent, bemused by what had happened. Now, as a first-aid box was produced, he showed signs of rising panic, lifting his hands towards his face as the meaning of the considerable amount of dripping blood became clear to him. The mouth trembled. From behind him bigger hands settled over his own, holding them firmly away from his face. Tears welled in his eyes before shoulders and the grey backs of heads hid him from view. Then he was on his feet, an arm round his chest, a hand holding a wad of lint over his left cheek. A barman was cleaning the bloodied table. The chatter rapidly resumed.

Craddock leaned across to the table where the man had remarked on the good fortune that had saved the boy's eyes. Craddock said, 'Do you know that lad's name?'

'Do they call him Sandy?' the man asked, looking round the table. One of his freinds nodded, and said, 'Lenny Parkin's lad.' They went on talking about accidents at work, and rates of compensation payments.

'Will you use that?' Hector asked Craddock.

'Possibly.'

'A little slice of life, so to speak.'

Craddock shrugged. 'It somehow fits the occasion. The place.'

'It could have happened anywhere.'

'The setting. The blokes' way of dealing with it. Seems all of a piece.'

'Good entertainment.'

'Hector, the kid's gone away with half his face off.'

'Exactly.'

'You think I should forget it?'

'Not at all. Go ahead and entertain.'

'You're a hard man, Hector.'

'I just want you to recognise what you're doing for what it is.'

There was a pause. Hector asked, 'Why did you want to know his name? That's *not* something you're going to use, is it?'

Craddock slowly shook his head. 'That private gallery of portraits we all collect inside here,' he said, tapping the back of his skull. 'I'd like to have names for them all, if possible. It isn't.'

Sandy Parkin's face, unscarred, filled his mind again as he sifted among the jabbering grey drinkers. Then abruptly he was seeing the eyes, the eyes with the flies in them; too big for the shrivelled features; the eyes so big they were too heavy for the children to carry. They were the living-dead children whose flesh had dried and cracked and flaked to dust. He was carrying one, but not in his arms because the child was too brittle and might disintegrate; so he made a scoop of his two hands, and even then some of the dust-skin fell through his fingers. He was telling the mission priest about the village where he had picked up the child; where there was no one but the already-dead and the living-dead; where he had stumbled from one horror to another, sickened but still taking his notes; where he had seized on this one child, knowingly not at random but at a loss to know why. No two children were quite alike, even dead ones, the priest said . . .

'Sorry, what? Didn't hear you, Hector.' Craddock leaned forward and Hector repeated his question patiently.

'I asked you what you've got lined up next.'

Craddock made an elaborate show of stretching back in his chair, hands behind his neck. 'A bit of time off,' he said. 'Roy Llewellyn's asked me if I'd like . . .'

'What's the favour *this* time?' Hector's interjection was sharp, harsh. Its aggression surprised Craddock; he simply shook his head. 'I bet there will be,' Hector said with the same forceful animosity.

Craddock leaned forward again. 'He's an old mate. It's ages since we met, and he happens to have this place . . .'

Hector started brushing with a hand at his canary waistcoat. They were such busy, flapping motions and Hector was so absorbed in them, as a display of disapprobation, he looked very like a ruffled bird giving its feathers a shake. It was an endearing sight. Craddock smiled and waited for the flourish to subside. Then he had to wait for the inevitable fit of coughing to pass.

'If philandering was an Olympic sport Llewellyn would be the permanent title holder. You and I have both helped him out, if you remember the incident . . .'

Again Hector's interruption had a bite to it. 'I've always hated salacious, hypocritical Sunday papers. That's all there was to that.'

'Well then, what's the problem?'

Hector sighed with tiredness and took off his spectacles to massage the pouches under his eyes. Lamely he said, 'Llewellyn isn't my cup of tea.'

'Do you see a lot of him?'

'Not face to face. Moves in exalted circles when he comes up here on safari.'

Craddock gave a puzzled shrug. 'If you don't meet him . . .'

Hector sighed again. 'Tony, you know how it goes. You meet people, who meet people, who meet people, who . . .' He returned Craddock's shrug.

Craddock said shortly. 'That seems quite a distance.' Hector was disinclined to respond, so Craddock pressed the point. 'A route as long as that, things can get a bit garbled.'

'Yes, I know.'

'Tell me what you've got against him.'

'I don't have any personal complaint.'

'But he's not your cup of tea. Obviously *somebody* has. What's he supposed to have done? Put somebody's schoolgirl daughter in the family way?'

Hector rallied in irritation. 'Nothing like that,' he said, and then added quickly, 'I don't *know* anything he's done. I've just got an impression. Ever since he first presented that winsome smile of his in Brinsley Bay I've had the bad feeling in the bones about him. I know he's a friend of yours, and you're entitled to tell me I'm a stupid old sod. But whether you do or not I'm telling you now I think you should watch your step with Roy Llewellyn.'

Then, of course, Hector coughed. Beads of sweat formed a rash on his high forehead and down his neck. He mopped up with one of the several handkerchiefs he made sure he always carried.

'You're a very stupid old sod,' Craddock said. 'I love you dearly, Hector. But you really are the most stupid old sod.'

Soon afterwards they left the club. Craddock called in on the betting shop to ask how business was generally, and received a guarded reply – 'Fairly steady, considering the bingo'. The bookmaker saw the bingo sessions at the club as a serious drain on family budgets. Lunch was eaten in the town, at a Chinese restaurant with a black ceiling and red flock-wallpaper, bearing portraits of Edwardian racehorses. The food consisted of hummocks of tufty vegetables of indeterminable flavour into which a few slivers of chicken had been infiltrated. Hector said he felt he had been put out to graze, and talked with a longing close to disbelief of his coming package holiday in Mexico where he would feast on avocado and guava. Craddock drove him back to the bed-sitter in Brinsley Bay, and they told each other to take care.

It was the last time they met. Craddock was to decide in due course that at the time Hector was probably aware he had only a few more months left.

CHAPTER FOURTEEN

There was a spell of about six weeks, before the final break, when Llewellyn's first marriage took on a reciprocal kindliness it had never before had. For that short while he and Valerie were thoughtful friends. Each made an effort to spend more time together at home. Llewellyn made a point of telling her how good she looked. They went to the theatre and the cinema and collected take-away suppers afterwards, rather than go to restaurants, so that they could discuss the shows as they picnicked with a bottle of wine in their own living room. They tried genuinely to take some interest in each other's work, and when they failed in the attempt they avoided rancour. They talked a lot about little Victoria: how like her mother she was in looks; how, they agreed, she seemed already to be showing also Valerie's nature, the self-contained determination. They agreed this was fortunate. It would have been worrying to have a daughter with Llewellyn's impetuosities, especially the sexual ones. Llewellyn hoped his infidelity had not hurt Valerie too much. She found it difficult to explain, but she was more annoyed with herself than with him on that score. She had never been stupid in the wordly sense and ought to have known at the outset what to expect. There had been times, when Victoria was tiny and needed constant attention, when she hated him for his flings with other women. She didn't now. Now she looked back on the seven years of marriage with only one major regret: she wished she'd started earlier. She was still adolescent on her wedding day, although not in years, and what she had enjoyed was the highly-charged adolescent's love affair. If only she had met Llewellyn at eighteen they would be having this sorting-out of their lives when she was twenty-five instead of nearing thirty.

They both knew well enough they were not going through a second honeymoon. Far from that. They were closing the books. The joint decision had been made long before it was mentioned aloud. Valerie could have asked for a divorce at any time in the past three years, because of her husband's adultery, and he would not have argued. (Prior to that she would have had equal grounds, although less certain information; and Llewellyn had a special fondness for her almost savage way of making love. It had cooled since.) But Valerie had no intention of making life hard for herself by striking out on her own with a small child. She waited for things to fall neatly into place, as she was sure – indeed, determined – they would. They had. Her part-time job, clearing up her employer's muddled paperwork as he bought and sold argumentatively on the 'phone, introduced her to a world whose politics she intuitively understood: the status-seeking hard bargaining of the market place, which appeared so normal and relevant to everyday life compared to the mysteries in which Llewellyn delved. She started with a small fish, but he knew bigger. Soon she was working for one, bright and twinkly little Mannie Burt. Mannie had an accountant, of course. The accountant had sons, one of which worked with his father. His name was David, and he completed the picture of Valerie's re-ordered life. Llewellyn sensed the arrival of his wife's next husband – he knew for Valerie it would have to be a husband and not a lover. The event was communicated in her change of manner. More ease. Relief, even. Problem settled. It was there in everything she did. She was about to make her new start. And because Llewellyn was also relieved they found it easy to be pleasant to each other. They were not unlike two passengers in an airliner who sit side-by-side through a rough journey and start to talk only when they are safely landed. Confidences can be exchanged about the experience past. The future is private.

And so during these six almost primly tranquil weeks Llewellyn and Valerie, who had excited but never liked each other, considerately disengaged.

*

By the autumn of 1969 Llewellyn had been divorced for three years and remarried for nearly twelve months. Mary, his second wife, was also a divorcee. But she was very different from Valerie. Mary's first marriage ended on a note of exasperation, not agreement. That is to say, *she* was exasperated. Gordon, whom she had wed not much more than a year before, was deeply offended by her leaving him. She knew he would be, and that pre-knowledge was part of her exasperation. She had told him with growing concern over the months that there was a grave probability the pair of them were incompatible, but Gordon's answer was to buy her something pretty on these occasions. A brooch. A pendant. Some roses. That was the trouble with Gordon. He was the kind of man who wanted to buy his wife flowers. The sight of the perfect blooms in the cellophane wrapping – all his presents came faultlessly packed – made her think of straw hats, buttoned boots, ribbons, bows . . . The imagery of childhood cinema, wherein true love never lacked a harvest moon. Before long the sight of Gordon had the same effect. Yuck!

It was not like that to begin with. They had met on a skiing holiday. Gordon was expert on skis, a swaggering athlete who tanned quickly. He swooped around her, full of daring on the snow, inviting admiration. She had never before been subjected to a man's self-advertising on such a scale. It amused her. And if indoors he proved not to have the same boldness of approach, there was something appealing in unexpected shyness. She went to bed with another young man during that fortnight, but not with Gordon; he did not ask.

If he had – and she wanted him to – she would have been saved the mistake of marrying him. Not because she would have found him unsatisfying in bed: in the event his sexual performance had some of the *élan* of his skiing – physical demand coaxed out the flamboyant in him. But she was too grown up to expect anything more of a little holiday whirl than the pleasure of the moment. It was precisely because Gordon had disappointed her in Vermont that she was receptive to him when she was back at work in New York.

A small parcel was delivered to the apartment she shared with her friend, Patti. Inside Mary found a little man on a little pair of skis, carved out of wood. With it was a note from Gordon, saying he had taken her address off one of her luggage labels and he hoped she wouldn't mind if he called her shortly with a view of taking her out somewhere. Both girls thought the little wooden man was a good joke, and when Gordon turned up at the apartment to collect Mary the following Sunday he found they had improved on his humorousness by sticking a blob of chewing gum between the wooden legs with half a toothpick emerging from it at the upward diagonal. When he reached out with poised forefinger and thumb at the appendage Patti smacked his hand and told him not to play with himself. He was embarrassed for a moment, and then joined in the laughter. In his jeans and sweat-shirt and lumber jacket, the holiday sun still in his skin, he exuded vitality; and that was a quality Mary much valued in young men at the time.

Asking herself, within six months of the wedding, how she had reached the absurd situation of being married to this man she was too bewildered to find a half-adequate answer. She even knew she had recognised the error she was making, before the marriage, the first time she saw Gordon dressed for the office. It was as if she had never seen a man in a grey suit before. She stared at him in wonder, which he enjoyed because he failed to see the accompanying alarm. If he had been in a black silk sheath and high heels Mary could not have been more alarmed.

Now young men in grey suits swarmed in New York, and Mary had no objection to them as a species. Some of them were thoroughly enjoyable company. She had met grey-suited lechers, moralists, drunks, wits, idlers, misanthropes, high-flyers, no-hopers, and shits, among others. The uniform did not necessarily constrain the wearer. But it did something very odd indeed to Gordon. She could not at first fathom what, except that it removed the heroic from him without a trace. Also there was an element of the child emanating from this changed being, when logically the formal garments should have aged him. She had an impulse to give Gordon a peck on the forehead and make a run for it. She did not, for a jumble of reasons. In the foreground was the simple, massive fact that the marriage had been agreed – had entered into the fabric of daily intercourse all around her. Every conversation, every greeting, every farewell, no matter how casual or brief, seemed to occur solely to facilitate the use of the word 'married'. *'When are you getting married? . . . After you're married . . . How about you, married! . . . When you've been married as long as I have . . . Hi, I heard you got married . . .'* The bells pealed day and night. As well as that she felt so weirdly baffled by Gordon she had to satisfy her curiosity. Then again, she was drinking rather a lot at that time – probably because she was worried about Gordon, she later realised – and doubt frequently was sluiced away with vodka and vermouth. (She was never inebriated by the standards of a seasoned drinker, as she was not at the age of twenty-three in 1958; she liked the tingle of unconcern that could be induced.) All in all she could truly say she let herself in for marrying Gordon against her better judgment. Or rather, in its suspension – *that* could truly be said.

But at least she was demystified on the subject of Gordon's character. The childishness carried right through the grain. She could hardly complain it was offensive. She told herself, and eventually him, there were probably girls around the country by the ten-thousand who would cherish such a husband, thanking the great marriage broker in the sky every night on their knees for the endearing innocence of the man's wants. But these wants, and this man, left Mary, the girl he had chosen – how the word stuck in her throat! – aching with an irritation rapidly taking on the virulence of diagnosable disease.

Gordon was stuck at that stage of development most boys reach at some time when they are besotted by their own proficiencies. Perhaps everyone goes through it. There is, for instance, the infantile thrall to the pronunciation of particular words: *acupuncture, testicle, precipitate, venereology* . . . Or a single phrase of melody has to be trilled to satiety. Gordon was well past all that: by five or six years, Mary assessed. He was at the model-making stage; the cleanest-kid-in-the-class stage; the pleasing-his-elders stage. That was why he looked so eerily young in his grey suit: he wasn't going to the office, he was going to school. He had to be spotless, because that was the phase he was in. Before breakfast he had to go through his physical training programme, because he was in love with his capacity for God knew how many press-ups and squat-jumps and he had to tell his superiors the numbers he reached. He had to do his nightly stint of wooden model-making, so that he could take the newly-finished models to show. He was, and for ever, The Boy Who Wanted To Please.

Mary had no wish to hurt him. But it was impossible to avoid. How could she not ridicule him? But he was so wounded she had to force herself to stop that. Straight talking about an apparent mismatch prompted the presents and the flowers in their maddeningly perfect packaging. It was when she found herself sobbing in public on her way to work that she decided enough was enough, and to Hell with the big, harmless, pathetic, overgrown brat.

The brat took his time over divorcing her. She saw the spitefulness in this, but accepted it as the price of perverse folly – something her Baptist upbringing in Lancaster, Ohio, had warned her to guard against. For once she acknowledged the deacons knew a thing or two. And she congratulated herself on having taken care not to get pregnant. That would have been folly on the grand level. There were times, during and after the marriage, when she imagined herself mother to a brood of little Gordons – all offspring would be boys, beyond question – and the conjured fate made a stalactite of her backbone. Condemned to a lifetime of child-minding . . . She phantasised nightmarishly to produce visions of male limbs and torsoes and genitals ever multiplying and magnifying and crowding in on her, towering over her, always with the piercing shrillness of a hundred squabbling small boys. Two hundred, three, four . . . The noise tore through her head from temple to temple like a drill. And every face was Gordon's, smooth and dimpled and tanned and smelling of after-shave. *'Look what I can do, mummy, and I'm only forty-four . . .'* Mary was in no hurry to remarry. She applied herself to her job, and prospered. The competent commercial artist became a style-setter.

★

'I think you're Anthony Craddock. I'm Mary Llewellyn.'

She had not given Craddock time to say yes or no. Clearly she was not the kind of woman to be abashed should she introduce herself with an expansive, welcoming smile to someone who had never heard of her.

'Hello,' he said. And then belatedly, so that it made her laugh, 'Yes, it's me.' It was a strong laugh, from a woman with a slender but firm figure all in white; shirt with short sleeves, and slacks. The teeth were very white, her hair was a rich cluster of tight curls so blonde they might have been shampoo bubbles. The skin of her arms and face and throat was golden. It was very American skin, to go with the voice; exposed to the world with total confidence.

'Roy sent me to meet you. He's got some meeting he didn't expect, or he'd be here.' She caught a questioning look in his eyes. 'Well, you know Roy. He never stops.'

'I thought you were on holiday,' Craddock said. His voice was studiously middle-class English and not quite his own. This was partly because he had developed a habit of emphasising his Englishness to Americans until he came to feel at ease with them, and partly because he had downed several whiskies while waiting for his flight at Heathrow and more in the plane. The words required careful separation.

She smiled. 'I am, one hundred per cent. But you know Roy.'

'Well, it's jolly good of you. I believe it's quite a tricky little drive, isn't it?'

The strong laugh rang out again in the general babble and clatter of the small airport building, as arriving and departing passengers collided in the glazed disorder that marks the package holiday. 'I love it. All these little old cars held together with string, and bouncing around these crazy roads – I'd be driving whether Roy came or not. Have you got all your stuff? I see you travel light.'

Craddock had one suitcase, a bottle of whisky in a cardboard container with a loop of cord to carry it by, and a light raincoat whose usefulness was in its pockets which bulged with two thick paperbacks, half a dozen packets of small cigars, copies of *Time*, the *Times Literary Supplement* and *Films and Filming*, and two small notebooks, virginal. She set off, dodging slickly through the lurching throng. Craddock followed in a patient straight line, pausing now and then for a gap to appear among the bodies and luggage. It was a patience acquired by necessity in thicker, noiser, hotter, more odorous crowds than this. But he was feeling the heat uncomfortably in the confined space, and was relieved to emerge in the hard sunlight of outdoors. Mary said, 'Hey, let me take that coat. Oh, I *see* – not so light, after all.' She held it draped over her two arms folded in front of her. 'You ought to try a shoulder bag. No, really, they're so convenient. That's the car, the green Vauxhall.' She pronounced it *Vokesharl*, which momentarily baffled him so that he stopped. She turned, immediately sensitive to his puzzlement, and in the glare of the sun the lines around her eyes were surprisingly deep as the gold skin creased in another snatch of laughter. It was an older, more interesting, more likeable face than the one that had greeted him. The glare toughened it; put tensions into it. And there were freckles around the nose he had not noticed before. 'I know. I mean the green *Voxorrl*,' she said, rolling an intruding 'r' with a resounding vibrato. It made him smile at her for the first time. 'Roy's told me a hundred times. Really I'm quite anglicised, you know. I say "lift" instead of "elevator", and "tube" instead of "subway", and I can put *petrol* in the car and ask where the ladies' *loo* is. Yes, I'd say after two years I'm handling the language pretty well. It's just some of the proper names I goof on all the time. But that's not English, is it – goof?'

Craddock changed the suitcase from left to right as he said, 'Filmgoers' English. I suppose "fluff" is in more common usage.'

'But that's an actor's word, isn't it? As in "to fluff a line".' She was looking at him earnestly, absorbed in the developing discussion. Craddock liked the incongruity of it: a sweating, half-drunk Englishman with a suitcase and a carton of whisky, and a cool American blonde awkwardly burdened with his misshapenly weighted raincoat – there they stood outside Luqa airport, within minutes of their first meeting, solemnly launched into etymologizing in the full heat of afternoon. British soldiers and airmen in starched shorts and tunic shirts materialised in some number at this point and were forced to make a detour round the immobile couple, which added to the oddness of things.

'Yes, you're right,' Craddock said. 'But a footballer can fluff a shot at goal, or a student can fluff his exams.' The suitcase changed hands again. She nodded slowly. 'The word "goofy" in English means slow-witted,' then he went on, 'but it's a term we'd use quite affectionately. I mean it's different from calling somebody "stupid". Come to think of it that makes a connection between your "goof" and our "goofy". Both to do with blundering, aren't they?'

'That's right. Is there a noun? I mean, can somebody be "a goof"?'

It seemed the most profound question Craddock had been asked in his life. The two pairs of eyes held each other's deep, silent concentration. More soldiers deployed past them, some giving the rooted couple inquisitive glances, and then looking back for a second examination to see if the statues had moved. 'I'm really not sure about that,' Craddock answered at last.

She said, 'I don't think we can match up your "goofy". It isn't "dumb". That's too tough.'

He was seized with inspiration. 'What about "dopey"? An American "dope", I would have thought, is exactly what an English "goof" would be – if we have the noun, that is.'

She nodded with her head on one side. 'Thanks. *Now* I've got your "goofy". Right, "dopey". Right. Like this?' And she let her mouth hang slack and shuffled her feet and shrugged her shoulders in a passable imitation of tongue-tied gaucherie.

'Exactly!' Craddock said.

They smiled in triumph at each other, and then both were startled by the blaring of a car horn. It sounded again before they located its source: a little open-topped vehicle with a narrowing bonnet and running boards, which Craddock recognised as a Morris Eight. He had not seen one, as far as he could remember, since his teens. It looked cherished. The driver, one of the starched soldiers of commissioned rank, returned Craddock's amiable smile with a miserly twitch of the lips. Then he levered himself so that he could peer round the windscreen, and said in the authentic tone of the shires and Sandhurst, 'Do you think you could move just a touch to your left, sir. I'm *trying* to get out of this car park.'

Mary began to giggle. 'Sorry, Colonel,' she cooed. The soldier was a lieutenant, Craddock noted, and he put his heels together, tucked the whisky carton under his left arm and gave the two pips a quivering salute before trailing after Mary towards her car. The weight of the suitcase, the burn of the sun and the day's whisky all contributed to his stagger towards the lieutenant's Morris as the engine was gunned. He righted himself and gave the young officer a sheepish grin.

'Thanks awfully,' snapped the lieutenant. Craddock was tempted for a moment to hurl the carton at him. But it was only for a moment.

As he joined Mary, opening the boot of the car he said, 'For English "twit" read American "jerk". Right?'

'And "twat" in both languages.' The lid of the boot banged shut on the suitcase and the far from light raincoat which, pressed to Mary's middle, had induced dark sweat stains on her previously snow-white outfit. As his eyes settled on them she plucked at her shirt with both hands and pulled it outside her trousers. There was a glimpse of a gold midriff.

'Do you know "berk"?' Craddock asked.

'Yes, "twat" for more polite society.' They got into the front seats of the car.

'Not polite at all, as a matter of fact.' Craddock gave her a smug smile, and she arched her eyebrows at him, deepening the lines across her broad forehead. 'You know what I mean by Cockney rhyming slang?'

'As in "Apples and pears" equals "stairs". Yes, I like it.'

'Well, "berk" derives from "Berkshire Hunt". Got it?'

The laugh yelped high, a single squeal of pleasure. 'Love it,' she said. She produced a pair of sunglasses with huge octagonal lenses and bright red frames, and with a wide grin reversed the car in an arc and at a speed that, combined, sent the vehicle slithering on its baked wheels. Then she propelled it forward just as vigorously.

Craddock braced himself for what he anticipated would be a thrilling ride, however short, to the luxurious seclusion Llewellyn had promised him in an unpronounceable snick of Malta's east coast. Being with Mary was markedly exciting, in itself.

Book Three

CHAPTER FIFTEEN

Of all Craddock's memories of Mary that first meeting was by far the most frequent. It was so pleasant. Others were weightier, some of them troubling. But the recollection of that quick rapport, a rare event for a man as wary as he, had the insistence of favourite music. Even now, nine years later, he could smile, unembarrassed, at the unaffected silliness of their introduction.

'Still full of Christmas spirit?' The mini-cab driver was fat, amiable and loquacious. The flesh of his neck overhung his collar. Cigarette ash gathered in the folds of his jacket and erupted from them in little dusty clusters whenever he shifted his position. He was a chain smoker. Equally he was addicted to cricket. As a regular driver with the cab firm Craddock used on account, he knew Craddock's business and much of his lifestyle and, so the man believed, his nature. He saw Craddock as the sporty type, in spite of being on the quiet side, who would always appreciate the flourish of little-known facts concerning cricketing heroes of the past. Craddock had allowed this false notion to persist because he knew that, holding to it, the driver would chatter contentedly about twin left-handed medium-paced spinners, or whatever cricketing arcana enthralled him at the time, without needing any responses beyond the respectful 'Really?' or 'Did they?' or 'Good Lord, did they really?' This was a driver who would always want to talk about *something*, whereas Craddock was a passenger who often – very often – had no wish to speak at all. Listening to a droning monologue on cricket, a sport Craddock found boring, was preferable to being drawn into unwilling argument. 'Nice to see you all smiles,' the driver said. 'You know, facially you're a dead ringer for a wicket-keeper I'm sure used to play for Glamorgan. I've thought it before and forgot to mention it. I just can't put a name to him. Like you, not the happy-go-lucky type. But when he smiled you knew he'd got something worth the effort. I just can't get that man's name. Johnson, Jepson, Jessop, Jenkinson . . .'

It was Boxing Day, shortly past noon. In the typical chill pallor of urban English Christmas the streets were just coming alive, traffic and pedestrians both diffident in their late start. The fat driver waited tolerantly as three adolescents, two girls and a boy, crossed the road in front of him at a set of traffic lights which turned to green as they stepped off the pavement. The boy and one of the girls steered a metal-mesh trolley acquired from some supermarket. It twisted awkwardly on its little wheels. In it lay the necessities for wandering through the lost days of festival: sleeping bags, a few cans of beer, assorted bottles. The second girl had a blanket round her shoulders, both hands gripping it under her chin. What little could be seen of her face was a thin grey, and sharp like the remains of a broken window pane. She did not look at the car. The pair pushing the trolley found themselves for a moment facing Craddock and the driver directly, and they stopped with clouded eyes fixed with the effort of co-ordination. The girl wore a long coat of artificial fur, the boy an imitation army combat jacket. 'There they are, God help us – the hope of the nation,' the driver said, and cigarette ash billowed as he shook his head and sighed with the hiss of a deflating tyre. The girl in the fake fur broke the deadlock by timidly raising her right hand and twiddling her fingers and smiling in greeting. Craddock felt touched by the gesture: she looked so frail, perplexed. But before he got his own hand above the dashboard in response her mood had changed. Her hand turned and two stiffened fingers jerked upwards in contempt. She and the boy swung the trolley back on course. The driver said, 'Would you believe it? For no reason whatsoever. Doing away with National Service was the worst thing that ever happened to this country.'

Craddock said, 'It never applied to girls.'

There was another hiss and another billow of ash. 'Some night those little buggers had, from the look of it. Drugs. Got to be. I can see him now, that bloke. Had a funny way of sticking his elbows out. Jefferson, Joplin . . . ?'

Craddock had phoned Llewellyn on Christmas Eve. It was

the first time they had spoken to each other for over four years. Craddock had to use the ex-directory operator: the number he tried to dial, also ex-directory, was out of date. 'I haven't sent you a card this year, Roy. I thought I'd 'phone it in. Thanks for yours. How are things?' He had decided coldly to take the opportunity of Christmas to renew contact. It was not until he started to make the call that he realised with a spasm of alarm he had no idea whether Llewellyn would be at home or possibly out of the country. But even as the thought came he knew he was right to assume his old friend had not gone away. If he had Llewellyn would have written a note to say so on his card to Craddock. Such little messages had become the token communication between them: tiny pieces of personal information, just sufficient to strike an echo of intimacy – to show they had never admitted any rift in their regard for each other. There had been a drifting apart on the natural winds of life. No more than that. These little Christmas notes would refer to, for example, Llewellyn's chastening double hernia and forthcoming trip to China; Craddock's first visit to a health farm and overtures from a megalomaniac Italian film producer. 'Mary and I off to (wherever) for Xmas binge' would certainly have appeared on Llewellyn's card this year, had such a holiday been arranged. In fact the message was intriguingly informative in a quite different way: 'Rather think Christmas '78 will be my last in govt office. Not resigning, old son. Suspect boot up collective botty imminent. Oh, happy day!'

Yes, Lord Llewellyn would take his call . . . 'I'm fine. Mary's fine. Terrific to hear your voice. It's absurd we haven't seen each other for so long. Let's *do* something about that. Listen, Boxing Day, lunchtime, what are you doing?'

Craddock had been prepared for more difficulty in effecting a meeting. He was ready to propose taking Llewellyn and Mary to lunch – perhaps a little jaunt out of town, to give the offer a sense of festive impulse the harder to refuse. To that end he tried to pitch his drinking, invariably heavy on Christmas Eve in order to anaesthetise him for most of Christmas Day, at a less ambitious level than in the past. He wished to be unashamedly sentimental, which would amuse and so persuade. Drunken incoherence would be ruinous. But Llewellyn's spontaneity did all the work. Llewellyn even answered the question Craddock was not, at that moment, ready to ask. 'Tony, I must apologise for not letting you have our new telephone number. With family and friends Mary and I shared the job of ringing round. All I can think is we both thought we'd got hold of you but in fact never did. Simple as that. Sorry, old son, really.'

Craddock was numb with wine about an hour after putting the 'phone down: and Christmas Day slipped by like a compressed convalescence. Sober now, he was nervous at the prospect of seeing Llewellyn and Mary again. Until the driver mentioned it he had not realised he was smiling to himself. As the car followed the driver's private route to Hampstead – the smug side-street navigation of the professional – Craddock's thoughts darted from past to present and future without connection. He recognised the process by which his mind avoided facing a prime worry, and did not resist. He was driving a Japanese truck in Botswana, along a road as rutted and holed as a dried river bed, and feeling heroic about it. The lovely Liz Ellison was stealing a scene from an enraged actor in rehearsal of one of Craddock's plays by absently taking off a sandal and scratching the back of her neck with it. It was time to say 'Did you really?' to the driver. Peter Franklin had not 'phoned him from Manchester and he had been disappointed, although they had made no arrangements to speak. Peter would be picking at roast turkey and a mound of vegetables with a look of agony being denied utterance. Presumably Peter *had* gone to Manchester. But for Peter's arrival in his life would he ever have met Llewellyn and Mary again? His mind had stopped performing tumbles and had focussed. But not on Llewellyn, who was the prime worry. Was he?

The car stopped at Llewellyn's house, which used to belong to the late Richard Goddard.

*

Goddard suffered a cerebral haemorrhage late in 1973. It happened in his room at the House of Commons when he was alone, reading constituents' letters, and he died within three days.

His death caused much turmoil. Only weeks before he had achieved a personal triumph at the party conference, emerging from that 'morass of mendacity' – his own private description – as the undisputed favourite to succeed Harrison as Leader. His own speeches bore the assumption of leadership and others' reinforced it, either by support or hostility. The vehemence told all. Harrison said nothing in public to indicate he was quitting the field. But, by its devious route, the blueprint for the near future found its way into the hands of the political commentators and became fact in the public mind. Harrison would resign in good time for Goddard to establish his authority and then steer the party back into Government at the next election. Harrison would wait for the opportune moment to relinquish the leadership: one day in the bleak mid-winter, when the general discontent among the populace was blackest and the idea of change, *any* change, most welcome. *The day of deliverance is at hand, my people. Harken, I beseech you, unto this your new prophet appointed by ME in my selfless regard for the public weal* . . . (Goddard performed a little speech along these lines, cleverly mimicking Harrison's voice, for the amusement of a few friends less than a week before he died.)

There were those present at lunch with Harrison, when news of Goddard's death arrived, who thought they saw a grin tremble on his lips in the instant before he dropped his head into his plump right hand. Perhaps, though, they considered on reflection, it was actually the beginning of the grimace of shock the removal of the hand revealed as Harrison struggled to speak. 'Poor old Dick,' he eventually said. 'That's cruel.' And then the lips twitched again with emotion, and again he had to employ the concealing hand. He delivered a panegyric on television in which the phrase 'my friend, the late Dick Goddard' brought an affecting catch in his voice. The words opened and closed the obituary, and appeared twice more during it, and when he uttered 'late' the word lingered before a little intake of breath enabled him to continue. One other phrase, although spoken only once, was floated on the air with the same resonance. This was 'that rare figure, the man who cannot be replaced'. Among colleagues and journalists exchanging notes on the eulogy there were several to agree they had not heard Harrison speak with such relish for ages.

Harrison's displacement was frustrated by Goddard's dying, as Harrison well knew. There was indeed no one else to step into Goddard's shoes – and then Harrison's. There would be claimants, of course; a scurrying of lobbyists would lead the reporters on a chase through the old familiar warren, as first one rabbit then another popped his head above the pack to invite acclamation. Harrison could not possibly resign now and leave the party open to a display of personal power-seeking. Dignity in bereavement had to be maintained. It had taken months of bargaining among the factions to secure Goddard's succession; and only when Harrison saw the certainty of defeat, if he tried to fight his rival off, did he concede. Now, in a muted turbulence or regrouping – the more serious contenders for the future leadership were grateful for the distraction provided by the jumping rabbits – Harrison was begged to stay on. He made the cardinals beg, reminding them they had convinced him he was a spent force. It entertained him greatly to put them through this demeaning performance. There was another little pleasure to savour: he could expect to be Prime Minister again.

*

Goddard's widow, Ursula, had always kept herself at a distance from the party; in a physical sense, that is. In terms of information she was as close as anyone. Typing and editing Goddard's private diaries gave her a view of party affairs no one guessed at. The constituency officials were never fully at ease with this small, calm woman whose dark eyes and dark hair seemed to lose no gloss over the years, while Goddard turned fully grey and showed signs of a stoop until he deliberately set back the big shoulders and aimed his jaw at a gathering as if lining up person by person for precision-firing. The subtleties and stealth of London were abandoned when Goddard stumped the country: he tended towards rather dated old-soldier language, such as 'mowing them down' and 'going in with the cold steel'. It gave him a Tory-squire manner at odds with his politics and true nature, but seemed to please his constituents. 'They want a *gent*,' he said to Ursula when she giggled, 'so I shall give them one.'

The marriage mystified Goddard's circle. Before it – and after it, from time to time – he showed an enthusiasm for taller, paler, modish girls with the air of busy pleasure about them. Ursula was a country girl, the daughter of a Wiltshire farmer without much of a spread who turned to the selling and hiring out of agricultural machinery and quickly prospered. She presented herself for tutorials when Goddard was briefly a modern history don at Oxford. At first he felt he had to treat this shy little thing with the soft black eye-lashes extra gently, curbing his irritation at the straying in of such unsuitably fragile material. Then he found her questioning his comments with a softly spoken persistence that demanded he concentrate; even justify. It was a painstaking mind, at its best when dismantling and reassembling, and he was not surprised when she told him of her father's excellence as a natural, untrained mechanic. That was the first time she laughed at him, and he had to apologise for patronising her. He had no recollection of previously apologising to any undergraduate for anything.

He left Oxford when she was halfway through her second year, taking with him another don's wife – tall, fair and a salacious wit – whom he did not marry, although the woman thought that was his intention. The next time he met Ursula was at Broadcasting House, when he went to be interviewed about his newly-published study of his Fabian childhood and its earnest, dotty luminaries, and found her working as the programme producer's assistant. He could hear her voice behind some of the questions, which had him revising several of his more playful verdicts on major reputations – not at all what he had in mind when he welcomed the invitation to the studio. The producer thanked him for giving so much for so small a fee, and to a tiny audience; and Goddard said there was something about the corridors of the B.B.C. that reminded him of school and made him feel required to own up. The producer chortled, well pleased.

Taking Ursula to dinner the following night, Goddard asked why she had thought it necessary to make sure he got such a hard time of it. She said it was a petulant question: she knew he had more interesting things to say about Fabianism than in his frivolous book and she wanted to hear them. She added that the talk would do his reputation no harm, although the book might. They married three months later. Goddard was thirty-eight, Ursula twenty-four. It was 1952. Goddard, an M.P. now for seven years, enjoyed an excitement in Ursula's examination of him that was far more intense than any he felt in the conflicts of Westminster. He recognised her possessiveness towards him;

there was a degree of envy in it – his abilities were of a bigger scale than hers, and of a kind she would like to have. But it was an entirely private possessiveness, whereas other women had wanted him for their adornment. It was a highly sexual marriage. Goddard's vanity was too deeply rooted for him to resist an occasional affair, always quickly and sometimes callously ended. But as the years drew on he lost appetite although not for Ursula. It was quite early in their married life when, wanting to re-establish their special intimacy after being with another woman, he began dictating his diaries for her to transcribe with her own special freedom of emendation. He told no one else the diaries existed. Ursula kept the typed pages in stiff-spined files in a locked cupboard in their bedroom; and eventually a second cupboard was needed. She re-read the early files at random, usually when Goddard was away from her for any length of time. She took more pleasure in the words on the page than in Goddard's voice on the tapes, which were not stored. She and Goddard lived together on the typed pages. They were conjoined there.

Goddard's will was the simplest of documents. It bequeathed everything he possessed to his widow. It ignored the possibility that Ursula could pre-decease him. It did not mention their two sons. (The boys were aged nineteen and seventeen when Goddard died.) It was the kind of will a man makes when he has no wish to make one at all. Goddard had never wanted for money, and took no interest in it. Before his marriage his accountant, solicitor and bank kept things orderly for him; afterwards Ursula acted effectively as his business manager. Seemingly unmoved by his death she set about rearranging the family assets with the same brisk discretion she had shown in mixing a new list of investments once she studied the terms of Goddard's legacy from his public-spirited father, who owned shoe factories. (For example, money he had been required to spend on 'the encouragement of outdoor leisure pursuits' had lain unused, and gathering interest, because Goddard could not bring himself to consider the matter. Ursula found there was nothing to prevent the placing of the sum with a caravan manufacturer, profitably.) She had lived in the Hampstead house with Goddard for nearly twenty years, but felt no attachment to it, not even its furniture. She left his secretary to clear his room at the

Commons; all his papers at Hampstead, down to the last remnant of notepad, she sifted alone. No one was allowed to help; working in his study, she locked the door; she burned paper by the hour. What she retained she packed, again unaided and unseen, in tea chests.

She told her two sons, without asking for their views, that she was selling the house; she would buy a flat in London big enough for the three of them to stay in comfortably as required, but the family home would in future be a country house near Salisbury, not far from where she was born. She intended to set up a small publishing business, which she would run from there, specialising in social history and hoping to collect also a clutch of new authors and fiction. The boys were not greatly surprised. Their mother's life had always appeared ruled by books – she had been reading for one publisher or another for as long as they could remember; and of the two parents they had come to expect far more show of interest from their father, when they saw him during holidays. The older son was now at Oxford; the younger would shortly follow him from boarding school. Neither of them liked Ursula. They were old enough to realise she had been jealous of Goddard's regard for them. They did not expect to see much of her in Wiltshire. When she invited them to take their pick of whatever books they wanted from Goddard's library, before the removal men came, they found the shelves already fissured. They took nothing. It occurred to Nicholas, the older boy, to ask whether she would take Goddard's desk and chair to the London flat or the country house. She said all the study furnishings would stay where they were: Roy Llewellyn had been delighted to take over the house with this particular room preserved as he had always known it, except for its books, and she preferred to start her new life in fully new surroundings. The boys could transplant their bedrooms, lock, stock and barrel if they wished, of course, and she could see they did. The younger son, Martin, shouted at this point, 'You're bloody mad!'

CHAPTER SIXTEEN

'Hi, I'm Lee and I'm flying.' The girl who opened the door to Craddock was around twenty and American. She wore an outfit something like a musical comedy gaucho's, with bright green trousers overlapping shiny black boots just below the knees. 'I'm in charge of coats, but watch where I put it because one more glass and it's anybody's – I mean your coat. At least I *think* I mean your coat. What's your name?'

The air was filled with loud, shrill pop music of a decade ago: electric guitars and a frantic falsetto 'Yeah-yeah, yeah-yeah'. Laughter and jumbled chatter mingled with it. Figures crossed the hall from one open doorway to another, drinks in their hands. 'I haven't slept for three days. You English and Christmas! Nobody warned me.' She took him by the hand and led him to the doorway straight ahead, where clearly the bulk of Llewellyn's guests were. She stood just inside the room and yelled, 'Mr Anthony Craddock, my lords, ladies and gentlemen.' There was a ragged cheering.

Craddock felt incongruously sober. He was sure for a moment he had come to the wrong house. Then two arms were round his neck from behind and he smelt expensive and delicate cosmetics. Mary's voice said, 'Tony, Tony, lover, hullo.' And she kissed him under his left ear before he turned round to look at her.

She was thinner; gaunt, even. She wore velvet and silk, orange and lemon. A sense of declared wealth, of money spent for effect, came to him straightaway. He had never received that impression from her before. It was not that she was over-dressed, over-groomed, over-jewelled; she was not. But there was a care expressed in how she presented herself that was new to her. The Mary he used to know would have given the day a laugh by wearing something out of place – a sprig of plastic holly in her hair, he remembered on one occasion. Today she

was showing impeccable taste. She did not in the o/
would have got in her way.

'You look different,' he said, and wished he c
managed something else. But he was caught off bala__

'You don't. I think I even recognise the suit.'

'It's my winter party-going suit.'

'How do you mean – different?' She looked hard at him and then found somewhere else to look, adjusting the collar points of his shirt so that they settled more neatly under his jacket.

'More . . . English,' he said. It was the truth, of a kind.

The brightened eyes shot back at his. 'At *last*. I thought at first you were complaining.'

He lifted his hands, intending to embrace her. But she inched away so that he could take her only by the shoulders. She let him kiss her lips by jutting her face forward. He found she was trembling faintly.

Craddock glanced quickly at the throng. 'I wasn't prepared for all this. Roy seemed to be talking about a little light lunch.'

'I know,' Mary said, and her face gleamed briefly with some of the exuberance he remembered. 'If *you're* surprised how do you think *he* looked when the hordes started pouring in. I thought he needed it. I've got enough champagne to flood the street, so grab yourself a bottle.'

She turned him round and put a hand between his shoulder-blades to guide him to the kitchen. This rear section of the ground floor she had rearranged from the Goddard's days. Walls had been knocked down so that now sliding louvre doors could be opened to make a huge room of what had been three. Craddock had a glimpse of pine pannelling and terracotta tiling and a console of cooking dials that looked complex enough for the cockpit of an airliner. Mary slid her narrow lemon arm into a glass-fronted refrigerator and gave Craddock his first drink of the day. He felt virtuous, he was so far behind the rest of the company.

'Aren't they decorative?' Mary took in the guests with a lift of one hand, without looking at them. She was more interested in Craddock's response.

He sipped his champagne and she refilled the glass as he made a rapid inspection. 'It's the chorus from *Jesus Christ, Superstar*,' he said.

'There *are* one or two dancers,' Mary smiled as she watched him savour the drink. 'Good?'

'Nectar.'

'They're not all *that* young. Some of them must be nearly as old as me. It's the design world; they like pretty colours. I've been very selective – a short-list of a dozen, with instructions to bring anyone guaranteed to brighten the place up. I'm sick of all Roy's . . .' She let an irritable jerk of the shoulders serve for words. Craddock saw her mouth tightening with anger. The lips worked hard on each other. She realised he had recognised bitterness, and in an instant the face relaxed and she went on in a throw-away tone, 'Well, that's politics and it's not a pretty sight.'

'Roy always gave it a lighter touch than most.'

She made no answer, instead found someone to wave at across the room: a girl with vermilion lips in a face dusted white as a clown's. The girl raised a cigarette high in the air with an arching of the eyebrows at the same time. Mary gave a quick shake of the head and the girl shrugged back before sucking lovingly on the cigarette. Obviously it contained not only tobacco. Craddock breathed in deeply through his nose, but the special sweetness was not there.

Mary said, 'Early yet. But there'll be plenty soon.'

'Anything harder?'

'Why, what's your bag, as we used to say when I was young and didn't dare?'

'Not for me. The alcohol's trouble enough.' Craddock held out his glass and she poured again.

'Real trouble? I mean *real*?'

'Outbursts. Most of the time I behave quite well these days.'

'Oh, that old moral view of yours. I told you years ago, that's your problem.'

There was a pause. Memories passed through both their minds like waves, and when they caught each other's eyes the moment was awkward.

She broke its hold by tapping the hand that held his glass. He put the drink to her lips and she squeezed his hand gently as she sipped.

'Glad you're here,' she said softly, so softly he was lip-reading against the din. Her voice rose. 'I'll find Roy. He'll be fondling some young thigh somewhere.' She gave him the half-empty bottle. 'Don't move.'

He nodded at the refrigerator, with its heaped bottles misty behind the glass door. 'No chance of it.' He watched her checked progress through the crowd. It was already more excitable now – arms draped round shoulders in shifting cuddles; several couples dancing. Mary took a kiss here, a mouthful from someone's glass there; and she drew deeply on a cigarette. Her movements looked tense, the body brittle. She was playing a part.

*

Craddock and Llewellyn sat in the study, where the noises of the party came to them muffled as if from another house. The voices had thinned anyway, half the guests having left. When Craddock and Llewellyn had gone upstairs the remaining visitors had reached the sprawling stage – heads in laps, feet on chairs. Two of the girls were collecting dirty glasses and coffee cups and imagined they were restoring order to Mary's abused kitchen. Mary sat in an armchair the colour of honeycomb and talked about the titles she was designing for a film, her audience two dazed young men cross-legged on the floor. The smell of marijuana was distinct in the air, but less so than a couple of hours earlier.

It was nearly dusk, and the reading lamp lit the area around the desk, at which Llewellyn sat. Craddock was in the chair by the window. A tray on a side table had the leftovers of their delayed lunch – cold turkey legs, salad, blue Stilton. They were sober, having never properly belonged to the happenings downstairs.

'I could have done without the hash,' Llewellyn said. And then, after a pause, 'As Mary knew bloody well.' He said it in a tone of resignation.

Craddock said, 'She always liked the odd joint, as I remember.'

'Don't mind that,' Llewellyn answered quickly, and seemed to change his mind about what he would say next. 'She can do what she . . . I don't like it taking the house over.'

He was heavier, the extra flesh more noticeable when he was sitting down than when moving with that habitual quick stride.

There was a grey filter over the shine of the fair hair, although he had lost none of that yet.

Craddock had asked about the crowd downstairs as a way of commenting to Llewellyn on the obvious (to Craddock, at least) disunion in the marriage. There was a time when he could have been more direct; might have asked simply, 'What's wrong?' But not now. He and Llewellyn were still being polite, although the last few minutes had brought signs that the old ease was returning. Their shared sense of taking refuge had helped.

What were the implications of the note on Llewellyn's Christmas card, suggesting he would not see another twelve months in office? Merely that the party would be out on its ear by the spring, said Llewellyn. Why was he so sure they could not win the election? Because they had behaved so much like a Tory government the electorate was likely to demand the genuine article instead of the copy – probably until Hell froze over, he suspected. It would be a happy release; he could return to the practicalities of business consultancy; the party generally could reapply itself to internal squabbling without the hindrance of having to run the country. Did he genuinely regret accepting his life peerage so that he could be made a minister? No, he liked being a lord; and as a matter of fact he thought he had done a little bit of good at the Home Office. At least a few people in prison were getting the books they needed for their study courses, whereas before they had not. There were other small achievements he could point to here and there, to do with ping-pong tables, allowable pin-ups . . . but had no wish to boast.

This touch of wry self-mockery on Llewellyn's part was new to Craddock. It seemed to connect with that tired note of submission, helplessness? . . . that had jarred when he talked about Mary's friends and drugs. He wondered whether to return to that. It was clearly a painful area for Llewellyn. Again, Craddock remembered, there was a time when he would not have hesitated a moment for fear of trespassing. He feared it now. He asked, 'Why did you take the Home Office job? It wasn't what you wanted, was it?'

Llewellyn shook his head, looking down at his hands clasped loosely in his lap. Then he looked up and said, 'Goddard died.'

He grinned when he saw the explanation was not understood by Craddock.

'Goddard was getting his team together. Harrison couldn't accept it – had to have his own men, naturally. I'm not talking about the big guns. They pick themselves, more or less, whoever's in charge. But Goddard set a lot of store by the junior ministers – thought he could get a lot more action out of them. He wanted us to run our departments like heads of divisions do in the multinational corporations. Harrison hated that – too many people making names for themselves; too many with a chance to snatch some limelight. That would be his first thought – he just can't help himself. His second would be that increased activity invites increased criticism, inevitably. Very bad, that; can't have chaps getting things done all over the place – bound to come a cropper. So he redeployed us, waiting until the very last minute, of course. Goddard would have given me industry; or half of it, anyway – special responsibility for the run-down areas. Rough job. But I was right for it. I know a lot of people. Special arrangements, special terms, deals with the unions – I could have done that. Exciting. Harrison thought my talent for image-changing – his words, not mine – ought to be put to work on the police and the prison warders. I was to reassure them, and the country at large, that we're not actually opposed to law and order. You see what I mean about Harrison's mind? The image he wanted me to change was *ours*, not theirs.'

He stopped short, as if he felt awkward. It struck Craddock that Llewellyn was not used to talking freely about himself nowadays. Once more Craddock thought of the past; and of Mary.

Craddock said, 'You could have turned the job down. It isn't unknown.'

Llewellyn shrugged.

Craddock persisted, but lightly, 'It isn't as if the money's that hot.'

Llewellyn shook his head, patiently dismissing the point as irrelevant.

Craddock decided to take a chance. 'Roy, there must be *something* in it for you. Four years? You could have resigned any time.'

'A lot of people didn't expect Harrison to stay the course. A new man in. A reshuffle. It looked on the cards.'

'I've never known you hanging about on the vague off-chance like that.'

'I didn't think I was.' Craddock got his second two-fingered gesture of the day, but this one came with Llewellyn's smile, the old winning smile of the past. 'Hindsight is about as much use as a cleft palate in politics, Tony.'

Craddock was moved by the smile. He knew Llewellyn was lying to him; or, at best, telling him only a little of the truth. Why did he not say that to Llewellyn? Why did Llewellyn know he wouldn't? The answer was the same to both questions. Because each man knew he was playing the part of the old friend, just as consciously as Mary was passing herself off as the blasé hedonist.

Yes, he was moved by Llewellyn's smile.

★

The telephone was ringing as he unlocked his front door. He ignored it. He was cold, dispirited. His living room had the particular melancholy that a wet winter night can impart the moment the lights are switched on and the room is at the mercy of the street. However brief that moment, before he could close the curtains, Craddock was made to feel his loneliness by it. Otherwise he was seldom aware of being lonely.

When the curtains were drawn and the electric fire was on he went to the cubby-hole under the stairs where Mrs Readhead stored the vacuum cleaner and the brushes and dusters and where Craddock kept his wine. There was no rack, just the cardboard cases the bottles came in. When he had opened a bottle of Beaujolais in the kitchen and taken his first sip the 'phone stopped ringing. He took off his sheepskin topcoat and stood in front of the fireplace, the glass in one hand and the bottle in the other. The warmth began to relax him. He thought the 'phone call was most likely from Peter Franklin. Yesterday he would have found pleasure in talking to Peter; this evening he wished to avoid it. He had no appetite for answering questions.

Just before he left Llewellyn's house he had arranged to take Mary to lunch next day. Would she remember? He could not tell whether she was as drugged as she appeared or exaggerating for effect. In either case she was doing it to displease Llewellyn more than for her own enjoyment. Presumably *that* had become a pleasure.

Halfway down the bottle he experienced a sudden surge of rage. One thought drummed again and again in his head: 'We were happy! We were happy! . . .'

It subsided. He felt exhausted. He carried the bottle and the empty glass into the kitchen, squeezed the cork back in and set the bottle on the floor in the corner under the sink furthest from the radiator. He swilled the glass under the tap and left it upturned on the draining board. He emptied the electric kettle of the water left in it from his morning tea-making; Mrs Readhead liked him to remember to do that, to stop the kettle furring up. The tiny domestic ritual was calming. He went to bed, and was soon asleep in spite of the noises up and down the street as friends and families came and left with jumbled bits of carols and children's screeches and shutting doors.

He woke twice: firstly when some people were pushing a car along the street, shouting and laughing as they tried to get the engine to start; secondly when his 'phone rang. He lay with his eyes open for some time after the ringing stopped; just long enough to question whether the voices in his mind came from memory or dream. Llewellyn's voice was saying, 'I've seen all I ever want to see of prison.' And his own said, 'We were happy.' Memory of course. He could rarely recall much of dreams.

CHAPTER SEVENTEEN

The rocks on the hill where the house stood were so bleached that the white building was naturally camouflaged. The narrow corrugated track did not carry on beyond it. Its back was to the land. Its main doors, windows and balconies looked at the sea which slapped and sighed in numerous little coves a hundred feet below. Two paths had been constructed down to the water from the wings of the house, winding among the cliffs with short flights of steps hewn out of the rock and stretches of handrail and small bridges and even a metal ladder lashed here and there. It was not possible to make a round trip, because both paths ended facing each other across a chasm. They ended at observation platforms which had half-circles of railings, waist high. Craddock and Mary used to race each other down to these platforms, taking the paths alternately because they were not of the same length and while one had the more broken steps the other had a ladder extra. The paths were narrow, and it was dangerous to hurry. They didn't care.

They would each arrive breathless on the platforms and grip the rails with a need for support that was not feigned. They were giddy with the exhilaration in the sun. Once they raced back up again. But Mary was far too light and quick uphill, and it was a non-contest they did not repeat.

Llewellyn never took part in the races. He watched once or twice from the terrace where the swimming pool was, looking anxiously for the two figures to emerge. The paths were visible from the house only in brief sections; but the two platforms were in plain view, and Craddock and Mary would each raise their clasped hands aloft in a victory salute to him regardless of who won. It was a gesture of reassurance. They were safe; all was well; they were having the time of their lives, and it was all due to him.

Craddock had the whole of September of 1969 with the

Llewellyns in Malta. It took only a couple of days after his arrival for him to feel the years peeling away. How long ago was it that his senses responded so readily, so incautiously? Had they ever?

He had known more exotic settings. India. South America. Africa. The West Indies. Peacocks, orchids, flamingoes . . . Nature being the supreme voluptuary. By comparison this was austere, but for the sun and the lucent sea.

But he felt avid. For the day; for company; for wine; for laughter; for food; for everything. And then there was languor – the delicious drowsiness of content in late afternoon, when the only sound or movement in the world came from the sea.

It was not an elaborate house; tiled floors, rush mats, Berber rugs, cane furniture – a mixing of English colonial and standard holiday villa. It was only three or four years old, but already cracks were showing in the plasterwork. The electricity supply wavered unpredictably. Llewellyn's promise of luxury had not been fulfilled, strictly speaking. But Craddock's body luxuriated, all the same. He was at ease, at home – at one with himself, as he told Mary his mother would have expressed it. Mary loved the phrase, and kissed his nose for it.

Llewellyn had rented the place from a friend whose name was not known to Craddock. When Craddock said he ought to pay his share Llewellyn waved the thought aside; he said the sum was peppercorn, in return for having trusted friends in residence rather than leave the house unused except by the insects and the servants. There were six bedrooms, three with their own bathrooms. A separate bungalow accommodated the local couple and their two daughters who maintained the house and its garden; they also grew vegetables as their own sideline on the scratchy soil in the five acres or so that went with the property. Mary relieved Craddock's concern privately by telling him that Llewellyn was in fact paying nothing. As Craddock could see, he was fitting in some freelance business during the holiday; the house came with the little job, whatever it was.

Llewellyn was frequently away from the house in the day, mostly in the mornings and early evenings, talking business. 'Arabs and Italians *and* Maltese politicians – that's talking,' he said. Craddock gathered he was involved in setting up a syndicate to build hotels. This held no interest for Llewellyn once he had left his meetings. He was able to put it right out of his mind and join Mary and Craddock in the fun of life.

They did not have to go far to find it. The rocky paths, the sun-traps and the pool kept them at the house most of the day. Craddock could not swim, and had always refused offers to teach him. He was a man who seldom showed much of his flesh to the air, and he had arrived without swimming trunks, beach shorts, suntan lotion – any of what he termed 'tourist paraphernalia'. Mary changed his attitude. He went with her into Valetta and on her persuasion bought the kind of stuff he would normally not even have looked at. He had trunks with stripes, denim shorts, T-shirts with film stars' faces on the front. And she taught him to swim. She coaxed and bullied. She swore at him and tickled him. Sometimes Llewellyn helped her. Craddock persevered in a spluttering near-panic. It was comic and tender. The three of them would end up in an embrace, laughing helplessly.

Mary made American-style sandwiches for lunch – the 'club sandwich', which put a plate of mixed salad and cold meat into layers of bread so that it challenged the stretch of the hands, let alone the mouth. Craddock had always found something gross in this, encountering it travelling, and would call for a knife and fork to be used in the formal English way – often just to see if it would amuse or irritate those around him. Now he munched from his hands with crude zest, sitting under an umbrella by the pool, reeking of sun lotion, his body going copper-coloured and his self-esteem boosted by it.

He was reluctant to get dressed. He read none of his paperbacks. He wrote nothing in his notebooks.

In the evenings they would usually drive the three miles back down the track to where it met the main road and there was a village, with the houses strung out around a rough crescent of low-lying coastline. There was not enough of it to be called a bay. Half a dozen families had fishing boats with small outboard motors. A few of the houses had been converted into holiday apartments for people who wanted sun and idleness but found no appeal in beaches. A start had been made on building a hotel, but second thoughts had put a stop to it and the framework stood roofless and sprouting weeds.

The village had three bars, but their favourite was Joe's Rainbow Restaurant and Bar. They were there by about seven o'clock most nights. Joe and his wife, whose name was Josephine and was consequently known to everyone as Mrs Joe, became nearly an extension of the household. Joe would turn taxi-driver as required, and on the days Llewellyn was working would often drive him to his meetings so that Mary and Craddock would always have the use of the Vauxhall. And sometimes Joe would be summoned to collect Llewellyn and bring him back, to join Mary and Craddock at the Rainbow. As often, though, a car dispatched by one of the business associates would convey Llewellyn, and now and again it would be an official government vehicle. Llewellyn never brought any of these associates into the Rainbow or to the house; Mary told Craddock he had promised to keep his work out of her hair, and had kept to it. Mrs Joe's great value was her cooking. At twenty-four hours' notice she would provide a rabbit stew or a vegetable pie or a chicken casserole. The local fish was a matter of chance, and Mrs Joe would 'phone the house, when luck was in, to be given her orders; she cooked it with thick wedges of chipped potatoes, not the matchstick kind that result from a shredding machine – her kitchen had no such device. She would do omelettes, and ham and eggs, and sausages and chips, on demand. The friends revelled in all of Mrs Joe's cooking, although most of it was of the kind they would normally connect unpleasantly with motorway cafeterias. But, as Llewellyn said, she had a knack for it. As Craddock said, it was attuned to the place. As Mary said, the woman was in her own home. Whatever inspired Mrs Joe, the friends ate like horses at the Rainbow.

They sat on plastic-slatted chairs of green, yellow, blue, pink. The floor was tiled in squares of the same colours. A rainbow was painted on the wall behind the bar counter with portraits of Queen Elizabeth, the Queen Mother, and the Duke of Edinburgh at its centre. They dated from the late Fifties. Joe had three other prized photographs in frames; the pale, bony Henry Cooper in his days as British and European heavyweight boxing champion; Stirling Moss, the pale British racing driver; and the pale, bony English soccer team which won the 1966 World Cup championship. Joe was short, plump and swarthily mottled. He had never been to England, but he talked about it more than anything else. He read the English newspapers his customers brought into the bar, and kept well abreast of the sports news. He had worked for five years in Australia, driving trucks, which had left him with a distinct Australian whine in his English vowels and a passion for fast, long-distance motoring – not, of course, available to him on the island, although he achieved alarming bursts of speed for half a mile or so.

He and Mrs Joe showed a kindly patience in the way they managed an awkward English regular, a sad drunk called Freddie, ex-army with the tattered remains of an acquired officers' mess accent. He did his twice-daily rounds of the three bars, half-shaved and with rips in his trousers and buttons missing, always making the Rainbow his last call because he knew it was the only place he could get a drink if he had spent the allowance his wife gave him for each little outing. If he seized on a stranger and cadged a drink Joe would make sure the customer got a compensatory round on the house later. Joe would 'phone for Freddie's wife to come and take him home; or, if Freddie was excessively drunk, he would give him a free taxi ride to save the woman the embarrassment. There was a solicitude of a special kind here. Freddie was not good for business; he was no roguish old beachcomber worth a tourist's snapshot and a glass of wine for the privilege; he was a nuisance. But Joe explained things with a shrug and the comment, 'Some people make mistakes.' He was putting a case for compassion in a wider context than merely Freddie's addiction. The friends recognised this when they saw the man's wife, who was a big surprise – a lithe woman with an artist's smock and her grey hair in two plaits. Misalliance. Poor Freddie and the handsome, cultured, still-young wife who painted saleable water-colours took their place in the friends' daily lives.

So did the retired psychiatrist from Birmingham, another of Joe's regulars, who entertained with old George Formby songs complete with the gormless grin. 'She wouldn't turn me down/ She's not a girl like that . . .' He played the ukelele solos with solemn concentration and would stop and go back to the beginning if he made an error. He had taken his retirement early, a bachelor. Most of Mrs Joe's vegetables came from his garden, where he was to be seen weeping and sweating as he hoed and raked. He was allowed to believe this grief – or was it penance? – went unobserved. Sometimes, to ring the changes, he did tricks with playing-cards in the Rainbow instead of his George Formby songs. Joe and his wife had two children, a girl just into her teens who was already a bossy little waitress in the evenings, and a boy of six with a mass of black curly hair which he would allow only Joe and Craddock – to Craddock's amazement – to comb before he was put to bed. Everyone else hurt him when they did it, including Mrs Joe, he said. It was quite a little ritual, accompanied by a tape recording of Judy Garland singing 'Somewhere Over the Rainbow.'

The friends did not feel as if they were on holiday. They felt they lived there. They talked of little else but the house, the village, the villagers, the Rainbow, its customers, Joe and Joe's family. They knew a lot of the details of villagers' incomes and budgets. They talked for long stretches about the best ways of adding some prosperity to the place without disturbing its unsophisticated self-containment. They never came to any conclusions on this matter. It weighed about their minds like a family problem which would have to be met one day – but there was plenty of time yet.

Glimpses of their own lives appeared in response to curiosity, usually prompted by some casual mention of a place or a person unfamiliar to one of the three. In fact most of this exchange of information was between Craddock and Mary because of Llewellyn's absences; and the two had known each other for such a short time, although it was hard to believe. So Mary learned something of Craddock's slow progress out of local newspapers and then his sudden acceleration once he was sent abroad and he found a subject to excite him. The third world. The *wealth*, for a writer, of injustice, misery, vivid misfortune. This experience had acted like a spring-release on his latent capacities, she gathered. Now he mixed sport and films and television and glossy magazines into his working life: he was much on the move; vague dissatisfactions had begun to gnaw; he supposed he should decide to concentrate, perhaps to settle – actually buy a house; he was coming up for forty. And Craddock learned something of Mary's diverse flair in designing record sleeves, book jackets, advertising posters. She had been drawn to England by the vivacious innovations in pop music, pop fashion, pop art; and had stayed to make a name for herself in this brash world. The money rolled in; life was quick and smart. She met Llewellyn at a party in Chelsea – where else? – and he wasted no time in picking her up. She had assumed she would never remarry, but the two of them found they were seeing so much of each other there was an urge to commit themselves formally. They had decided not to have children; after all, she was now thirty-four and had no longing to be a mother; she believed in doing what seemed right for her; other avenues of work were inviting, stage design for one and then what? No, a good marriage was one thing, running a family something else.

Llewellyn thrived in his imprecise function, on contract to Harrison's government but not a politician in the titular sense with a constituency or administrative department to tether him. Mary was glad he wasn't in politics in the true sense. Llewellyn laughed at this and said he was in it up to his eyeballs, and that was why he was a man fulfilled at last. He explained things for her and Craddock one afternoon of exceptional heat as they lay at the pool. They were in the state of half-reality that takes over sometimes with sun and indolence and privacy, so that all conversation is faintly puzzling, faintly unwanted, faint. 'When your father talked to you about the first world war, Tony,' he said, 'did he tell you about the men who specialised in no-man's land? They were strange characters. They were fascinated by the space between the lines, the dangerous ground where most people hated to be. They'd always volunteer for reconnaissance. They got a kick out of picking their way through the mines and the craters and all the booby-traps. And what they liked doing best of all was leading somebody else through. One foot wrong, and goodbye. But they loved it. A bit of swagger in it. No drudgery. And useful, of course. Important. That's what I do in politics. I guide and steer through the minefields. In and out among the fine print, the accepted procedures, the regulations designed to ensnare and frustrate . . . it's a bloody wonderful game.'

No more than glimpses. Nothing to disrupt their guiltless triviality.

The month was an age to Craddock. He had never got so far away from his past. But when it was over he was caught by surprise, the time had gone so fast.

On the friends' last night in the Rainbow Joe led the singing of 'Auld Lang Syne'. They each hugged Joe and Mrs Joe and kissed the children, the boy asleep on his sister's knee. They attracted a full house.

*

They made a number of arrangements to go away together again. Long week-ends. Fortnights. Full months. They managed only lunches, dinners, and once or twice a Sunday that stretched through a nostalgic afternoon to a little foray into bistro-land for spaghetti and plonk.

They were all so tied up. Their free time would not coincide. All travelled a lot. There were occasions when one or another had to cry off with jet lag or some briefly prostrating infection brought back from abroad; the stomach and the throat were the vulnerable parts. As time went on the phrase 'ought to be able to fit something in' was used so often they became self-conscious about it, and would smother it in mocking laughter down the 'phone.

Craddock saw Llewellyn and Mary separately, and there was a sense of being dominated by the absence of the third. The main form this took was in a compulsion to talk about the absentee but then to feel inhibited so that questions were left unanswered, and more were not asked. Both the others told Craddock that for this reason and that – most of all there was work – they really saw little more of each other lately than of him.

Eventually, of course, they would have to face the problem they all knew was there. But this was never said. So there was no confronting. No rift. A drifting apart, nothing more.

CHAPTER EIGHTEEN

Mary said the table was too big. The place felt too masculine – too much starched white linen. She didn't want fillet steak or turbot – any of that masculine kind of food. She could sense the waiters didn't like women. She wanted a very cold dry vermouth and some melba toast. It was this sort of place that made her pine for New York, or Las Vegas, or Acapulco, or anywhere that was vulgar and brassy. English good taste was creeping back into the national life, she'd noticed, like some old disease. Stiff-upperlipitis. A resurgence of male chauvinism. She said she wasn't joking, it was a country of dyed-in-the-wool reactionaries. Craddock had never brought her to a place like this before, which proved her point. She'd have another dry vermouth, and could they make this one cold? For Christ's sake, the room was cold enough . . .

Craddock let her burn away her tension, waiting for the alcohol and the tiredness she was suppressing to bring her down to an approachable level. He had chosen the restaurant because it was roomy and Mary was unfamiliar with it. He had assumed she would be raw at the nerve ends – if she was able to face lunching in public, at all. He did not want to risk running into some of her friends at one of her favourite places. In that event she would stay high, keep playing her part. None of the right questions would be raised. Pain would be averted.

But she was being the original all-American bitch. He was paying a high price. Her voice had a tremor which she tried to disguise, or banish, by talking over-loudly. She spoke in snatches. In the pauses she turned in her seat to stare at a waiter or at other customers until they were forced to look back at her. Her mouth was squeezed so tightly when she was silent he was prepared for blood to ooze from the lips. At these moments her whole face compressed, the lines around her eyes and the bridge of her nose like clusters of needles. She looked older than she was. He could place her age at forty-two or forty-three. These fierce introspective grimaces added ten years. He knew she was bitter with disappointment. Possibly she was also ill. The eyes pleaded and raged in random order.

After the third vermouth she let Craddock persuade her to inspect the hors d'oeuvres trolley. Halfway through eating her meagre selection she said quietly, 'Jesus, Tony, sorry about that. I can be a terrible old cow these days.' He sliced at his smoked trout, taking too long to answer, and she added, 'I wish you'd shown a bit more surprise.' When he looked up he saw a tiny reminder of the amused challenge that he remembered used to light up her face. It was a sad moment.

'I was surprised you made it here,' he said. 'You're entitled to whatever sees you through.'

Her shoulders sagged. The hand holding the fork rested weakly on the table. She gave a sigh which trembled, and he looked for tears in her eyes. But when she looked back at him the face had hardened again.

'Yes, that's right,' she said. 'Good phrase. Whatever sees me through.'

So they began to talk. That is, Mary did. In the early stages Craddock had only to interpose now and then, bringing her back when she strayed into a new area before he was ready.

'I'm a clever woman,' she started. 'I've been told I'm brilliant. I don't know if that's true. Anyway, what does it mean, brilliant? Just a word people use. I'm in a business where people don't know what they want till you give it to them. I'm not afraid to. That's all. It's kept me pretty near the top, and they still want me. I'm clever. I'm tough. But I have to keep telling myself that. Doesn't match up, does it? The last few years have been . . . well, you said it last night – I look different. I knew you'd notice. I didn't know if I wanted you to. Most people don't. Clever. Tough. Mary doesn't change. But when it comes to you, Tony . . . yes, that's something else. As if you wouldn't notice. Big joke . . .

'The work doesn't bother me. I mean, it's getting a hell of an effort, but it isn't the *work* doing that. How did you think Roy was looking?'

Craddock said, 'I'd say he's put on ten, twelve pounds.' But she was not interested in that, and overlapped him.

'Clever. Tough. But I can't handle Roy. No. Roy's got me beat. Roy bothers me . . .

'What is it about Roy? A beautiful man. Well, you know that. Remember how much sheer life he had? That's what hit me about him first. God, what he must have been like when he was twenty-five. Well, you know that as well. He can still turn it all on. Press the button for all systems go. All right, he's beautiful and he's one of those men who just can't help making the world go round. I mean, he makes it move under your feet. You know that. It doesn't happen so often these days, but he can still do it. But he's other things too. There's an old-fashioned American word for one thing he is. In the language of the old Hollywood B-picture, he's a heel. Let's face it, where women are concerned he's a heel in the *style* of the old Hollywood B-picture. But I never cared too much about that. I mean, just getting his kicks. Some of the other things . . .

'Why don't I walk out on him? Or we could break up by mutual agreement. Why not? No kids. Independent incomes. We don't want to. That's why not. But I don't understand it. There's nothing left in the marriage, except we sleep together once in a while. That's when we happen to be home at the same time and we both feel it's due . . .

'He's going to destroy me. Why can't I tell him to go and screw himself? He knows what he's doing. It can't go on for ever. But he won't let me talk to him. Imagine that, Tony. Me, the silent wife? That's what I mean when I say what the hell is it about Roy. No other man or woman on earth has ever stopped me talking . . .

'You shouldn't have broken with us the way you did. You could have helped. He'd have cared more about me just because you did. And if you'd been around to show it . . .

'You were in love with me. Funny old-fashioned expression. But it's true. In love with me, and you'd loved Roy most of your life. And there were your moral scruples, and your inhibitions, and your worries about how it would all end, and so you just dropped us. Did you convince yourself it was a noble sacrifice? A far, far better thing I do this day etcetera. Sorry, sorry . . .

'I wanted you, Tony. Roy would have turned a blind eye. You know he would. You must have known it then. I suppose that would make it worse for you. Hadn't been clear on that before. But I can see it now in your face. Once we spell it out it goes like this. Getting into bed with Roy's wife with Roy's approval comes awfully close to making love to Roy. And that's not the way you wanted to think about him. I mean, you'd been fighting it off for too long. I've blamed myself for not making it more plain how *much* I wanted you, once upon a time, but it would never have made any difference, would it? Poor Tony. And me, of course . . .

'And then there's Roy. Do you think he hasn't missed you all these years? He's needed you. How did you think he looked last night? How about . . . would you say troubled? Yes, he's got plenty to worry about. Deep trouble, Tony. Shit your conscience and your hang-ups. You should have stayed around. We needed you. You could have done some real good. Helped your friends – people you belong to. But we got too close and you couldn't take that . . .

'What brought you back? Funny thing, when Roy told me you were coming to the house I'd got a glass in my hand and nearly dropped it. Sheer excitement. What brought you back? Do you want to help? It's a mess . . . Such a mess.'

It took time for her to prise these reproofs and admissions out of herself. She swung between weariness and a cold intensity, and there were breathing spaces when she asked about Craddock's work and let him lighten the atmosphere with anecdotes about actors. They ate and drank. Her strident behaviour when she arrived made sure there were inquisitive glances after she stopped it. But the eavesdroppers got nothing more.

He asked her, 'Do you know what kind of trouble Roy's in?'
She did not answer.
'You said he's in deep.'
'He is.'
'*What*, though?'
She licked the tip of a finger and used it to pick up a few crystals of brown sugar spilt around the bowl and then placed them on the rim of her coffee cup. She paid great attention to this exercise.

Craddock said, 'Politics? Personal?'
She was irritated. 'All the same, isn't it?'
'Not always. Even a politician has his private . . .'
'Roy. We're talking about Roy, not *a politician*.' She inter-

rupted quickly, cleaning her fingers on the tablecloth with a vigorous scratching for emphasis. 'He's never out of politics.' She added softly, after a pause, 'And it isn't just some woman – he'd tell me. I've advised him in the past.'

'You're saying, on this other business he's told you nothing at all?'

She agreed with her silence.

Craddock had to take the plunge. 'There may be nothing to tell – that you don't already know. It's just the two of you. How much hash do you smoke? How many times do you whistle up that rent-a-mob you had in yesterday? How hard do you work at getting at him? What else are you on, apart from hash, Mary? You asked me twice how I thought he looked. He looked to me like a man whose wife's giving him a rough time. All right, you can say you've got every excuse for that. But if you're providing all the trouble, don't invent some mysterious murky secret he's supposed to be carrying round with him. That's just to let you off the hook.'

He could see he had hurt her. But, then, she had started the day hurt. He could not be sure if she was defeated by the truth of what he had said or simply by her own fatigue. The reference to drugs had certainly hit home. It brought a strange twist of the mouth and clenching of the eyes from her for a moment: a wince, but also something defiant suggesting contempt for the outsider.

Now she shook her head weakly, looking away from him. He noticed for the first time how the skin under her jaw was developing the slack folds of middle age. The sight affected him far more than had the hard lines of aggression he had seen earlier. He remembered her running and laughing.

He had to clear his throat before he could speak. 'Do you want some more coffee? Brandy or something?'

She giggled faintly. 'A sniff would help. But I'll settle for a brandy and a taxi.'

*

When she came back from the ladies' he could see she had been crying. She did not attempt to hide it. They were putting their coats on in the little entrance lobby, and she said, 'Don't look so worried, I'm not going to make a scene. I love that expression –

quintessentially English.' Her coat had a high collar, and she retreated into it so that her face was softened by shadow. 'I hope I didn't spoil your lunch, Tony.'

In the car taking them back to the Hampstead house she said nothing, and kept her eyes closed most of the way. Craddock asked her once if she was all right, and she gave a little nod and a hint of a smile.

He was glad of the respite. There was a light rain, and the drops clung to the car's side windows to make them almost opaque, more protective. The wipers' metronomic action on the windscreen was comforting. For a few minutes he felt pleasantly drowsy – unconcerned. Just for a few minutes.

As she unlocked the front door there was the humming of a vacuum cleaner somewhere upstairs. Craddock was aware immediately of how clinical the house seemed in comparison with the disarray of the day before. It was bigger than he had thought. The hall had a rosewood floor which he knew without asking was part of Mary's improvement of the place. He had not seen the upper rooms, except for Llewellyn's study; but judging from the ground floor he doubted if there was much of the house that had not been reordered since she and Llewellyn moved in.

Mary went to a 'phone on the wall and pressed one button. Craddock tried to remember the last time he was in a private house with an internal 'phone system, but could think only of hotel bedrooms and office blocks. She said 'Tony's here' and put the handset back on its rest straightaway. 'I'm going to get some sleep. Work tomorrow,' she said to Craddock, and then gave him a quick kiss on the cheek, as if by habit and not expecting him to respond. She started up the stairs, one hand on the balustrade. Looking up at her, Craddock saw thin legs, a hunch in the shoulders, the hand gripping hard enough for support to make it tremble. She could have been a cripple.

Llewellyn appeared on the first landing, and she passed him without speaking. He called down, 'Take your coat off, old son. Aren't you stopping?' He was using the accent of childhood, not accurately. Craddock gave him a grin, dropped his coat on a chair and followed him to the study.

The vacuum cleaner had been switched off, and Craddock would hear a woman's voice talking in awkward English. She sounded agitated, and he thought he heard the words 'silly' and 'doctor'. Distinctly, Mary's voice overwhelmed the other. She said, 'Shut up. Shut your mouth!' A door banged.

Craddock asked Llewellyn as they settled in their chairs. 'Did I hear the sounds of industrial dispute just then?' He hated his own facetiousness; but the incident could hardly be ignored.

'Concepta's Portuguese,' Llewellyn said. And then, 'The house was a tip this morning. I've hidden myself away in here all day.'

It sufficed for the moment.

'I remember a line or two in the papers when you bought the house,' Craddock said. 'Gossip column fodder – Dick Goddard's altar boy buys the rectory, or some sneer of the kind.'

'Yes.'

'What was the appeal?'

'Well, the place was never put on the market. You know how Fleet Street thinks – for private sale, read *secret*. They were bound to root around it a bit. God knows what they expected to find. Perhaps I used my evil influence to wheedle it out of his widow for peanuts – that was going the rounds in a vague sort of way. A long way from the truth. Ursula made me pay through the nose.'

'Roy, you misunderstand me.' Craddock was genuinely surprised. 'I can see why they had to look for a story. I meant, what made you buy the house? Especially since it cost a packet. Sure to, a place this size. A wonder it didn't break the bank.'

Llewellyn thought a little before he said, 'Don't forget Mary's always made good money.'

Craddock nodded, and to fill in the silence said idly, 'Everyone needs a roof.'

'It all started for me here,' Llewellyn said. His tone was different. There was simple, unemphatic emotion in it. 'I wanted to own this room.' He smiled, embarrassed, at Craddock. 'Can you understand that?'

'A sentimental Royston Llewellyn? A likely story.'

'No, not sentimental. Well, a bit of that, I suppose. But it was more a sort of joining up the ends of the circle. As I said, this is where it all got going for me.'

Craddock ventured, 'And now it's finished; is that what you're saying?'

'I bought the house four years ago, remember. Four years and eight months.'

'Finished *then*?'

'It's the wrong word. Completed – that's nearer.'

'But you told me you didn't get the job you wanted. Harrison fobbed you off.'

Llewellyn shrugged. 'Yes, he did. But forget the job. Nothing to do with it. The moment Ursula first mentioned selling the house I knew I wasn't going to let anyone else in. Ghosts. Echoes. Goddard taught me a lot.'

'It all sounds a bit mystical. You amaze me, Roy.'

'Well, think of it as exorcism.' Llewellyn spoke with a throw-away forbearance. 'The need to be my own man. What better way than moving in with the ghosts?' As Craddock pondered this Llewellyn added with a wistful relish, 'Some wicked plots have been laid here.'

Craddock exaggerated his eagerness, to underplay it. 'Please. Tell me more.'

Llewellyn yawned. 'Party manoeuvrings. They mattered desperately at the time, of course. Just water under the bridge.'

'Is that all I get?'

Llewellyn was sitting at the desk in his tall old leather chair – Goddard's chair, of course – as he had all the time they talked the day before. It seemed to Craddock the chair gave him confidence, security; he had never needed to borrow these attributes from furniture in the past. Llewellyn half-rose to turn the chair a little so that he could stretch out his legs and rest his head in the leather wing. He affected a look of benevolence which came across to Craddock as disagreeably coy.

'Does your novel have a title?' Llewellyn asked.

'Something like, "Whatever Happened to Jerusalem," with an exclamation mark.'

'You don't mean that, of course.'

'All right, what about "Arrows of Desire"?'

'So it's all about the crumbling of ideals. The young hero seduced by fame and the good life, abandoning responsibilities. Meanwhile back in his home town the pinched faces of the unemployed hang over their bowls of thin gruel in the soup kitchens. He's a poor lost soul, the tiresome git, and makes a pilgrimage of rediscovery – self-regeneration by sharing the poverty of the noble proles he left behind. But it's too late. He forgot the golden rule, Never Go Back. They shun him in the streets. They *stone* him in the streets. But there's this old flame he put in the family way when he was the hope of the valley – it's got to be set in Wales, this – and now she's grey and withered. She alone befriends him and takes him to her bed. The roof falls in just as he's giving her one.'

Craddock said, 'No, it's a contemporary novel.'

'Ah. No Welsh male voice choirs?'

'I haven't got a title,' Craddock said flatly, wanting to steer the conversation back to seriousness. 'That's probably why I don't know exactly what the book's about. I've never written a play without deciding on the title first. It defines intentions. I want the novel to answer some questions. Why do people want to *be* politicians, now there's a general public assumption they're all bent? Is that the new attraction – the tawdry glamour of the gangster?'

Llewellyn gave a short loud laugh.

Craddock went on, 'Well, let's make it the petty thief with aspirations. The country's always had a soft spot for the daring villain, as long as he doesn't bash anyone over the head. You do *know* you're all on the make according to popular opinion, do you? I ask because I know some of you older hands tend to live sheltered lives, cut off from the daily communion of the streets.'

'You're gunning for us, are you, Tony?'

'Seriously . . .'

'I should hope so.'

Craddock let the silence hang a little and then asked, 'Can you remember a time when there was as much distrust of politicians?'

'No, I share it,' Llewellyn said.

CHAPTER NINETEEN

Craddock had declined any alcohol at Llewellyn's house. Now, as he walked in search of a telephone kiosk, he longed for the taste of whisky and water. Llewellyn had been surprised he did not want a cab, but Craddock said a walk to the nearest tube station would do him good. For the first five minutes he was, in fact, glad to be on the move out of doors. The rain had turned to a flurry of snow, but that had stopped and the air was now sharply cold. To begin with it was refreshing, and he took long gulps of it down into his lungs and stomach; he felt he was cleaning his system of a sour coagulation. But he found he had to be careful of his stride, because the pavement glistened with frost and he slid a little until he checked his pace. And once the dry, still cold fastened around his head, and in particular clamped on to his temples, he had to make a determined effort to relax and banish a spasm of dizziness. Yes, he needed the salve of whisky. A pub with a telephone would serve ideally. But there was still a quarter of an hour to go before opening time. He slithered again and lifted his arms to help his balance. He stood still for several seconds, breathing steadily and waiting for calm to return. He was glad he had the street to himself. He thought he was going to vomit, and he held on to the small iron gate of the house he had stopped by. He recovered. Seeing his white hand gripping the gate he was reminded of Mary, dragging herself up the stairs with the support of the balustrade. Well, one clear image was less disturbing than a teeming of phrases and looks. The knot in his stomach eased. He moved on up the slight incline of the street towards the lights of the main road. He would find a 'phone there, and a drink.

★

It was nearly two hours later when a taxi delivered him to the house where Peter Franklin lived. It was in one of those terraces of three- and four-storeys in the more bedraggled part of Maida Vale. Wanderers' land. One of the mainstays of the London growth industry known as Light Removals.

The nearest street lamp was along and across the road, and he had to feel his way down the steps to the basement flat until he reached the dim light coming from a curtained window. He caught his ankle painfully against a dustbin before he found the door. There was no bell and no knocker. He fumbled in the blackness of the doorway until his hands located the letter-box. He pushed the flap and it stayed back, springless. A soaked doormat sucked at his feet. In a rush of exasperation he smacked repeatedly at the door with the flat of his hand, at the same time bawling Peter's name. He was making so much noise that he was unaware of footsteps or any other sound until the door was abruptly opened inwards as he thumped it. Momentarily he was off balance, and he half-stumbled into Peter.

'Oh, I see. I wondered what had kept you,' Peter said. He leaned back against the wall to take Craddock's weight. Craddock righted himself with a hand on Peter's chest. He was conscious of the texture of heavy new wool before he took in with his eyes that Peter was wearing an obvious Christmas present, a polo-necked sweater which draped him from the thin shoulders lopsidedly. The sight amused him, and his temper softened as he watched Peter close the door.

'Perhaps you'll grow into it,' Craddock said.

Peter gave him a tolerant half-smile. 'How many have you had?' He walked past Craddock as he spoke.

The question irked Craddock, and he was immediately aware again of his damp toes, chilled hands; and the dull, deep ache the day had implanted. He was standing in a small oblong hall, a door to his right, another facing it, a third straight ahead and which Peter had left open as he went into the room. Craddock opened the door at his right hand: a kitchen crowded by its gas cooker, refrigerator, a sink with an antique of a gas water heater above it. An unshaded lamp was on, and he saw the window was the feeble source of light he had been grateful for in the yard. He winced at the greasiness of the walls and the curtains – they were plastic, with a pattern of trees stamped on them, which took his memory back to bed-sitters of nearly thirty years ago. He switched the light off.

'Don't do that – leave it on.' Peter had reappeared. 'Discourages the mice. The bog's in there, if that's what you're looking for.' He pointed at the opposite door. 'You sometimes have to give the chain two or three pulls.'

'I can believe it.' Craddock snapped the kitchen light back on and shut the door with a bang. He went towards the doorway Peter stood in.

'Were you looking for booze? I haven't got any.' He turned and Craddock followed him into the main room.

It was warmed by a big gas fire, plainly new, and half lit by wall bracket lamps with little brown shades of the kind found in 'Tudor-style' hotel bars. Rush matting covered the floor. There was a big table with a scored top which belonged to a Victorian kitchen, and a tall angle-poise lamp threw a pool of light at one end of it where Peter had been working; a packet of typing paper, a scattering of handwritten pages, an open notebook, his tape-recorder. The table also bore piles of newspapers, magazines, books, a half-empty bottle of mineral water, a soup bowl full of cigarette ash and ends, a dozen or so packets of cigarettes arranged in the way a child makes a castle out of toy bricks, some letters with their envelopes paper-clipped to them in the method of a newspaper office, a few Christmas cards in a heap and not on display, a telephone. There were a couple of faded blue moquette armchairs, a portable colour television set; on the mantelpiece above the gas fire more books and a transistor radio. The walls had some old paper with vertical stripes, and gashes and holes left by the fittings of previous tenants here and there. A bead curtain divided the room, although enough of the strands were missing for a double bed, a wardrobe and a straight-backed chair to be visible. The chair's partner, with a rush seat, was at the table beside the angle-poise lamp.

Craddock unbuttoned his sheepskin topcoat, and Peter took it from him and ducked through the bead curtain to throw it on the bed. Craddock gave a little snort of a laugh. 'Those bloody beads. I wouldn't have thought it of you, Peter. I'd say call-girl, approximately nineteen-fifty-eight.'

Peter was lighting a cigarette. 'I'll take your word for it. They came with the place. The bed's mine. And the telly and the lamp. All the rest . . .' He dismissed it all with a shrug of indifference. He sat in one of the armchairs.

'How do you describe it in your letters home to mum?'

Peter said wearily, 'Oh, Christ.'

'How *was* mum, and all that up there in Manchester? Yuletide yuck well up to the mark?'

Peter looked at his watch. 'I should have known when you 'phoned me from a pub. You're pissed.'

'It's been a long hard day.'

'When do I get to see Llewellyn?'

'It's been a *very* long hard day.'

'Pissed.'

Craddock sat in the other threadbare armchair. 'You've got a little study in English anthropology here. Metropolitan man as seen through the artefacts of a single dwelling unit, say 1898 to 1978. Eighty years of household attitudes. Do you think the B.B.C. would take a radio talk on it?'

'Why don't you just sod off home and cuddle up to another bottle?'

After a few seconds, in which he took off his tie, rolled it like a spool round his fingers and put it in his jacket pocket, Craddock said straightforwardly, 'I couldn't mention you to Llewellyn. It wasn't the right time.'

'When *will* it be?'

'Don't know. Maybe next time I meet him.'

Seeing the quick glint in Peter's eyes he went on hurriedly, 'There's nothing fixed. The point is we're talking again. Picked up where we left off.' As a rueful qualification he added softly, 'More or less.'

Peter saw no reason to acknowledge the change of manner, except by changing his own. 'How did he strike you, after all this time?' When Craddock delayed answering Peter put in, 'You look as if the meeting knocked you about.' And as Craddock still delayed, 'A very hard day – your own words.'

Craddock said, 'Personal stuff.'

Peter dug in, as Craddock knew he would. The light voice flicked like a whip. 'What upset you? Have you got some doubts about him now? Not the same good old Roy?'

Craddock had to deal with that. The words spilled out, and he stammered a little, which had happened rarely since infancy. 'That's not the way to think about him. He was never just good old Roy. That's not Llewellyn. We're not talking about some king of the dirty stories in the lounge bar. He's always got some laughs out of life. Dead right, he has. He got laughs out of *people*. Never scared of *anybody*. Don't give me that good old Roy rubbish. He was never a mindless glad-hander. He had things he wanted to do. It isn't easy getting any real changes made in this country. Llewellyn was never patient. He found his own ways. Who plays to the rules, anyway? What rules *are* there any more? People like you – your generation, you *children* – come galloping around baying for blood, but you never stop to think you might owe something to a man like Llewellyn. If it wasn't for men like him . . . Who do you think gets the new universities and the polytechnics built? The red lecturers? The professional unemployables? We need people who can make things happen. That's what Llewellyn did.'

He had been leaning forward, glaring at Peter. His voice rose almost to a shout. All the time Peter was motionless, the brown eyes unfaltering as he took in Craddock's anger. His cigarette had burned to his fingers, and now he dropped it on the matting and squashed it with his foot. There was a faint smell of burnt straw for a moment, and it drew Craddock's attention, breaking his mood. Earnestly he said, 'Peter, that was a stupid thing to do. This room would go up like a bonfire.' He let his head loll on the back of the chair and closed his eyes.

'So it's true. Llewellyn's bent.' If Peter had waited a couple of seconds longer Craddock would have been asleep.

'Is that what I said?'

'Sounded like it.'

'I don't have any information.'

'You *must* have something.'

'Nothing.'

Peter lit another cigarette. In the quiet of the hot, grubby room Craddock's eyes would not stay open. He heard Peter exhale; a long dry rasp of exasperation. An absurd fantasy sped through his mind; the angle-poise lamp turned on his face and Peter's voice reaching a scream with, 'We have ways to make you talk.' He giggled softly, and the silly fancy went away. He forced his eyes open. Peter was standing by the table with his back to Craddock. The laughter had not been heard, it seemed. Perhaps it was part of the daydream. He sat upright and gave his head a shake.

Peter asked casually, 'So why did you bother to come round here?' He reached for the bottle of mineral water and turned to face Craddock before he drank from it.

Craddock was doubly bemused: by the question itself and by Peter's need to ask it. Some of the water trickled down Peter's chin and dropped inside the floppy neck of the over-big sweater, making him shudder as the cold liquid met his warm skin.

'I'm reporting in,' Craddock said. 'The conscientious leg man.'

'Reporting in what? Sweet bugger all, according to you.'

'Didn't you want to see me? I know you've been 'phoning.'

'And you didn't bother to answer.' The accusing tone was a relief to Craddock.

'I'm sorry. Am I welcome now?'

Peter turned back to the table and put down the bottle. From among the mound of papers and magazines he extracted an object in a paper bag with a bookseller's name repeated diagonally all over it. He held it out to Craddock with a stiff thrust of his arm, as clumsy as a ten-year-old with shyness. 'I got you this,' he said, and then sat down flicking the hair off his forehead.

The book was a collection of photographs of Provence, mostly street scenes: market days, boule players, a family at lunch in a courtyard . . . The unconcerned self-absorption was beguilingly caught in the pictures.

Craddock murmured, 'Thanks, Peter. I didn't know I'd ever talked to you about Provence.'

Peter shrugged. 'I was looking at your bookshelves . . . I thought we might go some time, if you feel like it.'

Craddock noted that the gift bore no inscription – of course.

CHAPTER TWENTY

The dining car, like the train, was two-thirds empty. Craddock bought the full, cooked breakfast, feeling under an obligation to the stewards. He saw them counting heads, doing their mental arithmetic. A ten per cent tip on tea and toast wouldn't help much towards the cost of launching the new year. Also the ceremony of the fried breakfast seemed to be part of the privilege he was buying. The first class traveller on a journey north . . . First class travellers were the ones who completed their business and returned without delay. The stewards managed to convey that in return for his privilege he had responsibilities to discharge. Eating sauté potatoes at eight-thirty in the morning was one of them. Another was to accept the stewards' reassuring sympathy . . . 'They don't get the winters they used to up there . . . With these air-conditioned trains and the central heating up there now you won't hardly notice you've left London.' There were three stewards: two Irishmen and a Scot.

Up There . . .

They had identified him: placed him in the order of things. He was one of the fortunate. He lived and worked where it was desirable to do so. Whatever connections he had with Up There were impersonal, profitable. He would visit Up There when necessity couldn't be denied.

Craddock's memory produced a radio voice from some distant time and place: 'Foreign visitors are advised to remain indoors, particularly after dark . . .' And he had to admit to himself he felt as if he was going to another country. London had a way of conditioning its captives. He had no special fondness for the city: in fact he never thought of it as an entity, as a *place*; it was many places, and there were odd bits he held strong feelings for or against. For example, he now loathed the Piccadilly Circus-Leicester Square bit, for its ingrained foulness, whereas once he had found the gamy parade stimulating.

The muddle of shops and the muddy little park near his house he liked, after six years, possessively. Before Parton Street there had been two other addresses in London, not counting a succession of brief tenancies when he first moved to the city and was finding his bearings. Nearly half his working life, and all his childhood, had been spent Up There, or thereabouts anyway – certainly it was all Up There to him now. He was one of its emigrants, and he watched the old country make way for him, in his plunging sealed train, with the wonder of recognition. Yes, it seemed much the same as ever. The brick and concrete got darker, generally speaking. It was to do with industry. So did people's clothing, and indeed overall demeanour; for the same reason. High ground appeared – real hills, with their tops cut off by cloud. He used to walk on them, embalmed in wool and oilskin. That was in a previous life. He drank pints of beer, got about by bus. He had preposterous ambitions to be a writer who lived in London and travelled all over the world . . .

He had stayed in the dining car for the whole journey, and as he got off the train, carrying a light grip and with his sheepskin coat over his arm, one of the Irish stewards said to him considerately, as a seasoned voyager should, 'All the same, I'd put that coat on if I was you, Sir, you'll need it up here.'

*

He was met at the station by an ex-reporter called Phil Simms, usually known as Simmy, who was now George Birtles' public relations man. That is, he was a partner in the public relations agency Birtles had taken over in the building of his company, which he called the G.B. Group. The letters G.B.G. were everywhere around the district, on delivery vans and glassy showrooms and workshop gates. G.B.G. were in the prefabricated buildings business, the double-glazing windows and doors business, the small pleasure-boat business, the office equipment business, the rising damp and dry rot business, the land reclamation business, the holiday coach-tours business, and, of course, the public relations business, which seemed to be the flagship of the line. G.B.G. Promotions took first place in the list of companies in white capitals on a black plastic board in the entrance hall of the office block to which Simmy took Craddock. The two men had known each other twenty years before, and Craddock noted that Simmy still had the same compulsion to seek out his own reflection in any surface that would function as a mirror, such as a shop window or the glass panel of a door as it stood at a particular angle. He would stroke the wavy black hair, lovingly, the head dipping into the palm of the hand, first to the right, then to the left. The hair started low on the forehead, and it was a slow transport of ecstasy for Simmy's palms up and over and down to the razored smoothness of the nape of his neck. Clearly Simmy was still making his weekly visit to the barber so that the famous locks should never need more than the lightest trimming. Simmy was wearing a suede overcoat with shoulder tabs and a belt. His shoes had raised heels. He was two or three years older than Craddock, with children in their twenties. The caressing of the hair had occurred twice in the car from the station – a journey of perhaps half a mile across the city – when Simmy managed to position himself to take advantage of the driving mirror. Birtles had sent his maroon Rolls Royce, with a driver in a dark suit but without a peaked cap. The registration number was G.B. 1.

'Greetings, old friend,' had been Simmy's welcome, and his left hand patted Craddock's shoulder as the right gripped for far too long. They had never been especially friendly. On the 'phone the day before when the meeting was arranged, Craddock had had to raise his voice sharply to deter Simmy from booking him into a hotel as a guest of G.B.G. Looking at Simmy now, as the lift took them to the top floor, Craddock wondered if the hair was dyed, and decided it was probably the faded white of the man's face that emphasised the blackness unnaturally. Simmy looked a sick old man, in spite of the young man's clothing and the boisterous reception. The hollows around his eyes were like old bruises. The eyes themselves blinked as if desperate for silence and dark. He kept straightening his shoulders and lifting his jaw. Since the effervescence of ushering Craddock into the car he had barely spoken.

They stepped out of the lift on to a maroon carpet with the letters G.B.G. woven into it in front of a desk where a girl sat. She had a magazine open before her and her fingers were entwined in her necklace. To Craddock she had the look of not having been disturbed for some time.

'Hullo, Louise, my pet of the year and every year,' Simmy

began, sounding mechanically operated, 'Mr Birtles is expecting me, with Mr Craddock, if you'd let him know pronto and without ado.' He walked to the back of her chair, reached over to fondle her breasts and carried on, 'Just having my fix. Louise understands.' He looked pitiful, as Louise saw just as plainly as did Craddock. It took her a few seconds to extricate her fingers from the necklace, and she used the time to decide on the right note: to stop Simmy making a sad fool of himself without showing to Craddock, the stranger, how familiar it was.

She said, 'You *are* excitable today, Mr Sims. I suppose it's party time in the air.' Craddock thought she had done rather well. He gave her a little smile before turning away towards a settee against the furthest wall. By the time he had taken off his coat and sat down she had pushed Simmy away and was dialling Birtles' office. Simmy was now removing his suede overcoat; underneath was a silky suit too light for the weather, too pinched at the waist. Craddock had a comic flight of imagination which presented Birtles, the horny-handed cock of the north, in the same creep's outfit. Perhaps it was the G.B.G. uniform? G.B.G., jee-*bee*-jee, *jee*-bi-jee . . . It was like the name of some kids' music programme on the wireless – Radio Prattle. Jee-bi-*jee*. The expression *heebie-jeebies* sprang into his mind. The jitters, the shakes, a touch of the vapours. Simmy could well be suffering from the heebie-jeebies. *Worried sick* would probably describe his appearance. A sad case, old Simmy. There was an altogether sad feel to the office. A Christmas tree leaned from the vertical in one corner, with its fairy lights unlit. Some of the Christmas cards which had been hung on lengths of string around the walls had fallen to the floor and left to lie there, although the place was so clean it looked unused. That was what was wrong about the office: the sense of inactivity. It did not connect with the renowned Birtles dynamism. Craddock had noticed that most floors of the office block were unoccupied . . .

'Mr Birtles will see you now,' said Louise, and Simmy lifted his chin and forced his shoulders back once more.

Two adjoining sides of Birtles' office consisted of floor-to-ceiling windows which could be slid open to give access to a broad balcony where a few evergreen shrubs stood in squat tubs, well below the height of the parapet to escape the cruel wind. Birtles was standing at one of the windows when Craddock and Simmy entered. He was looking out, with his rump resting against the back of a fat armchair, and he straightened and turned as he heard the door shut. But he did not walk towards them. 'Hullo, lads,' he said, and stretched out a hand at Craddock. Walking to grasp it, Craddock saw that this was Birtles' customary stance and procedure for impressing visitors. He was not posed, exactly; he was stationed to draw attention to the windows, the view, the eminence.

Craddock gave the due acknowledgment. 'A very elegant crow's nest you've got here, Mr Birtles.'

'Aye, it's been used by a few photographers, that balcony. All nationalities. This isn't the highest building, not by a long way. But it's got the ideal position. You can see what's been done from here. And a hell of a lot's been done. That's a new city out there. Made for the twentieth century.'

Craddock looked out at the rearing concrete and the bursts of traffic as the vehicles appeared on glimpses of flyover and urban motorway. A new bridge over the river made the old one, close to it, appear a toy – the plaything of some ancient eccentric with a love of iron curlicue. But what was that curious movement on the old bridge? People: people walking. The ancient eccentric had his successors. Only traffic moved on the new bridge.

'What you'd have seen from up here twenty years ago . . .' Birtles shook his head, 'We were in a sorry way then.'

'You forget, I knew the area in those days,' Craddock said.

'Of *course* you did, Tony. Yes, I do forget things nowadays. The years entering the bones – especially this one,' and he tapped his thick fingers on the top of his bald head. He gave a wide smile which creased his face into folds and lumps, reminding Craddock of an antique music hall comedian who finished his days in the region squeezing what laughs he could from jokes about loose false teeth. Birtles could almost have doubled for him, except for the clothing. The late comedian could never have afforded the custom-made tweed suit Birtles wore – and which put Simmy the more out of place. Birtles had the sagging paunch and the wasted chest. At fifty-six, his muscles had gone, and the gleam of the eye. There was something even in his gaze over the city – *his*, after all, by common acceptance – that promised a sigh: not of repletion, content, but of . . . what? It came to Craddock like a name forcing its way through memory's crowds. Submission. Incongruously, considering their many differences, Birtles conjured just the same air of weary surrender that Llewellyn had evinced after that grim Boxing Day party.

'Drink, Tony?' Birtles was gesturing towards one of the built-in cupboards, and Simmy was obeying the master's hand. 'I don't myself, but Simmy will keep you company whatever your pleasure.'

Simmy gave them each a grin over his shoulder, and looked at that moment, Craddock thought, positively lunatic with obsequiousness. He opened out two doors, and a cocktail bar complete with a miniature washing-up sink was there for plunder. Craddock hesitated, but not long, before asking for whisky.

'A novel about present-day politics, eh, Tony?' Birtles lingered at the window, held by the view without looking at anything in particular. He gave the impression of snuggling up to it, as a dog will lie on a man's feet. If he didn't pay the view enough attention it might go away.

'A background of politics, yes,' Craddock said. 'It's not one of those stories about burning ambition. I'm not much interested in the sort of man who wants to be Prime Minister.' He took the glass from Simmy. 'The idea I'm working at is more to do with the kind of chap who's always steered well clear of politics but finds himself forced in, because he doesn't like the way things are going.' Craddock was surprised at this clarity of purpose, and after a sip of whisky he carried on, inventing, 'Perhaps he's in a decent job – works manager or sales director, that sort of thing – and suddenly the whole work force is laid off. Finished. The scrap heap. It's a traumatic happening for this one community. He wants to know how it came about that *they* were selected for this disaster. Because he's a logically-minded man. He belongs to an advanced industrial society. He's been taught to believe we make our own future. We study, attain skills, plan for security. Life is manageable – so we are taught. He isn't a Bolivian Indian letting fate have its own way. So this calamity hasn't come by chance. The politicians sent it – and he disapproves, to put it mildly. Perhaps he starts up a sit-in, a workers' co-operative. Or he dispatches a few letter bombs to Downing Street and other worthy targets . . .' He shrugged, feeling he had gone far enough; and feeling, also, the idea wasn't at all bad. He sat in one of the broad armchairs, uninvited.

'A novel of protest,' said Birtles. 'Aye, it's topical.' He gave that comedian's grin. 'Always has been in this part of the world.' He lifted both arms to take in the new city with a messianic gesture, if a tired one. 'I think I can say my own protest was constructive.'

'The understatement of the year, that.' Simmy drained his glass after this contribution and began a sly inching back to the bar.

'See about the lunch.' Birtles' instruction caught Simmy just as the right hand fastened on the whisky bottle. Simmy stiffened, and his chin jerked.

Birtles' voice dropped again as he spoke to Craddock. 'I usually have something cold brought in. Is that all right with you?' As Craddock nodded Simmy got another order. 'Fill up Tony's glass before you go.'

'Do you have specific questions to put to George?' Simmy asked Craddock. He approached with the bottle and the jug of iced water. Craddock could not summon the charity to sympathise with the man, although he realised Simmy must make these forlorn attempts to assert authority countless times a day. He ignored the question, as Birtles clearly expected him to.

'Roy said you liked your Scotch, Tony, come to think of it.' Birtles at last removed himself from the window, but not far; he sat in the chair he had earlier used to lean against as he scanned the roads and rooftops. 'We had a chat about you yesterday. He thought your book was going to be all about *him*. Made him a bit jumpy, but then, he's not used to being pumped like I am . . .'

'I'll see about the food,' Simmy announced, as if he were volunteering. Neither Birtles nor Craddock gave him a glance as he went out.

'You've always attracted a lot of publicity,' Craddock said.

'Thrived on it. Part of my brand of politics – important part. George Birtles the human whirlwind. The irresistible force to shift the immovable object. Nothing discreet about whirlwinds. Now Roy – there's a different case altogether. He always had the sublety – except where the girls came into it. Aye, Roy and his ever-rampant member. Nothing discreet about that, eh, Tony? But once he saw his own way in politics – kept out of the front line, forgot about being an M.P. up on his feet shouting the odds and all that daft fiddle-faddle down at Westminster . . . Once he got himself behind the scenes where he could pull the strings – very effective. He's been a good friend to this region over the years. Oh yes, Roy Llewellyn's had a hand in all this. We teamed up the day we met, Roy and me. You wouldn't say we had much in common from the look of us, would you? But it's what we *want* that counts – what we value. *Action* is what we value. A good team, Roy and me. Bound to make enemies. Can't avoid it.' There was another lumpy grin. 'So you're on a fishing expedition, are you? You're not the first. I don't know what you lads think you'll get out of it. What does George Birtles have to hide? Did George Birtles ever hide *anything*? But you don't make omelettes without cracking eggs. Aye, bound to make enemies.' He laughed and his head nestled into the soft fabric of the chair. Craddock saw that odd look of surrender again. 'What did you make of Simmy? Got himself into a terrible state, poor lad. He thinks he's going to end up behind bars with me. I keep telling him he'll be declared unfit to plead. He doesn't see the joke. Aye, the poor frightened lad.'

Craddock asked lightly, 'What does he expect the charge to be?'

He got a hurt look from Birtles. 'Now the word for that, Tony, is disingenuous. I was the centre of a great web of local government corruption. Don't sit there drinking my whisky and playing the innocent like that. You're insulting my intelligence. I told you, you're not the first. I've had a good half-dozen Fleet Street boys up here in the last three or four months – all wanting the general chat. They're going to do a profile, or they want a briefing on the economic prospects for the region – that's a laugh; how many more papers would *that* sell? Nothing gets written. They're just building up their files, ready for the day of judgment. I've been out of politics for three years now. Who's brought on all this nosing around? Somebody's making a quid or two.'

The tired, sighing monologue asked for no response. Birtles was not indignant. Craddock felt at a disadvantage in the face of this restraint. It was rather like sitting out visiting hour with a hospital patient. The visitor tries not to notice the sick condition, the pain, for fear of causing further distress. Birtles reinforced the analogy by urging him to make more use of the whisky bottle, as a patient will press his gifts of chocolate and fruit on his tongue-tied callers. Craddock steeled himself and declined. This seemed to break Birtles' mood – probably Craddock's inner debate before refusing communicated itself, stirring the atmosphere – and he put a direct question. 'Who's paying *you*, Tony?'

Craddock could truthfully say, 'Nobody, so far.'

'The lone bounty hunter?'

'To get an advance on the book I need to put something definite in front of a publisher. I'm not ready yet.' He was still on the firm ground of fact; he could hear the self-assurance in his own voice and thought he had better put it to work while it was available. 'Why did you come out of politics? You'd been king of the castle so long, it must have been quite a wrench.'

'Oh, man, you've seen some of those old bags of sawdust lying around council chambers. I was determined I wouldn't end up like that – the local government caricature. Didn't I change the whole *nature* of running local politics? I made young men *envious*. They wanted to be where I was. They wanted the power I'd got. I was the *boss*, and I loved every minute of it. But I'd finished with it. I'd got a business to run. Wanted to build it up, make some real money. It was high time. I'd earned it, hadn't I?'

'You got out while the going was good?'

'Before I got found out, you mean?' Again the unbecoming grin. I'm the greatest public benefactor this city and this region has ever known. All your Victorian shipyard owners, coal owners . . . they gave the odd hospital, the odd school, laid out an acre or two of flower beds for the children of the deserving poor to skip through – those who weren't crippled with rickets. But compared with me? They were pygmies, those men. And the great social reformers – all the Webbs and Shaws and . . . and, yes, if you like, the great deliverers of the people, the Jimmy Maxtons and Keir Hardys – how many rat-trap slums did *they* stamp into the ground?' He could not sustain the burst of pugnacity. He stood and was drawn back to the windows, where all he had to do was to gaze out and his life was justified.

The building was so passive Craddock could hear Birtles breathing across the room: no, the sound was of sighing. Craddock contemplated his empty glass. Would another drop do any harm? Of course not, but the several more it might well lead to undoubtedly would. It was called getting the taste. It was some time since he last had one of his benders: the night before Liz Ellison brought Peter Franklin's name into his life – the best part of three weeks ago. It would be a kindness to himself to be spared any more of those demoralising hangovers: those days of enveloping, immobilising fear. His relative sobriety in this period was connected directly with Peter. It was because of Peter that he was now in this room with this decaying man . . .

'How long is it since you were last here, Tony?' Birtles was amicable, the pleasant host.

'Old Hector Brunskill's funeral. Nearly nine years ago. Brinsley Bay crematorium. There was quite a turn-out.'

'Aye, old Hector. Used to run into him from time to time. Kept his distance, as I remember. Lonely man, like you, wasn't he?'

'Well, as I said, he got quite a send-off.'

'You must be a lonely man, to come all this way at New Year. Your first visit in nine years, and all to pick up some background for a novel you're not sure you're going to write.'

Craddock said stiffly, 'Pointless celebration. I always ignore it, if I'm allowed to.'

To the sound of a faint rattling Simmy entered, pushing a serving trolley laden with plates of sandwiches, a bowl of salad, a bottle of champagne in a bucket of ice. Louise held open the door for him and then followed him in. Obviously, she was to act as waitress.

'He can't ignore New Year, can he, Simmy?' Simmy, bent over with his thin bottom in the air like an elderly cyclist, screwed up his face in obedient disbelief. 'That's what he says. He doesn't hold with it.' Birtles walked slowly to where Simmy brought the trolley to rest and tapped the neck of the champagne bottle. 'I bet this'll help change your mind. Roy said you're a different man with a few glasses of this stuff inside you. Simmy could find you some female company for the night, but

Roy said you wouldn't welcome it. If you want any other company you'll have to make your own arrangements, although Simmy can tell you where to look, can't you, Simmy?' The grin twisted, the eyes wavered. It was a half-hearted taunt, made almost apologetically. Birtles was straying out of his natural territory. There was pride. He could bully. But viciousness was outside his scope: he was squeamish about it. 'Here, let me,' he said, taking the bottle from Simmy's hands. He needed something to do, to cover his own embarrassment. Louise was busy with plates and knives.

This was where Simmy should have stepped in, either to press home his master's attack or convert it into innocent banter. The good public relations man should never let his employer flounder, but Simmy was lost in the struggle against his own disintegration; it was his daily round, the one and only task. Simmy squared his shoulders and lifted his chin and waited for the end. Craddock rose and held out a glass.

CHAPTER TWENTY-ONE

Peter's informant, Detective Sergeant Gavin Whittle of the fraud squad, had never mentioned Birtles. The curtailed enquiries in which Llewellyn's name figured had concerned another town; but Craddock was unfamiliar with it. Where would he start? 'Hullo, is that Councillor Blenkinsop? My name is . . . I don't know if you might have heard of me . . . I wonder if I could come and see you . . .' It was a hopeless way to embark on what Birtles had properly called a fishing expedition. Going over for a second time Peter's notes of his talks with Whittle – the sergeant had refused to be taped, with understandable prudence – Craddock could not help but remark on how flimsy Whittle's grounds were for so vehement a suspicion. What did he have? Other fraud squad men had also spoken of Llewellyn when talking about jobs around the country. All inquiries had been inconclusive. Llewellyn was not accused of anything: it was just that wherever there was a dubious housing committee or borough planning officer there was also Llewellyn. That was until four years ago when he had accepted his peerage and virtually gone to earth in the Home Office. But wouldn't Llewellyn's name crop up inevitably in the context of local authority planning and building? It had been his speciality, at his party's behest. In office and out the party had for years used Llewellyn's expertise as a go-between, a fixer, effecting liaison with Whitehall when the provincial supplicants needed it. Simply because he used to be friendly with Alderman this and Councillor that . . .

Peter had let him grumble on. It was late, stretching into the early hours after Peter had surprised Craddock with the Christmas present. They had been out for a meal in a cheap Greek place about fifteen minutes' walk from Peter's flat. Craddock was invigorated by the cheery casualness – the customers were mostly around Peter's age, and there was much noisy embracing, with kisses, of the tubby couple who ran the place. The charcoal sizzled; the retsina put a tingle in the mouth. Peter, on this occasion at least, showed no unwillingness to eat. He got a kiss on the top of his head from the owner's wife when she delivered the kebab. He had been there a few times before, although the last time was several months ago. He used to take a girl; he hadn't seen her for a while; she was a bit of a gypsy, like Liz Ellison, only not an actress; she had three or four languages and jobs came easily . . .

Craddock did not want to sleep yet. The day had been taxing, but he had dispelled the pain of it. He wanted to stay in Peter's company; to listen to his voice. They returned to the flat. Inexorably the talk turned to Llewellyn. When Craddock had reached the end of his complaint against Sergeant Whittle's poor case Peter said, 'But we've got beyond that now, haven't we? I mean, you *know*, don't you? I'm sorry. I suppose it must hurt. I mean, to have to face it. At last, after so long.'

Craddock had not answered for a long time. He sat in the armchair, his fingers scratching the worn moquette and picking at the greasy loose threads. Even in compassion Peter was not gentle: '. . . to have to face it . . . at *last*'. No more avoidance. Time's up. Condolences. '. . . I *suppose* it must hurt.' But there was no callousness in the face: at any rate not an adult's callousness, not a chosen indifference. There was inquisitiveness. He only partly understood. He imagined what he could of a particular kind of emotional wounding. Craddock searched the face and found a great deal of beauty in it: more than he had seen before. It showed more trust – and, of course, affection. And concern, which was the important change: concern for Craddock. It made the face stronger than when it was full of strain and suspicion. Objectively, Peter was right. Time was up.

So eventually Craddock said, 'I think I know where to go next.'

♠

The maroon Rolls Royce had delivered him to his hotel. Simmy, the cadaver, patted his shoulder and gave an over-loud splutter of 'All-you-wish-yourself' as Craddock got out of the car at the entrance.

A youth in chocolate and green livery came hurrying through the revolving doors and down the stone steps with chipped edges to take his one light bag. Simmy was going on, so Craddock gathered from bits of the cadaver's instructions to the driver, to deliver various gifts around the city to business acquaintances. The front passenger seat and the roomy carpeted floor in the back had the parcels, none of them large; they were plainly the bottles of whisky and brandy in their fancy cartons and the boxes of cigars that had become the standard tokens of goodwill in the conduct of trade and industry all over the country. Simmy's errands were unremarkable. There were the Christmas recipients and this other list of names to be favoured now. Mostly they were afterthoughts or Scotsmen. It was Friday afternoon, two days before New Year's Eve, and Simmy's calls would take him from office to office where men of his own rank would be expecting him. He would meet some of them again in someone else's office before evening fell; and during the weekend too. The talk would largely concern previous New Year gatherings in offices, and there would be special interest in who had puked in front of the junior staff and how many girls were believed to have opened their legs – even, indeed, how often. Simmy looked a wan runner for such an arduous task. 'Have fun,' Craddock said to him. The relief at seeing the back of Simmy supplied what warmth his smile possessed.

He followed the young porter to the reception desk, noting the moment he stepped inside the building the particular old-hotel smell of cigarette smoke and alcohol and ingrained dust and that utterly specific overlay which came from keeping the central heating at full power. Craddock knew it as 'radiator pong', a condition not recognised by the hotel trade. Craddock knew he would quickly stop smelling it, whereas he could never ignore the unpleasantly 'freshened' air of modern hotels – Simmy had tried to make him Birtles' guest in the town's newest. It was a smell that kept him awake at night, making him think of laboratories and white coats; and piped music would accompany it – somebody's velvet strings murmuring through the walls, familiar tunes from which all melodic quirk had been ruthlessly withdrawn. He had hoped – for some reason been quite confident – that the Old Boar's Head would not have gone that way; and he was right. It had withstood Birtles' rebuilding programme; there was a Preservation Order on the structure.

Inside there were the same mahogany and dulled gilt and floral Axminster and the lifts with latticed gates. He had a room with a high double bed and his own bathroom. All the rooms were with bath or shower now, the boy said as the lift creaked upwards. Mr Birtles' clients usually stayed at the Great North, the new hotel overlooking the racecourse, he said; the management had recently put a ban on women entering the cocktail bar unaccompanied at the Great North; it was some time since he'd last seen G.B. 1 pull up at the door; he didn't think Mr Simms was looking too well; there was a big dance-do on tonight in the main dining room, and tomorrow night of course, it being Saturday – and New Year, although there was always a dinner-dance on Saturdays – but the grill room was open until eleven; residents could have a T.V. set in their rooms, if they wanted.

Craddock liked the artlessness of the youth, who was trying to grow a moustache and had a boil on the left side of his neck so that he kept his head awkwardly on one side. 'Who's going to win the match tomorrow?' Craddock asked.

'We'll murder 'em, Sir,' the boy said. 'Three-nil, no danger.'

Craddock gave him a pound note, and asked on impulse, 'What do you think of Mr Birtles?'

The boy might have been delivering a committee decision, 'He's a good fella. That's what most of us think. Me dad always says good luck to him if he can get it.' Craddock smiled, and the boy added, 'Me dad's real hero is Ian Smith of Rhodesia. He always says *we* should have done a Rhodesia. Done a U.D.I. It's not on, though – not now. Because Mr Birtles was the only one of 'em with Ian Smith's stature.'

Craddock received this with a sage nod, and the boy left, assuring him the porter's desk was manned around the clock. Larry was the late night man; his own name was Clifford. Craddock expected he would recognise Larry. It was the kind of hotel where night porters made their homes. A decade was nothing in their lives.

Craddock's eyelids felt heavy. His mouth and throat were still trying to cope with the hot and faintly sooty air of the old hotel, more concentrated in the bedroom than downstairs. The window had net curtains as well as heavy old velvet ones. It looked out on to other hotel windows and a fire escape. He knew if he opened the window – if it *would* open – the room would grow cold but the smell would remain. The best course was the tried and tested one of patient acclimatising. He got half-undressed, washed his hands and face and gargled with a glass of water, having first swilled the glass under the hot tap. The bathroom was of grand proportions, presumably converted from a bedroom; but the bath and washbowl both had smears of grease; he decided to give the lavatory seat a vigorous rubbing with a pad he made out of sheets of toilet paper and soaked in hot water. When he had laid out his shaving gear, tooth-paste, tooth-brush, hair-brush and tin of talc – slightly medicated, the makers claimed – along the glass shelf under the shaving mirror he was already aware of settling into the place. He understood men who became night porters, he thought. Hotels, *some* hotels, the old ones of this kind, with their musty quietude not unlike libraries, *some* libraries, the old ones – such hotels could provide a sense of seclusion as of right not easily found elsewhere.

He lay on the bed in his shirt and underpants and put his mind to George Birtles: how the man looked, what he had said, how he had said it. During the sandwich lunch Birtles had enthused over his next Great Plan. He was intent on reclaiming a wide acreage of derelict riverside where now condemned sheds and warehouses rotted, and nettles hid old railway lines, and in the past year two small children had drowned in stagnant ditches and a prostitute had been found strangled in what had once been a timekeeper's office. He was to transform the whole fetid mess into the finest aquatic-sport-and-leisure complex in the country. There would be holiday flats and a youth hostel, swimming pools outdoor and indoor, a boating lake, a training school for yachtsmen, a restaurant, quick-food bars; the river would be cleansed of pollution and dinghy sailors would skim from Rivertown to the sea . . . That was his provisional name for his inspiration – Rivertown. He showed Craddock architects' drawings and artists' impressions and a model of the layout in colourful plastic. He already had leases on much of the land – unravelling the tangle of ownership and lapsed rental etcetera *was* an obstacle, he admitted, but with his experience he would master it – and talks were under way with several would-be investors, all in either the leisure or property business or both, who were no fools . . . He couldn't name them; he hadn't yet named them to anyone, although the local papers were clamouring; he wasn't yet at liberty to. But Rivertown would rise to the glory of . . . George Birtles had a new lifetime of service to give to his people yet. George Birtles wasn't finished until he was dead. He's never asked for gratitude, not George Birtles. But would there ever come a day in this country when men of vision were encouraged instead of hindered and hounded by the quibblers and the fusspots? (He never swore, Craddock observed, seizing at last on an elusive oddness in Birtles' speech.) The effusion had petered out on that note of aggrievement. Again, the sigh of acceptance . . .

Craddock put his feet on the floor and lifted the telephone beside the bed. The girl on the switchboard was giggling when at last she responded; but she got him his call without any delay. Peter's greeting had a skittish cheeriness which had to be accounted for.

'You sound as if you've been to an office party,' Craddock said.

'I *was* in the office and there *were* a few bottles being passed round.'

'Glad you enjoyed yourself.'

'The thing is, the editor doesn't much like that piece we wrote about you.' Peter was laughing.

'What? Oh, *that*.' Craddock remembered, after a second or two, the four hundred words he and Peter had put together for *Voice* magazine about his television plays. Was it only a week or so ago – nine, ten days? They had composed the piece in Craddock's house. Craddock had typed.

'He says – and you'll like this – there isn't enough Craddock in it. It *is* a good joke, isn't it?'

'I'm not doing a re-write,' said Craddock and he laughed with Peter. 'Isn't it hostile enough?'

'He says there's too much comment.'

'Always a failing of mine.'

'He means comment from *me*.'

'I did most of those bits, didn't I?' Craddock laughed again, scratching a knee as he sat on the edge of the bed. It was a childish habit going back to the cuddling and tickling of infant bedtimes.

'I nearly told him that.'

'Well, I'm sorry I made a balls of it for you, Peter.'

'It isn't *that* bad. He did say he liked my phrase, "baleful reticence".'

'So he should. Was that one of yours or one of mine?'

'*Mine*, you cheeky sod,' Peter shouted, and they both laughed. Then quietly Peter asked, 'How's it going?'

'I could do with that name from your friend Sergeant Whittle.'

'He didn't guarantee me one. Only that he'd ask around. See what turned up – if anything. It's delicate.'

'You're quite sure about Whittle, are you, Peter?' Craddock could hear the scrape of a match, and there was a pause as Peter sucked at the cigarette. He could visualise the puckering of Peter's forehead at the hardness in the question.

'What have you turned up?'

'Listen, Peter, have *Voice* paid Whittle money?'

'No.'

'You're sure?'

'We *never* pay. We just don't have the loot for cheque-book journalism.'

'So you're sure?'

'Yes. How could it happen without my knowledge? I'm the one he talks to.'

'There's the girl-friend. What's her name, Fran? She was his first contact on the paper, wasn't she?'

'Tony, it simply doesn't happen. What have you heard up there?'

Craddock told him about Birtles' visitors from Fleet Street.

'I think he's right about someone putting the bad word round.'

'It can't be Whittle. You picked Birtles yourself.'

'He could have his own reasons for deciding which name to drop where. That's always the trouble with tips, leaks – a devious business by definition.'

Peter came in swiftly. 'Doesn't make sense. Why would Whittle sell Birtles to Fleet Street when he's got a really big fish – Llewellyn?' Craddock's silence made its point. 'You think he *has* put them on to Llewellyn? Just came to *Voice* a bit late in the day? I don't believe it. Doesn't fit with Whittle. If you'd ever heard him talking about the papers . . .'

'Yes, you told me – the sergeant's a strange guy. I hope he delivers that name. I shan't be leaving the hotel tonight. If I'm not in my room I'll make sure they know at reception where I am.'

'Right.'

'I'm going to take a zizz . . .'

Peter overlapped him. 'If the papers *have* been tackling Llewellyn at least that explains why he doesn't want to talk to *Voice*. Was that the impression you got from him – under siege?'

'Pressure, of some kind. Outside the job.'

'You're hedging for him.'

'Wrong. The pressure could be entirely domestic, so I thought.'

'All right, you thought it *then*. How do you see it now?'

'He's waiting for something. You know how you wait for the result of an x-ray or a blood test. That kind of waiting.'

Peter said anxiously, 'Would he talk to the papers?'

'Not in this context.'

'You don't think one of them might have bought him up? For when the story breaks – the big exclusive.'

'He doesn't need money.'

'Not now, maybe. It could be different later, when he's in the dock.'

Craddock said sharply, 'No.' The rejection came from him like a reflex action. He went on quietly, 'You're jumping ahead of it all, Peter. Don't think about Llewellyn like that. It's the wrong way. Calculation: planning for contingencies – that's not him.'

'Well, as long as you're not out of date.'

'See if you can gee-up Whittle for that name. Cheers, Peter.'

Craddock put the 'phone down without waiting for Peter's reply.

It was dark now. Craddock took off his shirt, hung it over the back of the chair at the dressing table and got into bed. He lay flat, palms upwards, feeling the stress of the day in the ripple of pains across the small of his back. When he closed his eyes there was one of those brief spasms of shuddering in the neck muscles which sometimes alarmed him lately: sitting in a taxi or watching television at home, seemingly relaxed. He knew it was a matter of inner tensions manifesting themselves. He had started to think of it as 'that old thing'. Once or twice it had jolted him awake in the small hours, accompanied by a struggling for breath. Did he wish he were less introspective, less of a worrier – a private worrier – and able to release those tensions without the need for drink to unbutton him? He would need to be an altogether different man for that. He couldn't honestly say he wished to be. He was far from satisfied with what he had done; but he would accept what he was. The same went for Llewellyn. He was sure Llewellyn held the same attitude. 'Could be different later, when he's in the dock . . .'

Craddock rocked his head slowly from side to side on the pillows. He would never see Llewellyn in the dock. Peter was surely right in believing Whittle hadn't set the dogs on Birtles or Llewellyn. Who had? Whoever it was had been sparing with his information. From the sound of it he'd picked one paper at a time, spacing out the calls at his leisure over the weeks . . . Calls or letters? Calls were more likely, he felt, although he couldn't say why – he just felt this informant was a 'phone caller. Cryptic morsels. Tasty enough to send senior men on discreet inquiries. Discreet but harassing. Menacing . . . Birtles might be wrong about the financial motive – Birtles would think naturally of money. Wasn't there something more shadowy than that. The papers had kept it all to themselves. No gossip. Early days, of course. If the informant wasn't taking money perhaps the papers didn't know his name. Just a voice on the 'phone. Calling as the mood took him. Or her, of course. Anonymous tipsters were tricky. A paper could find itself on a fools' errand. There were people who got a thrill out of raising false alarms: fire engines wailing, police cars hurtling. Investigative journalists soft-shoeing. But in this case . . . Birtles' sigh would delight his tormentor. Craddock wandered into a faltering sleep.

*

The middle-aged waitresses in the grill room chattered to each other as they met on their journeys between kitchen and customers. It was a continuing conversation, all to do with the way a certain member of the management behaved, although the customers heard only snatches. Even so an unseen character was given substance and idiosyncrasy as Craddock's meal progressed from the melon to the cheeseboard via the fillet steak:

'Mind you, I said so the day he started. Those little piggy eyes . . .'

'Three clean shirts on, he had yesterday, Anita said . . .'

'Just let chef catch him. It's not his place, the mixing bowls . . .'

'I thought she was his mother . . .'

'He'll wake up *looking* like a bag of peanuts . . .'

'Anyway, he knows now as fish knives aren't for cleaning fingernails . . .'

'Name badges? I told him it isn't in keeping . . .'

'He'll do himself an injury with that sun lamp . . .'

When they found time they gave Craddock commiserating smiles because he was on his own. At most of the tables sat young couples; they were dressed up stiffly in the way young couples in London rarely would be for a restaurant. They took considerable interest in each other, comparing clothing and what food and drink were ordered. He was glad of the waitresses' chatter; they were the only people present who felt at ease.

He looked at his watch, aware that only three or four minutes could have passed since the last look. It was just gone ten. Peter had still not 'phoned him. In point of fact the waitresses' sympathy – generously accorded, in view of their troubling preoccupation – was not misplaced even if it was unsoundly based. He wished he were back in London. Suppose Sergeant Whittle failed to deliver tonight – what then? Craddock knew he would be greatly tempted to go home on the breakfast-time train. How long was he prepared to give Whittle? Another day? The prospect of a further twenty-four hours in this friendless place . . . That was to say he could think of no one here he wished to call on or even meet by chance. How he missed old Hector; although, under the circumstances, talk would have been bleakly constrained . . . Generally it was *friendly* enough, in the hospitable sense; that glibly repeated reputation was perfectly well-founded. But he was a stranger, and apprehensive. He must *not* over-dose himself with drink. Tomorrow was Saturday. He could go to the football match, provided he could get a seat. Once he would have relished the thought of standing on one of the steeply-raked terraces, absorbed into the chanting, snarling, tumbling crush of bodies, furious with pleasure and malevolence alike, but such discomfort deterred him now. Yes, if he could get a seat . . . But he knew he had no intention of going to the match; he was just letting his mind fill in time. He had no alternative but to hang around the hotel, waiting for Peter's next call. Suppose Whittle could not produce a name at all? Or wouldn't? He really ought to have met Whittle before anyone else. He had no sense of the sergeant's reliability. He was trusting Peter's judgment. Yes, yes, he was letting his mind amble back and forth over the same ground, filling in time. Again, he looked at his watch, and irritably held his sleeve over it. He could order another bottle of wine. Or a half. Or a glass of the house red. Or a slug of port. He could go up to his room and 'phone Peter. Christ, it was a stupid thing to do to come up here at New Year weekend. He would *not* stay longer than tomorrow lunchtime. Why hadn't he delayed? What difference would two or three days have made? He found himself sighing. Whatever was going to happen was imminent. He had been told so by Llewellyn, Mary, Birtles and Simmy, in their various ways. All right, he'd made the right move. He was entitled to feel miserable about it.

CHAPTER TWENTY-TWO

Peter's mistake was in not taking Detective Sergeant Whittle into his confidence about Craddock.

'A right cuntish thing to do,' the sergeant told Peter. 'For a bright lad like you – pathetic.'

Peter had to admit that the anger at his carelessness was justified. In asking Whittle to supply a name from a particular network of contacts, as a line of enquiry on Llewellyn via George Birtles, Peter had conveyed that he himself would be interviewing the man. This was not intentional deceit, but a failure to look ahead and see the facts Whittle would need. Whittle had no reason to ask who the interviewer would be because, as he told Peter, 'You've never mentioned any other fucker.'

The network involved did not exist on paper. It had no co-ordinator, no structure, no system of recruitment, no code-names, no funny handshakes as in freemasonry, no defined function. Its members never met to confer other than in twos or threes here and there over a drink or a meal, and then rarely. It was an expression in investigative terms of something uniquely British: the mutual-help arrangement known as Old School Tie. But this network was classless. In practice it was no more than a confidential information exchange, one which broke through the barriers of rank and department. A detective constable, with the proper recommendation, might privately make contact with a detective superintendent of another force, for example. Or a Customs and Excise man could take advice from someone in the Director of Public Prosecutions' office, without either man's own colleagues ever knowing. No one knew the size of the network. Some of its members might not have dealings with another for a year, or longer. It was not something that could ever be 'blown' or destroyed as a secret organisation because it would never be corporate. Someone's indiscretion could reveal connections between two people who had no official right to them, and both might then find themselves in serious trouble with their superiors – possibly even more so with their peers. But, as Whittle said to Peter, 'I could get the push, and so could the guy I've been talking to, for breaking the rules of the game. But if they burned our bollocks off neither of us could give them more than three or four other names. If I want to use the network I usually make one 'phone call. Then that guy makes one, and so does the next guy, and the next and so on. And probably what happens is I get a call from somebody who doesn't even tell me his name – he just says, 'I hear you want to ask me something.' I don't *want* to know his name. The fewer names the better. The vital thing is to be vouched for. That's what I was doing for you – for *you*, you stupid sod, not for somebody I've never set eyes on or said a dicky bird to and who turns out to be such a close old mate of Llewellyn's. The network's built on trust . . .'

But it had been founded – no one could say by whom or when – on the very opposite. Mistrust of fellow officers and superiors had led a few men to seek help and lay information elsewhere. The common bond was an obsession with catching law-breakers. As Whittle put it, 'I'm abnormal, I know that. That's what 'obsessed' means – three parts round the bend. And I bet that goes for everybody else in the network. We've fanatics. A secret force of vigilantes. The biggest catch of all is when you can blow the whistle on a bent copper – a top man. I'm going to do that one day. I'm going to hit some top brass in the fraud squad. I get a hard on when I think about that. Jesus, I want that so much. Suppose I nailed a chief superintendent mixed up in the Llewellyn case. Jesus, think of that!'

It was the measure of Sergeant Whittle's obsession with Llewellyn, as Peter recognised, that the detective had told him that much about the network. Under the circumstances he might have said simply, 'I've drawn a blank on Birtles' – which would have excluded Peter from some potentially damaging information. But the thought of Llewellyn in gaol governed his responses. He took a calculated risk, arguing aloud to Peter, 'I'm trusting you not to write a line about the network, not even tell your paper there is one. And that's in your own interest, because if you breathe a word you've cut off your access completely. But use it properly, and I mean sip at it like water in the desert, and it'll make your career. I've never introduced a journalist before, but I'm told there are one or two more. A very select little band. You're in, if you want to be. But for God's sake, *think* in future.'

And so at a few minutes past one on Saturday morning Larry, the night porter doubling as hotel switchboard operator, roused Craddock from a doze as he sat up in bed and said, 'Here's your call at last, sir. I expect you'd dropped off, hadn't you? Putting you through now.' Craddock had been half-right about Larry: they recognised each other, although last seen Larry was down the road at the Royal. He was now in the rich bloom of his calling as a night porter, secure in his sense of possession. Through the small hours the place was his own, its other occupants his charges to be humoured, reproved, helped, ignored at his discretion. Craddock had chatted to him with a carefully pitched formality and tipped him three pounds, which was neither generous nor mean; implicit was the promise of more should any special assistance be needed. Larry understood.

Peter said, 'You'll be contacted tomorrow – I mean today, Saturday, I mean.' He spoke slowly, on a curious surreptitious note.

'And thank the Lord for that,' Craddock said. He had been making notes about the chattering waitresses. The notebook was by his side on the bedspread, but he could not see his biro. 'Just hang on, I'll find a pen . . .' He leaned over first one side of the bed, then the other.

'Never mind. You don't need a pen.'

Craddock picked up the biro from the floor. Peter's voice was muffled by the bedclothes as the receiver pressed into them.

'Right, I'm ready,' Craddock said.

'That's all. Someone'll contact you.'

'Yes, I heard that. What's he called?'

'I don't know. He probably won't tell you who he is.'

'That inspires confidence.'

'That's the way they work.'

'Who?' Craddock heard Peter sucking on a cigarette, but afterwards he was still left waiting for an answer. Angrily he said, '*Who*, Peter? Why do you sound so bloody odd? The way *who* work?'

'People like this chap. Let's not go into it now. Just wait for someone to contact you.'

'Christ! What are we into? False noses? Poison-tipped umbrellas?'

'Tony, it'll be all right. Just wait for someone . . .'

'Don't say that again!'

'Look, Tony, they'll only do it their own way. Whittle's had a tough time fixing it. It's you who's the problem. Clearing you. All down the line.'

'Peter, will you please stop using this ridiculous language?'

'Sorry. I've been listening to it all night. But, look, it's true – because of your background, with Llewellyn, they had to be convinced you were safe. It was my fault in the first place. I nearly blew it . . .'

'Christ.'

'Sorry.'

'What time of day will this man with no name make his appearance?'

Craddock realised irritably that he had strayed into pomposity. But Peter was apparently too agitated to notice.

'I don't know.'

'I see. Are there any special instructions for me? Do I sit on the third stool from extreme left at the cocktail bar, with a Woolworth's carrier bag at my feet and reading the *Financial Times*?'

At last Peter's tone regained something of the familiar impatient intelligence. 'You can't expect me to explain all this to you on the 'phone – any more than the stuff you're going to get tomorrow could be passed down the 'phone. If it could, Whittle would have kept it all for himself and to hell with you and me. Whittle would give his right arm to be in your shoes tomorrow. But he can't go freewheeling around the country, trophy-hunting. Now I'm sorry about the touch of cloak and dagger, but they've got their reasons for it. Please don't piss about with this man who's coming to see you. I don't think Whittle's friends have too much sense of humour.'

Craddock was smiling now. 'Welcome back to reality,' he said. 'Quite a ticking-off. But you really did sound like amateur night out with MI5 when you started.'

'I told you, I've had a day of it.'

'You sound very tired.'
'Yeah, well . . . How about you?'
'Quite sober, Peter.'
'I didn't mean that.' The voice was suddenly gentle, and Craddock was moved by it. He needed a few seconds to steady his reply.
'Defensive reflex action.'
Peter said, 'I know. Look after yourself.'

*

The cold seemed to be binding him up in cheesewire. His ankles and wrists felt sliced by it. He remembered he once owned a hat made of artificial fur which he used to wear at football matches. As a child he had a gabardine helmet with padded ear-muffs and a strap which buckled under his chin to keep them in place . . .

He had been told to proceed down the coast to Brinsley Bay, where he would be met at noon at the top of the steps at the northern end of the esplanade. Very much a policeman's word, 'proceed' – comically so. Snatches of ancient scenes in the magistrates' courts of his youth flickered through his mind: I proceeded to caution the defendant, who replied eff-off-you-effing-Gestapo . . . The defendant was observed proceeding on his bicycle along the perimeter of the recreation field, where he exposed his private parts to the witness, Mrs Edwina . . .

What a strange persistence this unappealing little town exercised in his life. 'Bad vibrations' would be the vogue phrase for it – or was that term already as dead as 'gosh' or . . . what the hell did it matter? Roy Llewellyn had fought – or played at – an absurd by-election here; and Craddock had helped manoeuvre him out of a squalid little scandal in it. Squalid? Banal, perhaps. Dear old Hector Brunskill had died slowly here, and Craddock had neglected him, denying his real love for the man any expression, not even an occasional visit. No wonder the funeral was so painful – too late, too late . . .

Now, of course, it *would* be bleak little Brinsley Bay where he was to meet the nameless informant in circumstances of melodramatic subterfuge. He felt silly, as well as distressed by cold and memory. The sea was like black ice. Morning fog had not lifted sufficiently for the street lights to switch themselves off. He had been standing in the same spot for nearly fifteen minutes and not another pedestrian had appeared. As a party to a secret meeting he could hardly be more conspicuous. He muttered aloud, 'This is bloody daft.'

Instantly on cue, so that a grin of disbelief forced its way to his lips, a car stopped at the kerbside abreast of him. He looked at his watch, partly to hide the grin. He heard the car door shut and looked up as the driver walked the few steps to him. He was a man in his middle fifties, wearing a bluish tweed overcoat with a woollen scarf and a tweed hat. He had a thin pepper-and-salt moustache, and he was tall. His brown brogues had a deep shine. Craddock thought immediately of an actor, in costume, on location: trim, staid respectability assiduously composed. Then a snippet of overheard conversation, its source long forgotten, sprang to his mind: 'They don't make queers like that any more.'

The man said, 'Mr Craddock?' The eyes were a silvery blue and stood out under straight brows as if ready for polishing in a soldier's button-stick. Altogether, now he was close, he looked very soldierly, and he added to the impression – or impersonation? – by looking at his watch and saying, 'Twelve-o-seven. I've kept you hanging about. I have to blame the fog.' Craddock recognised the voice that had told him on the 'phone to go to Brinsley Bay. It was a confident voice of the kind, Craddock thought straight away, that was mostly used in direct question and answer. A badgering voice. Craddock forgot about actors. He had a feeling he was not going to like this man much. They shook hands. As Craddock expected, the man crunched at his knuckles with unnecessary strength. A badgering show-off. Seeing him wince, the man said, 'I can see you're cold. Not surprised. No gloves, nothing on your head, footwear too light. You're not equipped for bracing Brinny. Hop in the car. We'll go and get ourselves a noggin.'

'Thanks.' Craddock said, achieving a smile with some effort. He got into the front passenger seat. His movements were stiff with cold. There had been no heating on the grubby local train, which smelled like a recently sluiced urinal, and had much the same dampness.

'I don't live here,' the man said. 'But I possess a little place. Not a fisherman, are you?'

'No, never really . . .' Craddock murmured.

'Love it, myself. And it gets me time off from the wife. She can't take Brinny in the winter. A real southern girl, my wife. Guildford. Not that I'm a native of these parts. I suppose you can tell by the accent.'

'I couldn't place it,' Craddock said.

'That's travel. The university of life . . .' Craddock glanced quickly at him, to see if he was making a joke. He was not. 'Same with you in your line, isn't it?'

'Yes, I suppose so.' Craddock heard the forlorn indifference in his own voice and added quickly, and over-brightly, 'I was born in the Midlands . . .' He was ready to give the name of the town and of all the other towns he had lived in, but his voice now sounded shrill, as if it belonged to a stranger, and he rummaged in his pockets for his handkerchief and made a show of blowing his nose instead.

'I'm a Salopian, a Shropshire lad, the genuine article,' the man said, as Craddock sank his face into the handkerchief, trying to shake off incredulity and irresolution. 'But I was never going to follow the plough. Went for a soldier. The Royal Corps of Military Police . . .'

What else? Craddock thought, reluctant to uncover his face.

'That's the Guildford connection – where I met the good lady. A few years ago now, of course.'

Craddock nodded vigorously and put his handkerchief away, taking time with the buttons of the sheepskin coat.

'Nearly there,' the man said. 'The wife calls it the slit-trench. She hates it.' He smacked his hands on the steering wheel, with a shout of 'Ha!' The sound was akin to a laugh, so Craddock gave the man a grin. 'Oh yes, the good lady lets me get on with it in Brinny,' the man said, and Craddock watched his lips twist into a leer.

They had driven out of the town, and the road narrowed and veered inland a little. The street lighting was left behind. Bedraggled hedgerows, looming in the fog, marked out some glum farm fields. 'The badlands,' the man said. He turned the car into a lane, and then took another turning along a track of mud and loose gravel. He stopped at a bungalow which Craddock could see at a glance was built of a mixture of pre-fabricated cement blocks, wood, and corrugated iron sheets. Even in the mist the paintwork around the windows, the guttering and the front door, with its opaque glass panels, gleamed new: a grating purple. Craddock did not need the man to tell him, 'Some chap ran it up himself just after the war. Quite a lot of these kind of shacks dotted around still. You couldn't do it now, of course. Couldn't get planning permission. I've made a few improvements – like this . . .' He backed the car into a lean-to, which had a concrete floor and green perspex roof and sides. 'I'm proud of my car-port. Did it solo.' There were concrete flagstones leading to the little corrugated iron porch. Craddock remembered the spotless brogues.

'Keep that coat on for a few minutes,' the man said.

The front door led straight into the living room. 'Just till the place warms up.' He lit a Calor gas-fire which stood on little wheels in the fireplace. 'There. Before you know it we'll have a fug in here like an orderly room. Those old coke stoves – they were the things. Boil a kettle, do a fry-up . . . Did you have any military experience?'

'Yes, the regulation two years' National Service. I remember the coke stoves. You're right. Who would have survived without them?' Craddock remembered his winter days of army life with no pleasure. He adopted a note of false enthusiasm.

The man clapped his hands together, a mannerism Craddock had always found irritating. 'Well now, make yourself at home.' He pointed to an armchair. 'Like old times, my little clubhouse – don't you think?' He turned and went through a door which slid open on runners. There was a kitchen beyond it.

The man was right. To Craddock the place was all too grimly like old times. In its furnishings it could have been the corporals' club where the off-duty hours had dragged by night after night thirty years before. He was sitting in a bulky armchair upholstered in some form of green plastic; another was on the other side of the gas heater, whose faintly sickly smell was already threatening to give him a headache after the lacerating cold of the last two hours. At a table – with a grey ex-army blanket draped over it! – were four wooden chairs which could be folded for stacking. His memory juddered with glimpses of figures in khaki playing table tennis and swearing over card games. He remembered the taste of jam doughnuts and flat beer. But there was something far worse about this room, he found, as he looked round the walls. They were hung with military bric à brac: shoulder flashes, cap badges and other bits of insignia from the uniforms of many different units. The metal ones shone; the cloth pieces had been carefully mounted with adhesive on to strips of cardboard. They were all German.

The man came back from the kitchen. Between the fingers of each outstretched hand he held four small bottles of beer, the strong 'heavy brew' type. At least Craddock could not fault the choice of alcohol for the kind of day it was. 'Each one of these little jokers carries the kick of a double scotch. Up your street?' The man put the bottles on the table, and then took off his overcoat, hat and scarf. He wore a buttoned woollen cardigan. His grey hair was thin, but there remained enough for him to part it two-thirds-to-one. And he had cavalry twill trousers. He was every inch the ex-army officer; but Craddock knew he was not.

As the man produced two half-pint pewter tankards from a wall cupboard he noticed Craddock's gaze wandering over the Nazi insignia. He said, 'Not a bad collection, is it? A very fascinating body of men, our erstwhile foe. Deserving of much respect. I find a great deal of interest among some of our young people . . .' He laid a pointed emphasis on the word 'young' and for a moment a shadow of the leer Craddock had observed in the car hovered in his face. He went on, 'I believe you're a man who finds himself in sympathy with the young – the excitement in a young man's vitality, ambition . . .' The silvery blue eyes bulged a little more. 'Am I correct? Youthful company is the great stimulant – would you agree?'

'Or irritant,' Craddock said, and he smiled archly, the best he could do.

The man kept looking at him for a while, the muscles around his mouth not quite still. Craddock could sense his indecision. It filled the room. Then the man said, 'Ha!' which was the same unpleasant half-laughter as in the car, and he went to the table where he took the tops off two of the bottles. 'Nicely put, Craddock,' he said. 'My learned friend, I think we understand each other.' He poured the beer, the third and little fingers of his right hand held out crooked. 'I suppose it's time we got down to business – the nitty-gritty, as they say.'

Craddock was taking off his sheepskin, although he had an impulse to re-button it and dash for the door. As he expected the man seated himself at the table, and his voice took on the studied tone of authority again. 'We are concerned with George Birtles, and associates, shortly to be brought to book, so we hope . . .'

*

The train back to London had no dining car; not even a buffet bar. It was delayed for more than an hour while some youths were collared by waiting policemen at an unscheduled stop and statements were taken from several indignant passengers. The boys had rampaged up and down the train, swinging from luggage racks and bumping into people and squirting at each other with tins of Coca-Cola. They also set light to a lavatory.

There was a queue of at least a hundred at the taxi rank. Craddock hurried away to the nearest pub, reaching it ten minutes before closing time. He intended to 'phone for a mini-cab; he wanted to be home. The pub was like most to be found close to London's main railway stations; small, dim and packed with the maudlin drunk – the kind of people who gave the impression that they once, years ago, set out to catch a train but lost interest, and had settled for a perpetual musty twilight. The 'phone coin-box was jammed. He could feel the mixture of sick anger and exhaustion induced by the day turning into panic. As he stood at the bar, which dripped with spilled beer, he realised he was half-blinded by tears. The shock of it stiffened him. He squeezed his eyes tightly shut and then dried them quickly in the crook of his arm. He left without buying a drink.

Using the tube he got home an hour and a half later. He was unfamiliar with it, because he disliked being confined underground. The journey involved two changes of line. Trudging along one of the yellow-lit bending tunnels he came across a young couple – a youth and a girl of about twenty – lying face to face, apparently unconscious. From their positions it looked as if they had been walking with their arms round each other's shoulders before they had collapsed. Or had they been knocked down? There was vomit around them; also some splashes of blood. He paused. But the other people walking with him stepped over or round the couple, and he was swept along. He caught a guilty look from a woman who met his eyes in the awkward shuffling caused by the obstruction, but she scuttled away more eagerly than anyone else. He went with the crowd.

He had a bath when he reached home. Afterwards, hating the way the white and grey stubble made his face look so desolate, he shaved, although it was now nearing two a.m. He took the 'phone off its rest and went to bed.

CHAPTER TWENTY-THREE

Peter rang Craddock's doorbell shortly after mid-day, the second time twice as long as the first. The curtains at the living room window were open and he looked in at the familiar neatness. He had to press his face close to the glass, because the mild day was dull with low cloud. If Craddock was at home, and up and about, he would need some lights on. He stood back to look at the upper windows. The curtains were open, and there were no lights. For the third time he held his finger on the bell button. He was both worried and bad-tempered.

He stood with his back to the door, his hands stuffed into the pockets of his parka; it was unbuttoned and he flapped it irritably against his knees. The whole street was silent. Sunday, of course! He stepped over the low wall separating Craddock's minute front garden from its neighbour to the right and tried the bell. Hearing nothing, he used the heel of his fist against the door. He knew he was merely venting frustration because, as with Craddock's house, he could see no light anywhere.

He walked slowly along the street. Cars were parked, and there were families at home a few doors away, he found: children sitting on the floor watching television – a glimpse of a jewelled cowboy on a dancing horse. But he knew it was pointless to try these doors to ask about Craddock's movements; in the space of twenty yards Craddock was the type of man who became a very distant neighbour. Peter slouched on, trying to decide what to do. Should he find a 'phone box and call Whittle? Unwise, for the moment. Should he make for the garish red and black pub where he and Craddock had their first long talk? It could be no more than twenty minutes' walk away, and clearly Craddock had been known there, at least by the staff. But he remembered Craddock's teasing mood when protesting his liking for the place; it was an improbable spot to find the man today, under the circumstances. But what the hell were the circumstances? He'd had no contact with Craddock since their tired 'phone conversation two nights before. Aimlessly he crossed the street.

He was near its far end where it curved left and the houses changed style. They were bigger, with wide front doors and balconies at the main bedroom window. He had not been here before. He could hear music, the reedy kind of modern jazz which he had always disliked because he found it finicky and bloodless, and he could see the house it was coming from. Figures were grouped at a downstairs window with glasses in their hands. He decided he would walk past the house so that he would be far enough on the curve to see if this unknown stretch had a 'phone box, for future reference, and then he would go back to Craddock's house for one more try. He could sit on the doorstep, for that matter. As he passed the house with the jazz and the party he looked into the front room and saw Craddock looking straight back at him.

Astonished, relieved and angry at once, Peter was then further confused for a moment, thinking he had made a mistake and that the man he took to be Craddock was a stranger, since he made no immediate show of recognition. But there was no mistake. Craddock smiled and lifted a hand, palm flat, and then pointed in the direction of the front door. Peter made no move. Several of the group around Craddock rapped their knuckles on the window pane and beckoned at him. He saw Craddock speaking to the others and then move away from them. The faces smiled, the hands beckoned. He went slowly towards the front door. As Craddock opened it the music and chatter rolled briskly into the street. Craddock went towards him and clasped his hands on his shoulders. He said, 'Come inside, Peter. Have some breakfast with us.' There was cold, baffled resistance in Peter's face. 'Kedgeree, smoked salmon, hot croissants, champagne – anyway, almost champagne.' He squeezed Peter's shoulders. 'We don't have to stay long. Come on.'

'What the fuck's kedgeree?' Peter said, but he allowed himself to be ushered into the house.

Most of the people were in their thirties and forties, with a group of teenage sons and daughters who were taking around drinks and collecting dirty crockery with a giggling politeness. The clothing was conventionally casual: sweaters and corduroy mostly, with a flash of scarlet and a bold check pattern on a sporty shirt or two standing out among the quiet shades – the company had a freshly laundered air. The talk concerned summer holidays, skiing holidays, car engines, local property prices, the cost of school uniforms . . . Peter experienced an eerie fascination as he observed Craddock moving with smiles and ready comments through this alien world. Craddock had on a dark blue shirt and a jacket of grey corduroy and was as crisply laundered as anyone present – but then, wasn't he always when without the long old sheepskin? It was something Peter had not noticed before, and it seemed significant. Peter's impression of Craddock had been of an uneven temperament, an unpredictable veering: indecisive and tenacious, silly and precise, indulgent and unforgiving. The contradictions were what held Peter's attention. This cheery suavity belonged to a Craddock he didn't know. Peter was introduced to Doug and Yvonne, and Mac and Marje, and Si and Prue, and another Doug . . . He found his way into a corner and drank coffee and ate croissants and grapes. He mumbled to inquirers that he was a researcher doing some work for Craddock, indifferent to what conflicting identity Craddock might be giving him. First a Marje and then a Gloria tried to draw him into the body of the party, but he played the shy outsider – adequately, it seemed. In the downstairs lavatory, where he escaped for a few minutes, he found framed photographs of school Rugby teams, and there was the blade of a rowing oar on one wall. He had a spasm of exasperation so savage that he had an urge to seize the blade and smash the photographs with it. Instead he sat down and smoked a cigarette, watching the discreet turning of the handle on the locked door.

*

As they walked away from the house, and Craddock had acknowledged the last shout of 'All the best, Tony', Peter said to him, 'What was all that about?'

Craddock said pleasantly, 'Universal custom, Peter. New Year's Eve, friends and neighbours get together, a few drinks, a few old tunes . . .'

'For God's sake!'

'Good idea to have it at lunch-time. Saves all that embarrassing business at midnight. Linking arms . . .'

'I'd no idea where you were.'

'I wondered whether you'd call around. I was surprised you found me, though.'

'You stupid bloody . . .'

'I don't want any of that,' Craddock cut in sharply.

'Well, Christ!' Peter looked at Craddock's face and found it set tight. The bland urbanity of the past hour or so had been discarded. In the fresh air his eyes looked more shadowed, their whites more clouded than they had appeared at the party. Peter could sense the tension in him.

Craddock said more quietly, 'Just hold your water a minute. I'll tell you all about it.' They walked the rest of the way to Craddock's house in silence.

When they got there Craddock immediately opened a bottle of Beaujolais. He said he needed warming up after the walk without his topcoat, and he added, 'I couldn't take much of Doug's Spanish bubbly.'

They were in the living room. A reading lamp on top of a book-case lit it gently, and it was warm and quiet. Peter saw how well Craddock fitted this trim comfort – like his clothes. But he was glad Craddock had not brought the aura of the party with him, as he had feared he might as he watched Craddock take on the character of the crowd: that decorous babble about domestic trivia.

Peter said, 'Who *were* those people? I mean, apart from being the backbone of the country.'

'Don't sneer, Peter – some perfectly decent animals among them.'

'I believe it. Decent to the core. So smug. The whole thing looked like an animated Conservative Party poster – "A Clean Britain is a Healthy Britain. Vote Conservative for a Whiter Wash." Some rave-up you'd get in that crowd.'

Craddock grinned at him. He said, 'If you'd stayed long enough you might have got quite a surprise. You wouldn't have been allowed to skulk in that corner all afternoon. Once the booze got to work one of those respectable suburban mums would have wanted to have a look inside your flies. There's plenty of time yet, if you want to go back. A lot of interest was being shown in you. "Who's the pretty boy, then?" and all that.'

'What did you tell them?'

'You're my researcher.'

Peter gave a shout of laughter. 'I said the same.'

'I didn't think they'd believe it's the other way round.'

Peter hoped Craddock would now start talking about his meeting with the informant Whittle's contacts had provided. But Craddock was not ready yet. He needed a little more drink for that, Peter sensed. Also a little more ease between them. But Peter could not help in that respect; he had a complaint to make.

Craddock said, 'One or other of those couples gives a party every New Year. I've got a standing invitation, but that's only the second time I've turned up. As I say, that "Auld Lang Syne" stuff . . .' He shook his head. 'But when I looked at Doug's card this morning and saw they were kicking off with a late breakfast, it seemed just the place to go and hide for a while. A bit of undemanding small talk. Amiable badinage. Thought it might help to settle my very turbulent central nervous system. The last couple of days have been deeply unpleasant. Yesterday was a pig.'

'Why did you have to hide from *me*?'

'I just wanted breathing space.'

Peter listed Craddock's offences with quiet deliberation. Craddock was amused by the headmasterly manner, but kept a straight face. 'I had to ring the hotel to find out whether you'd left. You could at least have called me, just to say you were on your way back. I hadn't got the faintest idea what had happened to you. This morning your 'phone's off the hook, and after that you just ignored it – presumably, anyway, although how the hell am I supposed to know? And then you drift off to some geriatric knees-up – and still not a word from you. I happen to track you down, and all you say is you knew I'd come round here.' He sucked at the cigarette, his lips barely parted.

Craddock put in softly, 'I thought you *might* turn up here – that's what I said.'

Peter flicked a hand through his hair, a gesture of impatience. 'What's the difference? You let me chase you – that's the point. When one 'phone call was all that was needed. Didn't you think it mattered? Whittle's going crazy. He thinks you're giving the lot to Llewellyn.'

'Does he?' Craddock said flatly.

'Well, it's understandable. He was worried about you to begin with. He had hell's own job fixing the meeting, and then you do this hide-and-seek act. Wouldn't you expect him to be suspicious?'

'Are you?'

'I don't understand your behaviour. When *would* you have got in touch with me?'

'Probably this afternoon.'

'Probably? Thanks.'

'Depending on whether I felt lucid enough. Controlled enough.'

Peter looked at the wine bottle and then pointedly back to Craddock. With a shake of the head Craddock went on. 'No, not that. My meeting yesterday was a disturbing business. It left me in a very tangled state. The man . . .' He stopped, drained his glass and put the cork back on the bottle; it was about half-full. He had been standing with his back to the fireplace. Now he took his jacket off and went to sit in the second armchair in the bay window, across from Peter.

Peter asked, 'Did he give you his name?'

'No, you were right about that. No name, no 'phone number – not that I want to see him ever again.' He shook his head faintly, looking down at the carpet. Both could feel the change of atmosphere between them. The resentment had gone. Craddock smiled quickly at Peter as he lifted his head. 'I know I should have 'phoned you. You had every right to worry. But my mind seemed to switch itself off. I was glad to see you at that barmy party.'

Peter nodded. His face coloured a little; he could hear the fondness for him in Craddock's tone.

Craddock took a deep breath and let it out with a long sigh. He clasped his fingers loosely across his lap and began again, on a note of practicality. 'Well, this weird meeting . . .'

'Whittle's dying to hear about it.'

'You can pass on whatever you wish.'

'He's keen to hear it from you.'

'I'm not keen to meet him, Peter. I'm not attracted to him

and his friends. My feeling is they're not nice people.'

Peter shrugged. 'I'm sure you're right. Whittle himself says they're a mob of oddballs. It's isn't a moral crusade – not with him, that's certain. He's turned on by corruption.'

'Yes,' Craddock said softly. 'So is the man I saw yesterday.'

'I think I ought to 'phone Whittle – if only to tell him you've surfaced. I could say you're putting your notes together. Just to keep him quiet for now.'

'Why are you so anxious to stay in his good books?' Craddock asked curtly. 'He can't help you any more on Llewellyn. He doesn't know anything. He never did. All he ever had was suspicion.'

'I might need him again, though. His contacts.'

Craddock gave a little nod of understanding, and gestured towards the phone.

Whittle answered immediately. Peter said, 'Hullo, Gavin. Listen, Gav, it's all right. You'll love it. But he's got a load of stuff to sort out and get into some sort of order. Listen when shall I call back . . .'

Craddock watched Peter turn on his false mateyness, with a deliberately roughened accent, and saw a dexterity he had no liking for. But that was only one aspect of Peter's nature, he reminded himself. And indeed, as Peter put down the 'phone he reassured Craddock with one of his self-deprecating, shy smiles, and said, 'That was terrible, wasn't it?'

*

Sergeant Whittle did not interrupt as Peter retailed Craddock's information. He listened for the gaps as well as to the detail. He was thickly built. Aged twenty-eight he was made to look older by the vertical lines running down to his jaw and the dark lids of his eyes. It was not a gaunt face; it was fleshy. But its muscles moved under the flesh as he clenched his teeth, by habit.

Peter talked about George Birtles. The man was about to take the great tumble into disgrace. The income tax people would destroy him. They were after him for about £300,000 for unpaid taxes. Worse than that, there were the false declarations he'd made. Birtles was still putting up a great show of wealth. But a show was all it was. There wasn't a penny in his kitty. He owed debts all round the North. And he had misrepresented his financial position to numerous other businessmen, enticing them to invest in some grand make-or-break venture he called Rivertown – to do with a proposed yachting centre. To this end he had apparently forged letters. He had also misled these investors into believing he had secured various parcels of land and property when, in truth, he hadn't. By and large it seemed to be the old story of robbing Peter to pay Paul – over and over, backwards and sideways and then round the circuit again, until there wasn't a pocket left to pick. He was living on credit which came from a mixture of local goodwill for old times' sake and a measure of repayment for past favours. Some, if not all, of these favours were simply criminal. They had occurred during his days as the kingpin of regional politics, when he had pushed contracts in certain directions. Mostly, of course, they concerned the city rebuilding he was so proud of. Much of this malpractice was not normally the concern of the Inland Revenue investigative department, but the officers' inquiries into how the Birtles money came and went had led them into many areas; and a long way back. Birtles had been in business some years before he left politics. He began in public relations, and from the earliest days had worked for a number of the leading builders, planning consultants and architects involved in the redevelopments around the region. The fees paid to his company seemed now excessive, considering the modest services provided. When the tax men had finished with Birtles in the bankruptcy court there would be no other course open to the police but to arrest him on a host of charges; and, with him, several conspirators, because the business of bribery and inducement was essentially one of give-and-take. Among these, had he not died of a heart attack three months ago, would have been Big Ben Felden whom the fraud squad had suspected, although without linking him with Birtles. It was thought that Birtles would be gaoled for five years or possibly seven, because of his persistent abuse of public office. The half-dozen others – a couple of councillors of shorter careers, minor builders, an architect, two accountants; the list was not yet finalised – would go down for terms ranging from twelve months to three years, if the evidence was properly presented. A larger number of people had saved their skins by helping the investigation, and otherwise keeping their mouths shut about it.

'Is Llewellyn among that lot?' Whittle's voice matched him physically, heavy and quick.

'No,' Peter said, although he knew Whittle did not need the answer. Whittle had asked to help relieve his gathering fury. He was in the old moquette armchair in Peter's basement flat where Craddock had sat a few nights before, when Peter had said to him about Llewellyn, 'You know, don't you? I suppose it must hurt . . .'

Whittle was wearing his off-duty clothes, denims and a zip-fronted jacket. Peter had been surprised by how much a working lounge suit softened his appearance: disguised his nature, which had no softness. Whittle had brought a pack of canned beer, and he drank from one of the tins now. Peter lit a cigarette, and waited.

'He's going to get away with it,' Whittle said.

'He may not. Once the police are fully involved . . .'

'They are!' Whittle thumped the can on the arm of the chair and a spurt of beer fell on the fabric. He went on, 'In a different sense, they are. He's being protected. Somebody's repaying *him* a favour. Several somebodies, probably.'

Peter said, 'The top brass? With his job at the Home Office they're the ones he meets.' Whittle shrugged his heavy shoulders. 'You'd have a catch there – a shoal of whales.' He realised he had said it too lightly. Whittle's eyes had a glower as he looked up, and there was a faint twitching at the left side of his mouth. It was a brutal face for a moment. Peter met its look with a steadiness he did not feel, and shifted his tone. Earnestly he went on, 'What does it need to get the breakthrough there? What needs to happen?'

Whittle seemed mollified. 'You can plant something – fit somebody up. It doesn't have to be connected with what you really want to nail him on – it's just a way of turning him over. And then, surprise, surprise, look what this wicked bastard's been up to! The more senior the rank, the harder that is, of course. You might just have to wait to get lucky. Somebody retires, with his honours thick upon him, but he's got a bit careless in his old age and he doesn't clear his desk properly. Say the new man's an out-of-towner. He finds a bit of this and a bit of that left behind by his predecessor. Perhaps it's some poor *straight* sod's interview notes the old fucker buried on behalf of a friend. Or thought he had. Or it's the odd scrap of paper with some name on it and maybe a date and a few figures, and the new man wants to know what's all *this*, then? And he doesn't like the way nobody around the place seems to know anything about it. And he's an obstinate bleeder and he says there's the smell of bent money around this place and I'm going to disembowel that sanctimonious old bastard who's just walked out of here with his head held high, because that's my job in life . . .'

Peter could hear the yearning in the voice as Whittle pictured himself in action. Whittle, in turn, felt the cold inspection of Peter's brown eyes on him and was uncomfortable, because he knew he was not dominating this younger and less experienced man as he wished. He was being used. He took a gulp of beer and ended, sullenly more than aggressively, 'Like I said, you might have to just fucking wait.'

Peter nodded, and he remembered something Craddock had said about Llewellyn: 'He's waiting . . . how you wait for the result of an x-ray . . . that kind of waiting.'

'Llewellyn's guaranteed some very nasty publicity,' Peter said. 'He can never deny how closely he used to work with Birtles.'

Whittle said, 'I'd give a year's pay to see that pair slopping out together.'

CHAPTER TWENTY-FOUR

Sergeant Whittle had not been given a full account of Craddock's meeting with the military-looking man whose polished shoes gleamed in the fog. That was because Peter had not received a full account from Craddock. To satisfy Peter's curiosity, Craddock had described the man and said it was likely he worked for the investigative branch of the Inland Revenue, although probably not at a senior level, and added that they had gone to his little week-end bungalow at Brinsley Bay to talk. He had not elaborated further on the character of the man.

Llewellyn got the whole story.

They sat again in the study of the Hampstead house. Craddock arrived at eleven a.m. on New Year's Day, about an hour after 'phoning Llewellyn. Neither had been out the night before. Mary had, and was still asleep.

Craddock told Llewellyn about the collection of German military insignia and explained that the man's interest in the Third Reich did not stop there. He had his little library as well, the books of photographs of marching columns, blond young soldiers, blond young athletes, recruitment posters for the Hitler Youth. He had put together his own albums of similar material, pictures extracted from magazines mostly and with an emphasis on small groups and individual portraits of men of the Afrika Corps, often photographed from a low angle to enhance their heroic look. He had shown Craddock all these items with gloating pride, dwelling on those pictures he found especially exciting and wondering if Craddock agreed. Craddock said, 'He never suggested we should actually both get our cocks out, but he had a lot of trouble containing himself.'

The man punctuated his information on George Birtles with these offerings. Craddock was aware that if he made unsuitable comments about the man's pin-ups further information would be withheld. It had not been easy, once Craddock had exhausted his range of mute, appreciative facial expressions. He found the man much liked the use of the word 'lad', so Craddock also employed it, volunteering remarks such as, 'Intelligent face, that tall lad's got.' Eventually the man intimated that he was expecting two young friends to call that evening, on their motor-bikes, and hoped Craddock would stay to meet them. Craddock regretted that he had to get back to London. The man understood: Craddock no doubt had someone waiting for him.

Craddock told Llewellyn, 'I'm pretty sure I got what he knows about the Birtles business. I really don't think he knows exactly *when* it's going to break.'

Church bells were jangling nearby. It was Monday, so they probably indicated a New Year's Day wedding. The two men listened for a while, as if they knew about bell-ringing.

'You had, of course,' Llewellyn said flatly.

'What?'

'You had someone waiting for you. The kid from *Voice*.'

Quietly Craddock said, 'Not in his black leathers, with a skull and crossbones on his back.'

They met each other's eyes, which were more troubled than their voices.

'No. Sorry, I wasn't equating . . .' Llewellyn leaned forward with his elbows on his desk and sucked at his knuckles. He continued, 'That must have been pretty sickening up there. It looks as if the message passed down the grapevine about you got a bit garbled by the time it reached . . .' He paused and gave a tired grin. 'I remember you in the army – perpetual dumb insolence.'

Craddock said evenly, 'It's obvious the man was told "Craddock's a poof". So he thought, since it was his show – he was *paying*, if you like – he had a right to choose the entertainment. A sad afternoon.'

Llewellyn asked, 'What's this young friend of yours like?'

'Why don't you meet him and find out? He's asked often enough.'

'Do you want me to?'

Craddock shook his head impatiently. 'No, I can't see any point in it. What else are you going to give him except Llewellyn the adroit charmer? I don't think I want him to see that performance.' Llewellyn ducked his head slightly, acknowledging the reproof. Craddock said, 'I'm sorry, I was irritated by your question. You're not remotely interested in what he's like, are you?'

'Well, I don't give a damn whether he's a dwarf with warts or looks like something by Michelangelo. But I'd like to know what it is about him that has you stealing around the country digging for the dirt on *me*.'

'Perhaps it doesn't matter what Peter's like. Nothing to do with him . . .'

Llewellyn said quickly, 'Balls, Tony.'

'I'm saying I don't know for sure. He attracts me. Yes, that's true. As soon as we met we both knew we were going to get involved. But don't think I was *glad* when he asked me to help him pin you down as a crook.'

'You didn't waste any time. The jolly 'phone call on Christmas Eve – very sly.'

'Yes, I know. Not my way, normally . . .'

'Was your interview with Mary informative?'

Craddock raised his voice. 'The short answer to that is yes!' Llewellyn recognised pain as well as anger in the reply, and let Craddock continue more calmly. 'Let me try to clear up this other point. It *happened* to be Peter who pointed the finger at you, which meant I had to do something about it – it wouldn't have mattered what it was he wanted from me. But suppose it had been somebody else who came along with the same message, somebody who made no impact on me at all, or somebody I took a great dislike to. I believe I'd still have felt I had to act on it. Because it's to do with you and me, Roy. It isn't just a question of whether you're corrupt. A whole string of things follows on that. To begin with, do I care if you are? Have I always known it, or not let myself admit it? That would make me just as crooked. Do I care about *that*?'

Llewellyn said mildly, 'You sound like a man approaching fifty with an unhealthy compulsion to take stock. I can see it's true – you really do intend to write this novel.'

Craddock ignored the taunt. He said, 'Have I told you anything you didn't already know about George Birtles? I gather you keep in touch.'

'I knew he was in the shit financially. I didn't know he'd become a forger – assuming your man's right about that.'

'What about the other things – the ones that go back a few years? The brave new Britain built on back-handers. To quote George – "A good team, Roy and me". Where does that leave you? We're talking about your heyday.'

Llewellyn was curt. 'I was good at my job.'

'The one you once described to me as a bloody wonderful game.'

'I don't regret a day of it.'

'Birtles had his hand in the till for years. Did you?'

Llewellyn's two fists dropped hard on the desk. 'I got things *done*. I . . .'

Craddock cut him off softly with, 'I've already made that speech for you.'

'To your young friend, I suppose.' And he added politely, 'Thank you, old son.'

'Birtles delivered a longer version to me – as much on your behalf as his. If he's going to do a lot of that to the police, where does *that* leave you?'

Gently Llewellyn said, 'Tony, I am in the clear.'

'Mary says you're in deep.'

'You've seen the state Mary can get into.' The viciousness in the voice shocked Craddock. The picture of a hunched old woman dragging herself up the stairs filled his mind. He stared at Llewellyn, who saw the shock in his face and after a while gave a wry grin and said, 'You've never experienced marriage, old son. It's sometimes far from gentle.'

'She loves you,' Craddock said.

Llewellyn dropped his eyes and stirred uneasily in his chair. He stood up, wandered across the room to a window and then back to the desk, where he stood, not looking at Craddock. He said, 'The problem's heroin. She's been away once. But it's started again. She isn't a hopeless case. It hasn't gone that far.'

Craddock said softly, 'She was unhappy when we talked. But lucid. Most of the time she talked about you. Some complaints. But mostly worries. In deep, she said.'

Llewellyn's shrug was more of a nervous jerking of the shoulders, new to Craddock. 'We've had 'phone calls. She's taken a couple of them. She ought to be used to that sort of thing by now. We all get them. All kinds of . . . the heavy-breathers, the threateners, the flat-earthers. She used to laugh at them.'

'Are you talking about random calls? You're ex-directory. She'd still cope with that sort of thing. This is different, isn't it? Someone who knows you.' The shoulders jerked again. 'Blackmail?'

Llewellyn laughed and said, 'Sorry to disappoint you.' But he was uncomfortably on the defensive. He sat down again at the desk, waiting for the next question. He was like a man in a witness box.

Craddock asked, 'Have you been getting the same attention as Birtles from Fleet Street?'

Llewellyn shook his head sharply. 'I'm known to be very choosy nowadays about who I talk to.'

'Why didn't you simply have Peter Franklin told to piss off?'

'Why should I think it worth the bother?'

'It's the bother you've taken not to that's got him more and more suspicious. I can't say I blame him. It's bound to make him wonder if you're waiting for something to happen – something to make your mind up.'

'Perhaps I'm just busy.' But Llewellyn's continuing unease made the throw-away reply appear the more unconvincing.

'Why don't you tell *me* to piss off?' Craddock was surprised by the hard edge he put to his question, and it reminded him that his own nerves were stretched.

Quick to catch the atmosphere of the moment, Llewellyn found an engaging smile to go with his answer. 'Because I know you have nothing but my best interests at heart.'

'And there's also Mary,' Craddock said, not returning the smile. 'These 'phone calls – *do* you know who's making them? Why have they upset her so much?'

Llewellyn stared in silence at the desk top and then straightened in the chair, speaking unhurriedly. 'As the minister for cops and robbers I should be very careful about the company I keep, shouldn't I?' He waited for Craddock's nod. 'I haven't been. I don't think you're going to be amazed if I tell you there was a girl. She was at a party I went to – a few very senior policemen letting their hair down. It wasn't the sort of roast chicken and strawberry mousse affair they take their wives to.

There were a few highly privileged guests, sport and showbiz – the bookmaker, the football manager, the old boxer, the blue comic . . . such parties are like that. Nobody's there to discuss the defence budget or who's going to win the Nobel peace prize. There were girls. In particular, there was *this* girl. I saw a lot of her for a short while, just a few weeks. I've told you, I do a drudge's work. I was ready for the excitement. I knew she'd probably got criminal connections; of course I did. Cops and robbers have a lot of mutual friends. But she was too much to resist. I let her take me to meet some of *her* friends, and that, of course, was a silly mistake. Put it down to boredom. Insurrection. The 'phone calls started after I stopped seeing her. They didn't threaten – there was nothing to threaten about, except getting the girl to go to the papers. I agree that's quite nasty enough, because I can't share a mistress with a known criminal and stay in office. If she *had* gone to the papers I would have had to resign. Believe me, I'd have been glad to be rid of the job, but not that way. It wouldn't have done the party much good – or Mary, of course. The 'phone calls have been nothing more than gentle reminders that I've been indiscreet – an invitation to dinner, a little chiding for neglecting my friends, that sort of thing. Now that's *all*. Nobody's bought me. I'm not in anybody's pocket. Nothing more is going to happen about it. These people just have a little fun with me when they're feeling playful.'

'Why doesn't Mary believe that?' Craddock remembered her silence when he asked her if Llewellyn had explained what kind of trouble he was in. Craddock had misunderstood the silence, taking it to mean she knew nothing. He wondered now what else she had kept back while being so candid in her bitterness about other things. He knew that Llewellyn was concealing a lot; but he expected it.

Llewellyn gave that nervous shrug again. 'You haven't seen her at her . . . when she's at her most difficult, and even on our best days we're not too sure of each other lately, but I suppose you know.'

Craddock did not want the focus of the conversation to shift to Mary – at least, not yet. He asked, 'Can't your police friends get these people off your back?'

'There's no need for that. It's best left alone.'

'Well, not if Mary . . .' Craddock defeated his own intention in his baffled retort.

'Mary's a different problem,' Llewellyn said.

Craddock could find no way out of this, short of telling Llewellyn outright, 'You're lying.' And he did not feel on safe enough ground for that. He was in a morass of half-truth. On an impulse which was close to panic he got to his feet and started walking to the door.

Startled, Llewellyn asked, 'What's up, old son?' The voice told Craddock it was the first genuine response he had got since he arrived. But as he stood looking at Llewellyn's face he watched the expression make its small but conclusive change from concern to composure. Craddock was aware that he should be angered, but he was not; he had a strange feeling for a moment that he was a third person in the room, watching to see the conflict dealt with. He found himself delivering much the same kind of helpless, accepting sigh he had found so telling before in Llewellyn's behaviour, and Birtles'.

Lightly Craddock said, 'I just felt a bit claustrophobic then.' There was a grain of truth in it. 'It's happened a couple of times lately.' That was perfectly true, if he could define what he meant by 'it'. There was his desire to flee from the shack at Brinsley Bay; and the tears in the pub when he got back. And there was here, now. Disgust? Fear? Despair? Or was it nothing so grand, merely an understandable wish to be spared unpleasantness? Understandable or not, it wasn't being permitted. He heard himself sigh again.

'I told you years ago to watch the whisky,' Llewellyn said, and smiled.

'As you advised Birtles,' Craddock answered.

'Could you do with one now?' Llewellyn was being solicitous which irritated Craddock.

'Piss off, Roy.'

'One of us was bound to say it.'

Craddock was attracted by a sudden glinting of the sun at the windows and suggested, 'Why don't we get a bit of air for a few minutes? Show me the garden, like a proper host.'

★

For a few minutes they actually talked of gardening. Llewellyn identified species of roses, which Craddock thought very knowledgeable of him in their pruned, bloomless state. Craddock was reminded of rhododendrons he had seen wild on a hillside reaching twelve and fifteen feet, somewhere in Jugoslavia, he thought. Very self-sufficient, rhododendrons, Llewellyn commented. He took no credit for those on view; Goddard, or even his predecessor, had planted them. Craddock said he had a small electric clipper, for lawn edges, driven by a battery charged overnight, which he found ideal in his tiny back garden; it was mostly lawn, although he'd scattered a few daffodil bulbs around one year in a burst of enthusiasm, and even planted a lilac, which seemed to be doing well. Llewellyn was impressed by the image of Craddock planting a tree.

'What's going to happen about you and Mary?' Craddock asked.

'No telling at the moment.'

'Don't you care?'

'There are more factors involved than whether I care.'

'I'm sure you're wrong if you think she might leave you.' Craddock got a short laugh from Llewellyn, who also shook his head. Craddock persisted, 'I mean, when the drug thing's cleared up.'

'When she's her old self again? That what you mean? No matter what kind of crooked bastard I am, the lovely lady will not desert me – is that it? What a sweet old-fashioned way you have of looking at things, Tony.' He laughed again.

'I suppose it might depend on what *kind* of crooked bastard,' Craddock said.

'Thanks.'

As they turned Craddock caught the movement of a curtain at an upstairs window. He knew Mary had been watching them, and that she would not admit she knew he was at the house. 'I'd better be on my way,' he said.

'Have one for the road.' Craddock shook his head. 'Oh come on, for old times' sake. Goodbye to all that, and so on.'

Craddock heard more than was in the words, but didn't know what. Llewellyn grinned, and a gust of breeze stirred his hair, lifting it like a child's, and Craddock remembered Mary's trembling mouth as she said, 'Remember how much sheer life he had?' But Mary hadn't known Llewellyn as a child, which was how Craddock saw him now for an instant. The illusion was dispelled as quickly as the grin left Llewellyn's face, and he said, 'You deserve a drop of something for bringing me all this good news.' He walked past Craddock towards the French windows of the sitting room.

'My pleasure, mate,' Craddock called after him, and his voice was hard but had a catch in it.

Llewellyn called back, 'Come on, you need warming up.'

By the time Craddock had entered the sitting room and shut the French windows Llewellyn had poured two heavy measures of whisky and was holding one of the glasses out together with a water jug. His toast was, 'Thanks for the memory.'

Craddock said, 'Mary seems to think things might have gone better if I'd not drifted away.'

'Better for who?' Llewellyn looked him coolly in the face.

'For all three of us, I think she meant.'

Llewellyn's expression did not change. He said, 'Life took its course, that's all.'

The two men stood in the silence of the costly house, both aware that its appearance intruded on their memories.

CHAPTER TWENTY-FIVE

Ten days later Mary Llewellyn found her husband dead on the floor of his study.

She had been out to dinner with the producer and director of the film whose titles she was designing. She was quite buoyant, because her ideas had excited the two men. They were both younger than her by ten years or so, and she was pleased at the way she had been able to dominate the evening as a specialised practitioner. It was a film about mercenaries in Africa, and she was ingeniously making the silhouettes of guns and the explosions of shells dissolve into the actors' bodies and faces. She had not had much to drink, and it was quite early when she got home, not yet eleven p.m. The lights were on in the hall and on the stairs. She wondered if Roy might be home, and went to the 'phone on the wall. Beneath it were a small table and a chair. On the table, which was of mahogany with inlaid leather, stood a cactus in a copper bowl. There was an envelope with 'Mary' on the face, in Roy's tall handwriting, propped against the bowl. It was sealed, which she realised, afterwards, she should have seen as a warning.

She opened the envelope without haste, and unfolded the single sheet of Home Office ministerial writing paper. She read, 'Mary – Please don't go into the study. Dial 999 and tell the police I've killed myself. Sorry. Roy.'

She was halfway through reading the note a second time before she started running up the stairs. One of her shoes came off as she staggered, and she bruised her hands as she slapped them, one over the other like someone climbing a rope, against the balustrade. She had difficulty in forcing the door of the study open, because an armchair had been placed against it. This seemed to have been a late decision by Llewellyn when he was already drugged since the chair was not firmly positioned, and he could have jammed the door most effectively with that heavy furniture had he wished. She took in this point as she struggled, gasping; her mind was clear as she went through this frantic activity. She knew he would have used drugs – some of hers, because he had always resisted the prescribing for himself of anything beyond mild analgesics or sleeping pills as required sometimes. She could hear his voice telling her, 'You'll kill yourself one day with all this stuff you take.' She wondered which pills he had picked from the hoard of anti-depressants and sedatives in the small top drawer of her bedside cabinet. His handwriting had been remarkably undistorted. But she had always had trouble with it – the over-long tails and the high placing of the apostrophes tending to distract her attention from the individual words, because they often made up odd patterns.

She could not see him at first when she got into the room. She made naturally for the pool of light around the desk which came from the green-shaded reading lamp. He was lying hunched on his side, wedged between desk and chair. She knew immediately that he was dead. She knelt beside him, studying the figure. He was wearing one of his plain worsted suits – years ago she had discouraged him from stripes and weaves – with a shirt and tie; so he had been to his office or out somewhere on business and not worked at home during the day. He was casual about the house. Although, of course, if he held meetings in the study he usually put on a suit. He changed his clothes quite a lot. She reached out a hand to touch his face.

It was when the flesh made contact that her mind stopped working. She tried to embrace him, but collapsed, scraping her face against the side of the desk. She lay there, screaming his name, except that the scream remained embedded inside her. She started to choke, because her mouth and nose were pressed into the carpet. Her thin arms, which had managed to push aside the obstructed door, now trembled with the effort of raising her own slight weight upright. She had to use Roy's body to help her. It slanted in its wedged position, and she dug her fingers into the cloth of his jacket, climbing slowly upwards along his chest and on to his shoulders so that she could get her hands first to the seat and then to one arm of the bulky chair. She knelt there, becoming aware of pain in her knees, and on her cheek, and in her throat and chest. At last her voice broke through, but not with a scream. She spoke his name softly, then again, then more loudly, then more loudly still, again and again. When she felt able to she looked into his face, only a few inches away from her own. Because they were so close she could not see his features properly, and it seemed it was all that mattered in the world was that she should. With that moment of strength she got herself to her feet, and her mind came back to her. She did not look at his face but at the small plastic container on the desk. He had chosen the Tryptizol. She lifted the 'phone receiver, and it felt on fire because of the rawness of her hand, with its welts and bruises.

*

The quiet and calm of her voice, as she told him over the 'phone what had happened, made it the harder for Craddock to take in what she was saying. He wasn't used to hearing her like that, and he had just fallen asleep when she called him, towards one in the morning.

'. . . The police are here, and some people from his office have been sent for, and I've got my girl Concepta, and I'll be all right. So don't come over here now, Tony. I thought you'd want to hear it from me, and not get it from the newspapers or the radio – well, maybe it's too late for the morning paper, but I thought I shouldn't wait.'

'Yes, of course,' Craddock said, and added automatically, 'thank you.' He knew it was an absurd thing to say.

Mary said, 'But listen, Tony. There's going to be a lot happening. There'll be the inquest and the funeral, and maybe a lot more stuff. Well, I know there'll be a lot more stuff, and I'm going to need some help with that. So will you keep near your 'phone? I don't know whether I'll stay in the house. I might go away if things get – well, I think you know what I mean. I'd better go now . . .' Her voice carried on, but muffled, as she talked to someone else. The break gave time for Craddock to visualise Llewellyn's corpse on the floor of that room he loved. She said, 'I'm sorry, Tony, the people from Roy's office are here.' Her voice was suddenly stronger, but less controlled. 'They've sent some woman to look after me – looks like a wardress. I'm going to get rid of her.'

'Look, are you sure you don't want me to come over?'

'You stay out of it just now.' She gave a little gasp of a laugh. 'The place is crawling.' She put the receiver down.

Craddock shivered in the warm room. He went downstairs in his dressing gown, and turned on the electric fire in the sitting room. Opening the drinks cabinet and pouring a glass of whisky he found his hands shaking. He sipped at the whisky neat and it gripped at his throat so that he came close to throwing it up. He took the glass into the kitchen to fill it with water, and cautiously stood at the sink for a few minutes while he sipped the dilution. The shivering diminished, but the pit of his stomach still felt cold. He went back to the sitting room and stood by the fire. The last time he saw Llewellyn they had said goodbye standing with glasses of whisky in their hands – and Craddock had known it was the last time they would meet. There was nothing premonitory in that. Llewellyn had as good as dismissed him. It was up to Craddock to decide whether to stay dismissed. And he had, because he would not accept the humiliation of being lied to, and was unable to bring himself to tell Llewellyn that he knew it.

That was cowardice, if looked at objectively. But no matter how many times he had tried to be objective about Llewellyn he had always failed. He was more objective about himself, and as he calmed he recognised that he was relieved by Llewellyn's death. The banal phrase 'putting him out of his misery' recurred in his head. Llewellyn, who had lived by his own rules, had chosen his own penalty for breaking other people's – or rather for being found out. He remembered the impression Llewellyn had given of waiting anxiously; of waiting on events, decisions, outside his control. And there was the resigned acceptance . . . Craddock realised that Llewellyn had decided some time ago – weeks, perhaps months – that he would commit suicide if events fell a certain way. And with that thought came his recollection of telling Peter Franklin not to think of Llewellyn as a man who calculated, who planned for contingencies. 'As long as you're not out of date' was Peter's comment. He was, of course, in any objective sense. There was so much he wanted to know.

He placed his glass, still half-full, on the mantelpiece, and picked up the 'phone. On its long lead he could easily carry it to one of the armchairs in the bay window. He dialled from memory. When Peter answered, sounding drowsy, Craddock began steadily, without bothering to introduce himself, 'Hullo, Peter. You seem to have been right about Roy Llewellyn – at least, the one I didn't know . . .'

★

It was the first contact between Craddock and Peter since the day Craddock and Llewellyn last met. Craddock had then 'phoned to say he had to go away for a few days, not indicating why or where, and he would be in touch when he got back. Peter had not asked any questions, except to press Craddock on whether he was feeling well. Craddock said lightly that he'd felt a great deal worse after previous Christmasses and New Years. He did not mention his visit to Llewellyn.

The fact was that Craddock felt distinctly, if imprecisely, ill. He understood that the whole episode of his reunion with Llewellyn and Mary, ending on that chilling farewell, was bound to stretch him on the rack emotionally. But there were physical symptoms he was not sure he ought to associate with that. It was as he slumped in his sitting room after talking to Peter that he thought of Dr Chadbon, the sturdy, no-nonsense locum who had dealt with Peter's collapse. In spite of what he had told Peter he had made no plans to go anywhere – he was really asking to be left alone for a while, as Peter probably gathered. The image of Chadbon, burly with his silver curls, tending Peter like a trainer with a felled fighter, was reassuring. Half-dozing he imagined himself struggling to explain that he seemed to be dragging a ball-and-chain by his ankles; that he didn't have headaches exactly, but his head felt misshapen sometimes; that his back didn't ache exactly, but he was strangely over-aware of it; that he found memories of starving children in India, although familiar to him, much more troubling now than ever before – he felt a sense of shame at exploiting them to further his career, and this shame could hit him at times like a stone between the eyes . . . And Chadbon was listening to this recital with shrewd understanding – a man of the world whom nothing could surprise. Craddock fell asleep as Chadbon opened his mouth to begin his diagnosis.

At morning surgery the next day old Dr Fazackerly, who had now returned from his holiday in Madeira, smoked his pipe as he heard Craddock out. Craddock said he felt tired, his joints ached, and his temples throbbed. He made no mention of balls-and-chains or memories of scenes of famine. Dr Fazackerly looked down the patient's throat, checked his blood pressure, and put the stethoscope over his back and chest. He told Craddock, 'Come back in three days if you don't feel any better.'

Craddock went home and packed a grip with some spare shirts, underpants, socks, an extra sweater and an extra pair of cords, and 'phoned a hire-car firm. He didn't wait to stop his newspapers. He drove off with no set purpose, and when he came upon signs to Brighton he decided to take them. He found the unaccustomed concentration of driving quite soothing.

In the week that followed he ate two cooked meals a day. He took two hours' sleep in the late afternoon and still went to bed early at night. He walked for about an hour in the morning and again after lunch. He got wet and wind-blown, and was grateful for occasional sunlight. Never driving more than an hour and a half in any one day he dawdled along the South Coast, choosing the biggest sea front hotels, as far as Lyme Regis. All the towns gave the impression that it was early-closing day. He was sober. He was polite to waiters and barmen, but discouraged chatting. He bought a copy of *Dombey and Son*, because it was the one Dickens novel he had never read before, and found himself reading in bed for an hour before he got up each day – something he could not recall doing since childhood. He ignored the newspapers and television. His time seemed fully occupied. After five days he could see that he had put on a little weight; his face had some colour; he had no pains; the juddering of his neck muscles had stopped, and the twitching at his temples. He was satisfied that he wasn't ill. By the seventh day he was bored and realised that he must have been unwell not to have been bored earlier. He felt self-conscious that night, sitting in the hotel dining room with only Dombey and Son for company and probably twenty years younger than anyone else there, except the waiters. It was time he got back to work. It was more than a month since he'd written anything: a re-working of someone else's film script about competitive ballroom dancing – a melancholy little comedy which he doubted would reach the screen, which would be a pity because he admired its originator's observation and the producer's courage in spending money on it. He asked himself, at last, how serious he was about writing a political novel, which reassembled Llewellyn, Mary, Peter in his mind. He decided he wasn't ready for them, and escaped back into *Dombey and Son*.

But next day, driving back to London much more confidently than he had left it, he ordered his thoughts. He had first intended to tackle the conflict inside a Labour constituency party: young militants of the left trying to boot out the sitting Member and replace him with one of their own kind. There had been several such instances around the country in the last two or three years. But Craddock wanted to grapple with the personal confrontation, to treat the story like that of a family in turmoil, not of people wrangling over policy. That was before Peter Franklin had come along. Now Craddock couldn't avoid seeing the kernel of a plot with more dramatic, more surprising possibilities: a young investigative reporter and a successful career politician thrown into the ring against each other. Again he would concentrate on the personal: different generations, backgrounds, values, needs. The two men would fascinate each other, the young hunter and the master survivor. There was a book in that, for sure. But if Craddock were to do it he would have to re-draw his two main characters. He would feel too constrained if he had Llewellyn and Peter in the front of his mind all the time. It shouldn't be too difficult. The politician, to begin with, should be much more of a public figure – a frequent performer on television, for example – so that there was a big reputation for the younger man to challenge. He should be a Fleet Street favourite, the harder to attack. The reporter ought to have a rougher edge than Peter – should he be Scottish, perhaps, with a ready belligerence learned from the tenements? Suppose they shared the same eager taste in women . . .

At home Mrs Readhead, who cleaned his house, had stacked the accumulated newspapers and magazines on the coffee table in the sitting room, and the mail on his desk – an unappetising pile of buff envelopes with second class stamps. She had left him a note to say she had taken one telephone call, from a Mr Franklin, and she hoped he had a nice New Year. He realised he had forgotten to leave her week's money when he took off in his curious daze: he would need to apologise for that. Half the next day was spent on bachelor's chores: the dry-cleaner's, the supermarket, the delicatessen. Then he started to set down his outline of the novel, and the day afterwards he continued with it, concentrating on biographical detail of his two principal characters. He deliberately did not return Peter's call, so as to avoid thinking about him or Llewellyn. He worked into that night, as Llewellyn died.

*

In order that the funeral could take place without undue delay an inquest was formally opened and adjourned. A pathologist gave evidence that Llewellyn's death was due to an overdose of anti-depressant drugs, which was baldly reported in the papers and on the television and radio news – a matter of a few words, a few seconds. The interest the media showed in the funeral was in massive disproportion. The cremation service was private, confined to immediate family and close friends, at the request of the widow. So there were no Cabinet Ministers present – in fact, no governmental representatives except for members of Llewellyn's staff. They had the job of surrounding Mary, helped by detectives, as she made her way between the car and the chapel and the car and the house, and keeping the throng of cameramen and reporters at a distance she found bearable.

Llewellyn's father was there. He was aged eighty-four and fragile, although his eyes were alert and he had a snowy version of his son's springy hair. He was brought by his daughter and son-in-law, both teachers, with whom he now lived in Nottingham. Mary had discussed with Craddock how the old man could be kept away, to reduce some of the stress of the occasion. Remembering Llewellyn's father as a strongly-minded man – virtually self-educated to become a university lecturer in politics, and running his local ward for the Labour Party for nearly half a century – Craddock knew he would not be dissuaded. Mr Llewellyn had himself driven straight to the service and, when it was over, straight home again. He shook hands with Craddock and let him kiss him on the cheek. He surveyed the gathering of pressmen and knew its significance. He said to Craddock and Mary, 'They don't want all these pictures just because Roy committed suicide. I know that. There's a lot to come out yet about it all, isn't there? I expect it's to do with these sackings at Scotland Yard.' Neither Craddock nor Mary felt able to answer him. He said, 'Anyone who reads the papers ought to be able to see that.' And just before he left he remarked on the absence of parliamentarians, showing that he knew Mary's request for 'privacy' was a concealment of the true circumstances. 'I bet Dick Goddard would have been here, whatever Roy's done,' he said. He shook his head in a mixture of irritation and sympathy at Llewellyn's sister as the woman choked back a sob. She and her husband both looked at Mary with a bewildered hostility as they went, affronted by the attention the cameras were giving her. Llewellyn's father told them sharply, 'Don't blame Mary. What did you expect?'

*

The old man had read between the lines just as the newspapers wished him to. The news of Llewellyn's death had been in the hands of the media by the middle of the following morning. On broadcasts and in evening papers it was a separate item. So was another report, in later editions of the two London evenings, of a highly suspicious upheaval in one of the more glamorous departments of Scotland Yard. This was a section known colloquially as the sniffer squad, because its function was to gather intelligence about the underworld. All detectives did that, to some extent, in their daily work, but the sniffer squad was concerned with nothing else. It had a very free rein. It operated all over London, unrestricted by divisional boundaries, and it was specifically concerned with the movements of professional criminals: who was teaming with whom, or had parted company; an impending change of leadership in a particular gang; a gang's intention to annex another's territory; what disgruntled, or greedy, or tired villain might be ready to turn informer; what new criminal ventures were under discussion, however preliminary . . . The squad was the brainchild of the present Commissioner, who had held the job for the last five years. He wanted a form of intelligence corps which would keep out of the rough and tumble of inquiry and arrest. It would sift and assess its information, and report on the implications to the sections in the field, thus helping them to anticipate serious crime rather than toil in its wake. That, at least, was the theory.

The evening papers reported that the second-in-command of

the sniffer squad, a detective superintendent, had been suspended from duty, a chief inspector had resigned from the force, and an inspector and two sergeants had been transferred to other departments. The squad had recently acquired a new boss, brought in from one of the divisions, on the retirement of the first head, a Chief Superintendent Adrian Bell, who was nicknamed Professor Bell because he presented a scholastic manner with his glasses hanging round his neck on a piece of string. Both stories referred to the squad's controversial position within the Metropolitan force, detractors and supporters dividing roughly on whether it was an expensive waste of thief-catchers or a long-term deterrent.

By the next morning the national dailies had Llewellyn's death and the sniffer squad sackings in the same story. Adrian 'Professor' Bell and Lord Llewellyn had been close friends, often seen lunching or dining together, the reports said. Bell had been interviewed at his home in Lewisham and said how shocked he was by Llewellyn's death: the police of the whole country had lost a friend. The ex-chief superintendent was photographed in a suede jacket and carpet slippers, with his feet up in the picture window of his 'luxury bungalow'. The papers thought it relevant to say that his white Volvo estate car and his wife's blue Fiat sports saloon were parked in the drive. Twenty-four hours later the papers were able to record the pathologists's testimony that Llewellyn had died from an overdose of drugs; the following day, that 'Professor' Bell had been visited by the two senior detectives from the section which dealt with police corruption. Two days after that, on the morning of Llewellyn's funeral, the sniffer squad's former number-two was reported to have been similarly visited. He declined to talk to reporters.

Half a dozen of the press cars followed the black Daimler which took Mary and Craddock back to the Hampstead house after the cremation. Craddock remembered doing the same kind of thing years ago: laying siege to the bereaved did not enhance the self-esteem. It was a point Mary seemed to have appreciated. As they sat in the room with the French windows to the garden, drinking the coffee which Concepta had waiting for them, Mary said not unkindly, 'How long are those miserable sods out there expected to hang around?'

'They'll just dwindle away,' Craddock said. 'Their offices

have got the message by now that you're not going to say anything. But if you talk to any one of them they'll all come flocking back.'

'What about the police?'

'They need to be convinced you've told them what you know.'

'They've got all there is, for what it's worth.'

The two of them had little chance to talk that day. The night before Mary had 'phoned him, asking him to accompany her to the funeral – not just attend: she needed his arm.

As she had asked him on the night of Llewellyn's death, Craddock had not been away from his house in Parton Street for longer than a couple of hours at a time. For the first two days she did not call him. After that she 'phoned at all hours – midnight, noon, dawn – passing on what the police had told her, the questions they had asked; crying sometimes; chattering about the past; describing the laborious detail in which the detectives searched through Llewellyn's study, while ignoring the rest of the house, which showed they knew their man and the way he lived, and had their instructions. They were not to complicate their task by stumbling across his wife's illicit drugs. But she did not ask to see Craddock until the funeral. He knew she must be spending most of her time in bed. Her doctor was calling daily. Craddock was surprised when he saw her that she was comparatively steady. But she did not let go of his arm for a moment when she was on her feet.

With Mary's calls and the more coherent information brought to him by Peter, who had the benefit of Sergeant Whittle's gloating disclosures, Craddock was ahead of Fleet Street in assembling the story. In terms of fact it was simple. 'Professor' Bell and his second-in-command had been selling their criminal intelligence reports to the criminals. (The chief inspector, the inspector and the two sergeants now replaced had known what was happening but had not been part of the conspiracy, except by their silence. This, they expected with good reason, would earn them recommendations for promotion. It seemed that the inspector and the sergeants genuinely did not realise the extent of the racket, which was why they were allowed to retain their rank.)

Llewellyn was the middle-man. There was nothing whatever

unusual in his meeting frequently with Bell: it was his readiness to meet a wide range of senior policemen, familiarising himself with their problems, which made him – and Harrison's government – popular with the Police Federation. At least, it made the government less unpopular than it might be. Llewellyn conducted the transactions between the sniffer squad and the criminals through a solicitor whom, again, he met often; the lawyer had a special line in advising policemen in cases of complaint by civil rights campaigners and black activists, and the like. Invariably legitimate Home Office business was discussed at all these meetings. But among the paper exchanged sometimes were squad reports, which found their way to the criminals they concerned, and bundles of five-pound and ten-pound notes, which Llewellyn and the two detectives shared equally after allowing the lawyer his cut. Estimates of the sum involved over a period of two and a half years varied from twenty thousand pounds to a hundred thousand. The disparity reflected the large number of people in the criminal world the police had to interview and how little, for the moment, the known accomplices were saying.

The racket had come to light much in the way Sergeant Whittle had explained to Peter that such things happen, if somebody's lucky. 'Professor' Bell's successor eased himself unhurriedly into his new job and read his way back and through the files. He was impressed by the wealth of the information gathered – he had inherited a vigorous and able department. But when he set up an exercise to establish how much use all this cogent evaluation had so far proved he found the files uncommunicative. He became uneasy and realised that his mood was being interpreted as suspicion which, in turn, made him suspicious. One day he noticed that several more copies than were needed were made of one of his reports, and he asked the girl who handled the photo-copying machine why. She told him that Mr Bell always liked a few spares. She didn't know what happened to them. He tackled the chief inspector first and, too quickly, the man offered to resign . . .

Craddock asked Mary, 'Did you ever meet Bell?'

'Yes. Roy brought him to the house a few times. The three of us had some lunch here once.' She used both hands to hold her coffee cup. 'He was a cheery old soul. I mean that was his act – he wasn't so much older than Roy. He called me, "My dear." Roy could see I didn't take to it. Well, he knew I wouldn't before he brought the man along. This goes back two years. We were starting to fight then.'

She put the cup down and Craddock offered to refill it. But she didn't want more coffee, she wanted to talk. She sank back in the chair. 'I don't know if there was anything more I could have done. Not then, anyway. It was too late then. I guess I was just too busy. Roy got himself involved with the gangsters and Bell for the hell of it. Dotting old Harrison one in the eye for not giving him the job Goddard promised him. It's as stupid as that. And he wanted something new, a new game to play. I went to a couple of those parties with him, in the early days. Cops and robbers and girls. Yes, of course, the girls were a big draw for Roy. I told him he was playing with fire, mixing with those people. I never knew what he was doing. I just know it was bad. You know, at one stage I even thought of going to Harrison to tell him. I got this idea Roy was just trying to see how far he could go. And then, I don't know when it was, just some moment in the sober light of day, I knew he was in over his head. For the first time in his life Roy was in something he couldn't handle. And I couldn't handle that. I tried to tell you that day . . .' She trailed off giving him a weak smile.

'Yes, you got quite close to it,' Craddock said. 'I'm sorry, I wasn't much help.' He remembered their dire lunch just after Christmas: how ill she had looked – worse than now. He saw that Llewellyn's death had released them both from the intolerable. He could hear Llewellyn's voice saying, 'I've seen all I ever want to see of prison.' He told her the story Llewellyn had given him about the 'phone calls which had supposedly upset her.

She said, 'Bell and the others were getting pretty rough by then. They were desperate. They thought he could pull some strings. This new man who followed Bell, he'd put the fear of God into them. They said, "Don't forget to tell Roy it was all his own idea" – and stuff like that. I didn't know what it meant. When I told Roy he said I should stop answering the 'phone.' She laughed suddenly, with a quick bright ring, and then said, 'He never was *scared*. I mean he knew he was finished, but he was never scared. It just wasn't in him.'

'I know,' Craddock said. 'It was the thing I first noticed about him. We were eleven years old, at a new school, and I was so frightened I couldn't speak. Roy was the only one of us utterly unafraid.'

'Do you wish you'd never set eyes on him?'

He knew he ought to be able to answer immediately. But he found himself examining the question. Eventually he said, 'I can't imagine that.'

'You might have had a very different life.'

'I don't see why.'

'You think if it hadn't been Roy you'd have had to find someone else to tag on to, and then watch over, paying off your debts?'

He objected, 'There were years without any contact. Even before *you* came along there were a lot of gaps.'

She smiled, and said, 'You're here now, right at the end, helping to clear up the mess. You've paid your debts, Tony.' Her eyes closed and the lids twitched.

He asked, 'What are you going to do – about the house, and so on?'

'Finish my picture. Sell. After that . . .' She shook her head slightly, too tired to think further: not interested. Still with her eyes closed she said, 'Do you know what he did with the money? The police told me he used to send it all up to that funny little guy called Birtles. Some riverside investment up there. Wildcat scheme. Roy must have known he was just throwing the money away, so the police said. See what I mean? He'd run out of games to play.'

Craddock said quietly, 'The kind of criminals he was involved with aren't the playful type. They don't care who gets hurt, or how badly. He knew that, as well.'

She opened her eyes and looked steadily at Craddock. 'There isn't much left for us to admire, is there?' she said. 'But we both know that isn't the Roy we're going to remember. The one we'll make ourselves remember.'

He did not answer. In the silence the question he wanted to ask her grew in its cruelty and its importance. He had to ask it. 'Do *you* wish you'd never set eyes on Roy?'

She answered simply, 'Oh yes.'

*

Peter Franklin could not get rid of the nagging exasperation that he had been chasing the wrong story about Llewellyn. The truth had turned out to be more sensational, and appalling. But he still felt cheated, as he explained to Craddock, as if Llewellyn had laid false trails, deliberately inviting pursuit. 'Even *you* thought he was corrupt for all that time when he was mixed up with the planners and the builders and bent local councillors all over the place – well, eventually you did,' he said to Craddock, who could not deny it. 'It's as if he *wanted* the idea to get around – a kind of insurance against the day he really did get himself on the wrong side of the law. Everyone would be so busy doubling back through his past they wouldn't see what he was up to now. Do you think it's possible?'

Craddock was not prepared to dismiss the theory. He did not believe it was quite what happened, although he could see Llewellyn richly enjoying the sight of a team of Sergeant Whittles vainly, furiously trying to find the crime that never was there. But he no longer knew what Llewellyn might have been capable of. He shrugged and said, 'Could be.'

They were in the little Greek restaurant again. It was mid-evening and quiet. Craddock had been living mostly on lumps of cheese and apples and pots of tea and cautious glasses of whisky for the past week, and he had now ordered a huge meal: sucking-pig, potatoes and one of those big Greek salads.

Peter said, 'Do you think it could have been Llewellyn who tipped off the papers about George Birtles? I'm still on the same lines. He knew people would tie him in with Birtles. He might have thought he could gain himself a bit of time, at least, if he could get them in each other's way.' But Peter this time brought a vigorous shake of the head from Craddock.

'Simms,' Craddock said. 'I'd put my money on poor little Simmy. The dogsbody's revenge. He'd really know exactly who to 'phone around the newspapers, and he'd know better than to have them all turning up on the same train. Simmy isn't going to prison; he was just the errand boy. He'll have a lovely time when Birtles is safely put away and Simmy's in the limelight being interviewed in the cocktail bar of the Great North Hotel.' Craddock sipped at his wine, 'I wonder, if we made the effort, could we manage to talk about something else?'

Peter said, 'Why? If you're going to write that book you want the whole business milling round your mind all the time, don't you?'

Craddock looked at the brown still eyes, which made a challenge of the question. He said, 'I'm forgetting about the book. I can't see the point, if Llewellyn isn't here to read it.'